Beauty Beyond Darkness

The true story of one woman's survival against the odds

LILLA BENIGNO

*To my mother and my father and
to my children Caroline, Dean and Chantelle.*

To all my family in Melbourne and Italy.

To my close friends.

*To the community of Cairns, North Queensland,
my paradise.*

Beauty Beyond Darkness

Copyright © 2020 Lilla Benigno.

All rights reserved. No part of this book may be reproduced or transmitted in any form or by any means without written permission from the author.

National Library of Australia Cataloguing-in-Publication entry:

Creator: Benigo, Lilla, author, photographer.
Title: Beauty Beyond Darkness: The true story of one woman's survival against the odds / Lilla Benigno, (author/photographer).
Editor, Philip Newey.
Proofreader, Pauline Phillips.
ISBN: 9780994500106 (paperback).
Notes: Includes bibliographical references.
Subjects: Benigno, Lilla—childhood and youth.
Women with disabilities—Australia—Biography.
Women with disabilities—Attitudes.
Self-actualisation (Psychology) in women.
Women—Identity.

Dewey Number: 362.43092

Copy editor: Philip Newey.
Proofreader: Pauline Phillips.
Cover design and project management: Michael Hanrahan Publishing.
Cover art: Lilla Benigno.
Typesetting: Digital Print Australia.

Contents

INTRODUCTION xi

CHAPTER 1 1

Birth and horror of poliomyelitis.
March 27, 1958—six months old in Messina, Sicily.

CHAPTER 2 5

My years in the convent with the nuns in Italy, 1963–1968.
I was five years old.
I was eight years old when my father took me to Sicily
to see my family.
My first holiday—one that I will never forget.

CHAPTER 3 21

    My best friend Rita (who also had polio), 1964-1969.

CHAPTER 4 27

    My mother's visit to the convent—Drama, May 1970.
    I was twelve years old.

CHAPTER 5 35

    When we left Sicily to go to Australia, October 1970.
    I was twelve years old.

CHAPTER 6 53

    My mother—1971-1974.

CHAPTER 7 63

    My father—1971-1974.

CHAPTER 8 69

    August 1971—My encounter with pop singer Johnny Farnham.
    I was thirteen years old.

CHAPTER 9 75

    November 1974—Glen Waverly High School, and why I got expelled.
    The party that my older sister Isabella and I went to.
    I was fourteen years old.

CHAPTER 10 83

    February 1971-1972—My first suicide attempt. I was thirteen years
    old.
    My last suicide attempt that landed me in the
    Glen Waverly Rehabilitation Centre.

CHAPTER 11 89

*May 1973-1974—My first love John, and my rescuer.
I was nearly fifteen years old.*

CHAPTER 12 95

June 1973-1974—The trip to Mildura by train. On the run with John.

CHAPTER 13 105

*The beginning of my hell. My first rape by Rob.
I was fifteen years old.*

CHAPTER 14 113

December 1974—My second love Frankie. I was sixteen years old.

CHAPTER 15 127

*December 1975—The first pimp I met, Pete.
I was seventeen years old.*

CHAPTER 16 135

Three days after Christmas 1975—I was gang-raped by many men in one night. I was seventeen years old.

CHAPTER 17 141

April 1976—My motorbike accident. I was eighteen years old.

CHAPTER 18 149

*Living in the streets and pregnant.
The birth of my daughter Chantelle, January 21, 1976.
I was eighteen years old.*

CHAPTER 19... 163

The pain of adopting out my daughter sent me back to heroin and back living in the streets. I was nineteen years old.

CHAPTER 20... 173

Gang-raped by many bikers, 1977. I was nineteen years old.

CHAPTER 21... 179

Hashish party where I nearly died, 1978. I was twenty years old.

CHAPTER 22... 183

My third love José, 1979. I was twenty-one years old.

CHAPTER 23... 191

Selling my disabled body for heroin to stop the pain and turmoil I was going through.

CHAPTER 24... 199

April 13, 1980—The birth of my son Dean. I was twenty-two years old.

CHAPTER 25... 213

My best friend Carol. I was twenty-four years old.

CHAPTER 26... 223

Melbourne Odyssey House; and six months in Sydney Odyssey House. Altogether four and a half years of rehabilitation, getting off heroin. I was twenty-five years old.

CHAPTER 27 237

*January 28, 1987—The birth of my daughter Caroline.
I was twenty-nine years old.*

CHAPTER 28 249

*Keeping my daughter, learning to be a mother with all the
advice of my mother, 1987.*

CHAPTER 29 259

*March 1989 —First time at The Addiction Help Agency.
This place slowly restored me to sanity. I was thirty-three years old.*

CHAPTER 30 271

*Sexually molested by a priest two days before Christmas 1992,
and I was thirty-four years old when I was raped again
by a friend I knew.*

CHAPTER 31 279

1993—My new freedom called 'Gopher'. I was thirty-five years old.

CHAPTER 32 287

*Trauma while I was sleeping, my daughter was nine years old.
1996—Second time at the Addiction Help Agency.
I was thirty-six years old.*

CHAPTER 33 297

*Going back to school, at TAFE College—1997–2008.
My gift to my mother and my family, also to my children: my son
Dean, my daughters Chantelle and Caroline, and all the people
of Cairns.
Finally in 2008, I proudly received my 'Diploma of Visual Arts'.*

CHAPTER 34..309

My new life, my freedom and my happiness. Present moment.

CHAPTER 35..315

My disability—1958 until the present moment, 2019.

ACKNOWLEDGEMENTS..319

Thanking everyone for being there for me—2014.

Introduction

A FEW WORDS about this book.

These are my memories, triumphs, joys, despair, sadness, anger, fears… The tempest of emotions.

I experienced that for ten years. This is a story about survival. This book is the last step in calming the storm.

From the deepest, darkest pit—living on the streets as a disabled person and a drug addict, vulnerable, lost and bewildered—I rose above it all into a new and better world, a happier and functional world, the world I always dreamed of, at peace within myself.

Born in Sicily, struck with polio when only a few months old, forced to live in institutions for much of my early childhood, my life was turned upside down when the family decided to immigrate to Australia: a strange country, an unknown language, a foreign culture.

Dark times followed as I struggled to adjust to this family I scarcely knew, and as they struggled to relate to me. I have used the dark mines of these horrid memories to extract the strength and courage to look ahead.

Living on the streets of Melbourne at fifteen years of age, struggling to survive, stumbling around on twisted legs that needed callipers to give them strength… Drugs, sex, rape, depression and violence were my constant companions.

Finally I climbed my way out of the morass, finding support in Odyssey House, in Melbourne and Sydney. Then fleeing north, to Cairns, in Far North Queensland, where I found such tremendous support in the Addiction Help Agency (AHA), Alcoholics Anonymous (AA), and other groups and agencies.

This is my story. Perhaps my autobiography is not that important to many. But I don't care anymore what people think of me. I need to write. I wanted to write this story to express my pride for having made it; to make everyone see that, disability or no disability, I, too, have made it, all on my own. Yes, I am mighty proud of it.

It took me many years to write this book. So many tears, and almost as many years of procrastination. Now I understand why I had to do it. For years I didn't believe my story was good enough to be told. I thought, 'I am nothing. Who wants to read my story?' But then one day I thought, 'I am somebody. I am a survivor. I have learned how to speak my mind, my heart and my soul.' Now I would love my children to know my real story.

Mine is a story of courage, fear, disappointments, love, pain, a life story that is *Beauty Beyond Darkness*.

Chapter 1

Birth and horror of poliomyelitis.
March 27, 1958—six months old in Messina, Sicily.

BORN IN SICILY, a land of millenarian culture, in a family as vast and knotted as a fisherman's net after one night in a tempest at sea, I was struck by polio when I was six months old and ended up at twelve years old in the land of the descendants of scallywags.

The humiliation of my body by nature and the spiritual and physical rape by humans turned me from a beautiful creature into a monster.

My home town was Messina, the city facing Scylla and Cariddi, the two mythological monsters that swallowed all mariners. I was born on March 27, 1958. Messina, in the district of San Paolo, is a poor little town in Sicily, called Camaro Inferiore.

My mother was Sicilian, born in Messina too. My father was born in Arabic Tunisia. I was the fifth in the family. I had three older brothers and one sister. Later in life many other children came along.

Lilla Benigno, six months old, with Mum.

My mother told me I was a happy baby, smiling all the time, kicking my legs and laughing. But then one day disaster struck in my parents' lives—and mine. I was hit by poliomyelitis.

I was six months old at the time. My life and theirs changed tremendously. I was told that while my mother was bathing me, my little body suddenly started to collapse. My head flopped from side to side, my body broke out in a high temperature, and my mother called for my father.

My father rushed into the bathroom and saw my mother screaming out my name and crying. He glanced at my sick body, grabbed a blanket, and they both walked to Palermo Hospital. It was a long way from where we lived. There were no hospitals in Messina at that time, and they were too poor to get a taxi. I can imagine how painful it was for my parents, not knowing if I was going to live or die. After hours of walking they arrived at the hospital. Nurses and doctors helped my parents as quickly as they could and put me into isolation. Even the doctors didn't know what I had. They had to run many tests. But there was one doctor who knew about polio, and he gave the bad news to my parents.

They were mortified. They didn't know what to do. They had other children to look after and had no money to pay for expensive treatment. My mother reports that, while in the isolation ward, I was soaked by rain. It's hard to believe nowadays, but there was a leak in the ceiling above my cot that nobody had noticed. That night it poured for hours. Rain water poured into my cot and when my mother returned the next morning, she found a baby more dead than alive, with a very high fever. She screamed, the doctors rushed in, and I was taken into emergency in a last effort to save me. It was then that my father saved my life by giving me his blood.

Polio had hit me severely. It paralysed my left arm, and both legs and feet. My feet twisted in a way that made it impossible to walk, and many nerves in my legs, feet and arm were dead. I had no balance. I couldn't stand, walk, or even sit. My whole life I relied on my right arm, the arm that dragged me everywhere for years on end.

My parents were furious at the doctors and nurses. They felt lost. People were terrified of this disease. Children were the most vulnerable. Many would die, and the few who survived were prone to pain and humiliation. Adults too could catch the virus and suddenly become paralysed. Their life would stop: no more words, no more daily chores, no more looking after their own children.

When it hit teenagers, they were suddenly tied to a wheelchair and placed in some institution, their little faces struck by pain and fear. People feared most the fact that it was contagious. The vaccine for that plague— it is even recorded in hieroglyphics from the fifteenth century BC—was developed in 1955. Vaccination began three years later, but certainly not, in those days, in the south of Italy. My parents probably didn't even know a vaccine existed.

I stayed in Palermo Hospital for five years. I hoped I could recover some mobility but I was making little progress. I couldn't walk at all. My body felt dead. Only my right arm grew strong. To move around, I used to slide on the floor. That's how I 'walked' everywhere.

One day the doctor who had looked after me all those five years suggested to my father that it would be better to move me to a specialized institution. At first my father hesitated at the idea of sending me elsewhere, far from home. I know it was hard for him and my mother.

But something had to be done. I needed help to survive and to learn new ways of coping. I needed to get better. In the end my parents gave in, and the doctor gave my father a telephone number to call and make all the arrangements. I was too small to understand what was happening, but I knew something was wrong. My parents now had a way out. Finally there was a place where I could be well looked after. It was far from where I was born. We had to travel to Milano, to an institute for children with the same problem. My parents couldn't provide everything I needed. I was very sick, almost dead, but my father saved my life.

After World War II many people were trying to adjust to a new life. It was time to recover and make a better life. But there were no jobs and hardly any food. People were desperately looking for work, so they could provide for their families. My parents were trying to build a good life for the family. But this disease placed them in a terrible predicament. Poverty was widespread and, although my father was working at the time, we were still quite poor. The war left so many people scarred for life. Despite this, everyone was happy that the war had ended. It was time to rebuild and recover.

My parents made the best decision for me, so I could get the help I needed for my legs. They moved to Milano to be near me. I was too young to remember most of it, but my mother later told me how she made that decision with my father. I know how hard it was for them. They loved us all, but poverty left them no choice but to put me away in a convent with the nuns.

Looking back today, I still believe it was the best decision, or else I would have not survived. I wouldn't be here, writing this book.

I know my parents lived with a lot of guilt for putting me in the convent; but I also know it was the best thing they ever did for me.

Chapter 2

My years in the convent with the nuns in Italy, 1963-1968.
I was five years old.
I was eight years old when my father took me to Sicily to see my family.
My first holiday—one that I will never forget.

I WAS SENT to the Don Carlo Gnocchi convent in Milano. It was a wonderful institution. I didn't think so when I was little, but now I feel it was the best institution, especially in those dark years. From 1945, a plan began to take concrete shape to aid those suffering following the war. Don Carlo Gnocchi was named director of the Istituto Grandi Invalidi (Institute of Registered Invalids) in Arosio, where he received the first orphans of the war and the crippled children. The work began that would earn him the meritorious title of 'father of the *mutilatini*'.

This man was like a saint. He helped so many children with polio. Alone, he opened five institutions for millions of children who caught polio, and also for children who were injured during the war, with either arms or legs missing.

In 1949 the work of Don Gnocchi obtained its first official acknowledgment. The Fondazione Pro Infanzia Mutilata (Foundation

Painting by Lilla Benigno.

for Mutilated Infants), which he founded the year before in order to better coordinate care for the small victims of the war, was recognized officially with a presidential decree. In the same year, the Head of the Government, Alcide De Gasperi, made Don Carlo advisor to the Presidency of the Council for the problem of war mutilation.

From this moment, one new college opened after another: Parma (1949), Pessano (1949), Turin (1950), Inverigo (1950), Rome (1950), Salerno (1950), Pozzolatico (1951).

My father organized everything. I remember the very first time, being in my mother's arms, with her holding me so tight. As we turned the corner there it was, this beautiful, enormous place. It looked like a castle, but in a spooky way. I still remember the car, black and huge. We were both sitting in the back. When we arrived I saw so many beautiful flowers. The convent was in Pessano, Milano.

The year was 1963. I was five years old.

While I was looking at the flowers, I saw a man digging in the dirt, then the car stopped at the front entrance of the convent. I don't remember my father being there, only my mother. As we got out of the car I started to panic. My mother carried me and I could hear the sound of her stilettos, so loud. As she carried me, I was completely paralyzed. Neither my legs, my left arm nor my head were very strong. Sometimes I would flop from side to side. Most of the nerves in my body were dead.

My mother sounded and looked so nice. I stared at her. Every time she put on the red lipstick I wanted some too. When my mother put me on the floor, next to the nun who came over to greet her, I was scared. I watched them talking but I was too little to understand.

Suddenly my mother was kissing me and crying, so I started to cry too. She was saying goodbye to me. When I saw her walking away, I screamed very loudly, calling out to her until I was out of breath. The nun, seeing how exhausted I was, picked me up and showed me where I was going to sleep. She gave me something to eat and introduced me to everyone. I was scared, but I was happy to see other girls; no boys, only girls.

Those heels were very traumatizing for me. They gave me nightmares for many years to come. I missed my parents every single day. Although I managed to make some friends, I didn't understand why I was put in the convent. I was too little. But I felt that void, that emptiness inside, and sometimes when everyone was sleeping I cried, silently, making sure no one heard me; and praying so hard to God to send my parents back so I could go home. All those prayers went unanswered. I remember speaking one day to Sister Maria, a tall woman, with big eyes and gentle hands. She always patted my head gently when she knew I was distressed.

'Sister Maria, if I pray every night, really hard, will God bring my family back?' Poor Sister Maria! She tried to give me the answer I needed, not the one I wanted.

'Yes, Lilla, God always answers all prayers, even yours.' And with that, I kept praying and praying every single night; but inside I started to doubt everything about God. He was not answering my prayers, and I automatically believed He didn't like me, or couldn't hear me.

One year went by with no sign of my mother and father. I stayed in Cessano, Turin and Pessano. Later I also went to Parma for an operation. As the years went by I learned to adapt to this new life. No college I went to was better than another. In each I had my own bed, my own meals, and my own friends.

Physiotherapy sessions were the worst times. They were like torture. When it was my turn for physio I would hide, either under the bed or in the toilets. The very first time I had physio, one of the nuns picked me up and took me to the room where there were lots of children in beds. All of them were crying. The nuns would stretch their legs or their arms, and I could feel their pain. I was so scared.

I didn't want physio, but in the end I had to have it. I was too little to fight back.

When my turn came, I asked the nun if it was going to be very painful. She reassured me it wouldn't, then she laid me on a white bed. It was hard, and the pillow was wet from the tears of the little girl before me. Now it was my turn.

The nun put some powder on my legs and started to massage them. I was lying on my stomach, my face on the pillow. Then, slowly, she began to bend them. It was so painful, but I didn't cry. But when she bent my legs and tied a cord to hold my legs in that position, nearly touching my bottom, then put two bricks covered in a white sheet under them that was when I started to cry. I was screaming, begging her to stop. The pain was unbearable.

She patted my little head and said, 'I will come back in a little while and get those bricks off, okay?' A little while? What was that? One hour, or two, or three? I looked at her with tears in my eyes.

'It hurts,' I said, 'it hurts so badly.'

And the nun replied, 'It's for your own good. You will get better if we keep doing these exercises.'

And she left. I started crying so loud, calling out to my mother. 'Mum! Mum! I want my mum, mum, muuuuuuuuum!' The nun who had put me in that position came over and told me to be quiet. I was a bit scared of the nuns. I kept crying, but not as loud as before.

Some time went by, but eventually the nun returned and took the bricks off my legs. She slowly tried to straighten my legs, and I screamed at the top of my lungs. Then she massaged my legs, picked me up and put me inside a large cubicle. She strapped me in and shut the cubicle with my head poking out.

Later I found out that this cubicle was to help me to breath. The polio had affected my lungs too; not severely, but enough that I needed that cubicle. It did help. After each physio torture, that cubicle for me was like heaven. It didn't hurt, and I breathed much better every time I was put in it.

I endured this torture three times a week. I hated it, but it was good for my legs and my lungs. After a while, I grew used to it. Although I didn't understand at the time that it was for my own good, looking back now, I realise that that torture saved my life. Without it I would have grown worse. Eventually I would probably have died.

I was six years old when my little callipers were ready for me. One of the nuns came over to me. 'Lilla, your new callipers have arrived. Want to come and try them?' I was very excited, and of course I said, '*Si, si, si.*'

She took me into a small room where the doctor who had taken my measurements months earlier was happy to see me. He gave me a big smile. The nun put me into his arms and he sat me on the bed.

'So, Lilla, are you ready now to start walking?'

I was too excited and said 'yes' with a big smile. He carefully put on one little calliper and strapped my leg in. My shoe fitted nicely. I felt no pain. Then he put the calliper on the other leg. I still felt no pain. My new callipers were cool, and I couldn't wait to walk and even run. Instead the doctor told me I had to start walking very slowly, using a little trolley, and get used to the callipers. But as soon as they put me on the ground, I wanted to run. I immediately fell over.

The nun told me to take small steps until I got used to it, and I listened to her. I didn't want to fall over again. Next thing I knew I was outside this little room and walking up and down the corridor. I felt so tall, and free. I didn't have to use my arms anymore to drag me everywhere. Now I could walk.

And as I was walking, I suddenly heard my favourite sound. It was my mother's heels! She was coming to visit me. When I saw her I screamed out, 'Mamma, I can walk, I can walk!'

My mother cried and gave me the biggest hug, with lots of kisses. 'You are doing so well. It's wonderful. I am so happy.'

'Mamma, now that I can walk can I come back home?'

She picked me up, callipers and all, hugged me so tight, and said, 'Not yet, Lilla. When you get a lot better, then, yes, you can come back home.'

I was so happy to see my mother. I couldn't believe she had come to see my first steps. Looking back now I realise one of the nuns must have called her to let her know my new callipers had finally arrived. My mother came for this big event. She witnessed my first walk and cried with happiness. She stayed for a while. When she said good bye again, this time I didn't cry, because I was too busy learning how to walk.

Gradually I grew used to living with the nuns. I had my own bed, my own toothbrush, my clothes were always nice and clean, and I felt safe. I always felt safe with the nuns, perhaps because there were so many other girls like me, or worse, and we were treated equally.

Our days were very simple. Breakfast, lunch and dinner. Sometimes, if the weather was not bad, we would be allowed to play outside until it was dark. We could see the stars. Sometimes we would have competitions to see who could count the most stars.

Life in the convent was very hard at first. Later I found out my tongue was my biggest weapon. I would lash out with frustration and anger towards the other girls. On the other hand, I would gladly help the girls who were badly affected by polio. I always felt compassion towards those girls who found it hard to finish their tasks. Sometimes I would get their plates and put them on the trolley for them, as their arms were too weak; or sometimes a nun would ask me to help one of them eat, because they couldn't do it on their own. When I helped another girl, I always felt satisfied and happy.

There weren't many rules in the convent. We had to watch our swearing. And there were nits. I had short hair all the time, and when my hair started to grow a nun would put a fine comb through it to see if I had any nits. If I did I was sent to the head nun to cut off all my hair. I used to cheat. I would go to the toilet before seeing the nun, and put the comb through my hair over and over again, until all the nits disappeared. Catching nits was inevitable in the convent. It only needed one girl to have them, and it would turn into an epidemic. The only way the nuns could deal with this was to cut off all our hair.

Sometimes the nuns would take us for trips in the bus, to the beach, to play in the sand, without callipers. I remember one particular day as if it were yesterday.

A group of young children, myself included, were at the beach having a great time. The beach was in Turin. I had a red plastic bucket and a yellow shovel. I was digging the sand and putting it in the red bucket, with a big smile on my face. Suddenly the weather started to change, and I saw the tallest wave I have ever seen. I felt an arm scoop me up quickly, and saw other nuns picking up girls and running quickly back to the bus so we could go back to the convent. The nun who carried me made it inside just in time. Back at the convent they put us in a big room called 'sick bay'. Many children were in shock and the nuns too. But the nuns' quick thinking saved all the children.

We needed three buses, sometimes more, to go out. Once they took us to see the Tower of Pisa. I was so amazed. I couldn't understand why it would lean on one side. At one stage I panicked a little, thinking it was going to fall on our bus, but the nun reassured me that it would not happen.

The nuns always did their best to keep us happy. But some girls were so sad. They would cry a lot, especially at night. I used to wonder why they cried so much. I cried too, but I made sure no one heard me. I didn't want to be a baby like the rest of them. I learned to be tough in the convent, and I was getting a bad reputation.

The holidays were the worst time of the year for me. I would be so jealous of the girls whose parents came to pick them up. They were away for at least two months. They would return to the convent with lots of great things: bracelets, earrings, lollies, chocolates. Some girls had everything, and I wanted to kill them. I hated them all, but I wanted to be like them. I wanted my parents to come and get me, but they didn't. Another year. Waiting. Again they didn't come. The following year, same story. I waited for hours with tears in my eyes, praying and wishing that my mother or father would come and take me away for good.

I would watch all the other girls getting picked up by their parents. But my parents never came. At those times I used to feel very sad and lonely.

I wanted to be alone, and I would hide in the back of the convent, near a big statue of Mary holding the baby Jesus. I would sit and talk to her, beg her to send my mother, with tears in my eyes, holding my hands so tight, pretending that Mary was real, and pretending that she would hear all my prayers and see my tears. This was my hideaway. If anyone came there while I was with Mary, I would scream and tell them to go away. It was my spot.

I prayed and cried for so many years, always wishing that my father or mother would rescue me and take me home. To no avail. All this praying and wishing become annoying. I doubted God more and more. I began doubting everything the nuns were preaching to us. I started answering back to the nuns, and now and then I would cop a smack on the back of my head for answering back or being a smartarse.

I dreamt about being someone important when I grew up, such as a nurse or a doctor. I wanted to grow up really quickly, so I could have my own radio with my own music like the other girls. Music was my saviour, and the nuns knew this, because they allowed so many girls to have portable radios. I loved hearing the music so much, and I wanted one too.

I settled in quite well at the convent. I began to build some beliefs and healthy morals: never hit another girl, never steal, never tell lies, and never take another person's life. These beliefs and so much more helped me a great deal, later in life. But, of course, my anger and rage were doing the opposite. I would pick on other girls. Sometimes I would hit them, for no apparent reason; or I would pull their hair, especially those who used to go away with their parents, when they returned from holidays.

I lived in the convent in Pessano, Milano, for a few years. I loved it, but I was always naughty. Nearly every day I earned punishment.

One day I received the biggest surprise I ever wished for; my prayers in the end paid off. My father came to pick me up so I could spend time with the family in Sicily.

I remember the very first time I saw my father when he came to get me. He was talking to Mother Superior and I looked at him, thinking, Wow this man is very tall. I didn't recognize him until he was coming towards my table with Mother Superior. I was eight years old.

I was so excited I jumped off the chair. The chair fell backwards and I screamed out, 'Papa, Papaaaa!' I was the happiest little girl in that convent.

My father hurried towards me and picked me up, giving me lots of kisses. He smelled so beautiful. He was dressed like a business man, with a tie, a white shirt, a black jacket, long black pants and shiny black shoes.

My father was very handsome and so charming. Everyone who met him fell in love with his personality. He was extremely easy going and often quite funny. I loved him tremendously. When I was little my father was my saviour. My father was my hero. I had to put him on a pedestal so I could survive the loneliness I felt.

My father and I were on the train on our way to Sicily. This was the first time in three years that I was going home for the holidays, as so many others girls did every year. I felt sorry for Rita. No one from her family ever came to see her. But my excitement was way too strong. I wanted to go with my dad. I remember holding his hand and going up in the lift. I wanted to show him my bed, number eighteen. Each bed had a number. Under mine was a little suitcase, and my father helped pack some clothes and my toothbrush, and off we went. I was going home. I was going to Sicily to see my mother. I was leaving the convent, finally, and in my head I was hoping it was for good.

I was so happy. While I sat on the train I stared at my dad, and suddenly I asked him something I had wanted to ask for a long time. 'Papa, all my friends have earrings. Can I have a pair too, please?' He looked at me and smiled. 'Of course. I will buy you a pair as soon as we arrive in Sicily.' I hugged him again. This made me so happy.

I put my head on his lap and went to sleep. I didn't want him to leave me. I didn't want him to leave the cabin, and he didn't. He held me close to him. He knew I was so happy that he was taking me home. I felt like a princess.

Finally we arrived in Sicily, and my father kept his promise and went to the jewellery shop. He bought me a pair of gorgeous gold earrings. I loved them. I couldn't wait to return to the convent to show all my friends, especially Rita.

My family had moved back to Sicily. We arrived at the house in Fondo Pistone, Camaro Inferiore, a little town in Sicily. It was a small house, with bunks beds, a big table in the middle of the lounge room, and one bedroom for my mum and dad. In the hall was a big bed for my brothers. We girls, Isabella, Lucia, Stella and I, and Pippo, my younger brother, slept on the bunk beds in the lounge room. My three older brothers slept in the double bed in the next room.

My mother was happy to see me. She hugged me and kissed me. My sister Isabella was happy to see me too.

Dad and I were both very tired from the trip. 'Lilla, you can come and sleep with me if you are tired.'

'*Si, si*, I want to sleep.'

The trip had been very long. I took off my callipers very quickly, going under the blankets and holding my father tightly. I put my arm around his waist, not wanting to let him go, and went to sleep.

Suddenly I heard a baby crying. It was Adriana. She was so little. I saw Mum pick her up from the cot in the bedroom, then turned around, hugged Dad again and fell asleep. I had never met my new sister. Part of me wanted to get up and give her a hug, but instead I went back to sleep. I was very tired.

But when my father and I woke up, I wanted to see Adriana. She was only about two weeks old, and she was so beautiful. Mother carried her everywhere, and I asked if I could hold her. Mum let me hold her for a little while. She looked like a doll, big eyes and so pretty. I smiled at Mum. 'Mum, she's smiling. Look! Look!' And my mother smiled at me.

One morning I went to watch Mum washing the clothes. It was hard work but she made it look so easy. I asked if I could help. She said yes, so there I was, washing the clothes with Mum. It made me feel so wonderful inside. I had never washed clothes by hand before. I watched my mother and copied her. I felt united with her.

A couple of weeks later we moved house. My mother called this house '*Casa della pazza*' ('the house of the crazy lady'). It was a big house but the rent was low. It was on a hill, still in Messina, Sicily, not far from our old house. It had lots of stairs and big windows. I had to use both feet and arms to get around. This is when my hell began, this is when I become incredibly petrified every single night.

I remember an older member of my family coming in late at night, waking me up and taking me to the toilet with him. He was doing things to me that I didn't understand. He would give me *cento lire*, so I wouldn't cry, and was with him sometimes for hours. He would hurt me, and I was too little to fight back or to run away. He did this for many nights, and I was incredibly scared of him, I knew who it was but I was really scared of telling my mother, just in case she would send me back in the college forever, I was too young to understand, but the pain he put me through scarred me for life.

I remember when he would give me *cento lire*, and I would punch his head and beg him to stop, crying and sobbing so loud, I never understood how my parents didn't hear my crying, and then when he was satisfied, he would always tell me not to tell no one about it, and I was scared of him, so I kept it inside me for many years. My behaviour changed right there and then; I knew I was little but I was incredibly petrified, and I wanted to go back to the convent, but I was scared to tell my father and my mother what was happening to me at the time. To stop this nightmare, one night I went to sleep with my older brother, so I would be left alone by this family member, and that did the trick. He stopped, but it went on for a few weeks, and somehow I had to find a way for him to stop and I did.

Because of this sexual abuse that happened to me I started acting out in a real bad way that I didn't understand. I so badly wanted to tell my mother and my father, but being eight years old the fear of being sent away for good crossed my mind so many times, and I felt that maybe they wouldn't believe me. Instead I kept quite full of fear, and I started to withdraw from being an innocent child, into a little monster.

Mum and Dad wouldn't let me play outside because they were afraid I might get hurt. But my sister Isabella always stuck up for me. If any of the children called me names she would run up and scream at them. When I was little, Isabella and I were very close. I knew she was happy when I came home, and I loved being with her. She was one year older than me.

One day I went over to the little bed where my little sister, Lucia, lay. She was about sixteen months old, and was so pretty when she was little. I picked her up and slowly sat her on the windowsill, swinging her, from side to side. I felt she needed some air. We were both inside while Mum washed the clothes outside.

When Mum finished hanging the clothes she came inside and screamed. '*Lilla, non ti muovere tieni la bambina stretta, vengo e la prendo, non ti muovere.* [Lilla, don't move. Hold the baby very tight. I'm coming now.]' I was crying for help, but instead I was acting out in ways that seemed really crazy to everyone.

She grabbed my little sister, turned to me, screamed and slapped me. She thought I wanted to kill the baby, but all I wanted was to play with her. I had no one to play with, and because I wasn't allowed to go outside to play, I put the baby on the windowsill and sat her there, holding her tight. I couldn't even reach the window because I was very little myself. I could barely hold the baby, which was why my mother became really scared. She thought I was going to drop the baby out the window. She was screaming, 'Oh my God! She nearly killed the baby. Oh my God!' I felt like a little devil, but that was not my intention. I just wanted to play.

When my father came home he didn't hit me, but he really told me off. He was tired. He had just come back from work, and Mum told him the story. She told him I was evil, and that I tried to kill Lucia, but it wasn't true. That was the first sign of my acting out.

Of course, sometimes I was jealous of my sisters who were there, at home. I was jealous of my brothers too, but my intention was never to hurt them. I wanted to be part of the family, but because I was disabled I felt I wasn't. I wanted so badly to tell my mother what this family member was doing to me while everyone was sleeping but instead my behaviour became out of control in different ways. I felt a lot of anger, and I felt so alone.

After what happened with my little sister, I felt as though I was the naughtiest child in the world. Everything I did turned into disaster.

One morning the sun was shining, and Isabella and I were sitting outside our new big house, when suddenly Grandpa Franco, my mother's father, came out of his house. He looked so dapper with a walking stick, wearing a black hat, and dressed all in black. As he was walking past me and my sister I screamed out, 'Hello, Grandpa.' He looked at me, then put his hand in his pocket and threw me *cento lire*.

I caught it and screamed out, 'Thank you, Grandpa, thank you.' Isabella and I were shocked that grandpa gave us *cento lire*!

I went inside, so excited I wanted to tell Mum. With a big smile she said to me, 'Go and buy an ice-cream for you and your sister.'

I hugged her. 'Okay, I will, Mum.' Isabella and I went to the shop and bought the same chocolate ice-cream, our favourite. That was the best treat we ever had. We were both so happy.

But we were both tired of eating bread for lunch and dinner. It was hard for Mum and Dad. I was too young to understand why they had only bread, and now and then soup, but those were the only meals they could afford, especially now that the family was growing. More children and mouths to feed.

Being poor was difficult for my parents, but that was the life they lived at the time. I knew Dad used to work, but I didn't know what kind of work. I was too little to understand. Every morning very early my father would get up, and Mum would do the same. She would make him coffee, then he would kiss her, and off he would go to work.

Those couple of months I spent with my family were the best months in my life. It didn't matter to me if they were poor, or rich, it was the time I spent with them that made me so happy. Even though I was going through the turmoil inside me of what had happened to me, I still wanted to be with my family, I still didn't want to leave and go back to the convent, but I had to, I had no choice in the matter, because of my legs.

Sometimes I used to think, Why do Mum and Dad have so many children? Where do children come from, and why so many? But I never dared to ask, because in my mind just spending time with them was like gold. It was as though I was part of the family. And that was really what I wanted, instead of being sent away.

Finally my father took me back to the convent with the nuns. This time I was happy to be out of that house because I knew that this person would not touch me again. But I knew right there and then, that this had changed my life. I was scared all the time and my behavior became out of control, I was always in punishment. Part of me wanted to tell the nuns what had happened to me in Sicily but I didn't know how, I kept remembering his words, 'Don't ever tell anyone, OK?'

The worse acting out that I ever did was when I lied to a nun about having a stomach pain. When I came back in the convent, I was not the same Lilla anymore, I was full of anger, and I would lash out at everyone, even my best friend Rita. One day I smacked Rita on the head when we were fighting. The nun came over and smacked me on the head. I told her I had sore tummy, so she sent me upstairs to the sleeping quarters and told me to wait on the bed until the doctor came around. I didn't have any pains. I lied. I was eight years old.

The doctor came to see me, a man dressed in a black suit with a little black case. When he reached my bed, he touched my tummy. When he touched the right side, I screamed a little. I was acting. It wasn't sore.

Sister Maria, a middle-aged woman, looked as though she had no figure. Her black robe, with a big cross and beads, made so much noise every time she walked. She had a heart of gold. She always favoured the children who never went for a holiday to see their parents. I was one of them, but I was always so naughty, always wanting attention from everyone.

The doctor told Sister Maria, 'This little girl needs her appendix out.'

I wondered, 'What in the world is an appendix?'

Sister Maria was very nice to me, very sympathetic. She prepared my clothes and me, so that I was ready to go to the hospital. She carried me in her arms. I was going to get my appendix out, with no pain. I knew that I was doing that as a cry for help with what had happened to me in Sicily. This family member not only took advantage of my disability, but when I grew up I understood he did it to me because he knew I would be sent back to the convent.

I was too scared to tell Sister Maria that I was lying that I had no pain, so I kept my mouth shut and went along to the hospital. It felt as if I was going for a little holiday. This lie was my cry for help.

I was in hospital for about a week. The operation went well. I was sore for a while, but now my appendix was out, and I felt guiltier than ever.

Then I thought, Maybe it was time for my appendix to come out. I was scared to tell anyone, even Rita. I knew she had a big mouth and loved to gossip. I kept quiet. I never told a soul. I kept this secret for many years. Years later I had the courage to tell my mother and she was incredibly shocked.

I missed my mother and my father, but living in the convent became easier as the years went by and I felt very safe. When I started school, it was the best day of my life. I have always been so curious about every little thing, and I always asked questions of the nuns and other children.

I adored the smell of school. I loved my uniform, the little black dress with a big, white collar. We were only allowed to wear the uniform at school. When school was finished we had to take the uniform off and put on our normal clothes. I didn't have any clothes. The nuns provided them: jumpers, dresses, and underwear; toothbrush and toothpaste, and a little soap. I was good at school. I was eager to learn. In history I always got great marks, and the nuns would pat me on the back for my achievements. My first communion was such a big event. Dressed all in white, with a white veil, I felt as though I was getting married. The nuns told us that many parents would be there, but Rita and I knew our parents wouldn't come. I felt so sad. I didn't want to have this first communion. But when the big day arrived we were all excited.

Thirty of us, all dressed in white, walked down the aisle. The parents of the other girls were looking at us with big smiles. Suddenly Sister Maria, whom Rita and I loved so much, came over and gave us each a gold necklace, with Jesus on a cross. I couldn't believe it. Rita and I had been the only girls dressed in white, with no necklace of Jesus. I was so happy. Sister Maria made me feel so important. Now, walking down the aisle with everyone, I didn't care that my parents weren't there. Sister Maria was like our mother. She did everything in her power to make us happy, and we were. After the communion, fathers and mothers hugged their children. Rita and I watched this, feeling down because our parents weren't there. But we had the present that Sister Maria had given us. It was a big event for so many young girls and, in the end, it was a big event for me too. I could eat the body of Christ, like all the other girls.

I loved praying in church. Praying became my little weapon. I never told anyone how many prayers I said, but I prayed every night when I went to bed. I would talk to God as if he were my best friend. But of course, in the end I gave up. Praying didn't work for me. Was I really so naughty that God didn't answer my prayers? Yes I was.

Chapter 3

My best friend Rita (who also had polio) 1964-1969.

RITA AND I met under very strange circumstances. No one would talk to her. Rita had moles all over her face. Some were really big, some were small, and some looked like warts. The girls always whispered when she walked by, and I heard over and over from other girls how ugly she was. That used to upset me, because I couldn't see any ugliness in her. She was the only one who made me laugh, and she was very adventurous, just like me.

I was very popular. I believed I was tough, and never copped any crap from the older girls. Living in the convent taught me survival skills. I had to learn to defend myself, and that I surely did. Rita was not much taller than me and wore callipers on both legs, like me. One day Rita shouted, 'Who wants to have a race with me?'

I shouted, 'I do,' and quickly we both raced in, putting our callipers on, making our bed, and brushing our teeth. I won that race and Rita was not happy with me.

After breakfast the nuns would send us all outside to play, and I saw Rita sitting alone. She was always alone, but I wanted her to be my friend, so I

Painting by Lilla Benigno.

sat next to her—not too close—and started talking. From that time on we never left each other's sight. We were always together. We became best friends, holding hands… and always in trouble.

Sometimes, in the middle of the night, we would stroll our little bodies down the stairs while the nuns were sleeping, down into the kitchen to steal other girls' chocolate or lollies. Everything was an adventure. We were both cheeky and made a great pair. I was extremely rebellious. Behind the nuns' backs Rita and I got up to all kinds of tricks.

I became worse when I turned nine. My behaviour was out of control. I wanted to punch someone, or pull someone's hair, and I did.

Once, when we were extremely bored, Rita came up with the idea that it would be nice to see what was under the nuns' veils. Being young, I always wanted to know, so I agreed.

We ended up in the ceiling, above where the nuns were dressing or undressing, peeking through a hole. We honestly believed we were going to be punished by God. This was a sin. We knew we shouldn't watch the nuns change their clothes, but we were so excited. The nuns had short hair, and bound their breasts with an elastic boob tube. It was extraordinary. But it was too much for me and I forgot where I was. I coughed. Suddenly all eyes were staring at our hole, and Rita and I panicked.

We made a run for it, laughing so much. But one of the nuns knew our laughs quite well, and minutes later there she was, Sister Maria, looking for me and Rita. We ran outside and sat on the bench, waiting anxiously for our punishment.

Sister Maria was furious. From miles away she started to scream at us. Rita and I were holding hands, and Rita's grip became harder as the nun drew closer. We were terrified. We knew that what we did, although it was funny for us, was very wrong and sinful.

Our punishment that day was to go to our bedroom and go to bed with no dinner. But we talked and laughed so much that the time passed really quickly. Rita and I were very close.

We had an art teacher whose name was Miss Terribile. I didn't understand why that was her name, because she was so beautiful: long, blond, wavy hair, blue eyes, and the little make-up she wore made her look ten more times more beautiful. She was slender and very tall.

Miss Terribile had many problems with Rita and me. Once she put us both in punishment for hours, each in a corner, staring at the wall, because Rita and I had a big fight, punching each other on the floor. Rita had pulled my hair so hard that I started screaming. I punched her on the mouth but it wasn't hard enough, so I wanted to do it again, but Miss Terribile came to the rescue and separated us.

We were each put into a corner, away from each other, facing the wall, and stayed there for a long time. We were there for hours, until one of the nuns asked us what we were doing there. When we told her that Miss Terribile was punishing us for fighting, the nun told us that the punishment was over. Miss Terribile had gone home for the day. She had left about two hours earlier and forgotten about me and Rita.

But Miss Terribile was teaching us a beautiful play. We performed the play to show our parents how good we were. When I started learning the songs, I grew to like it, and was looking forward to the big night.

Rita told me that many parents would be coming to see the play, although I knew my parents wouldn't come. They never came for any important events.

I was so happy when the big day came. While we were getting ready, I looked out from behind the curtains, searching for my parents, but they weren't there.

About two hours later, when the play finished, the audience stood and clapped. We were overwhelmed by it all. I didn't want it to end. Those couple of hours on stage made me feel so alive and so important. I felt like a queen.

Some parents were shouting bravo to their children. Again I searched among the crowd, hoping to see my mum and dad, but they hadn't come. I was sad, incredibly sad. And I was so angry that I picked on other girls until one of them cried. For that I was sent to bed at 6 pm with no dinner. But that night Rita came in and gave me some bread. I was very hungry.

Rita and I spent so much time getting into trouble. Negative attention was better that no attention at all. We were both so sad all the time. We couldn't understand why our parents never came to see our special events. Sometimes we would take it out on each other. Sure we were close, but sometimes I couldn't stand her. It depended how I was feeling. I honestly believed my mother and my father didn't love me because I was disabled. Later in life, I understood why my parents couldn't come, but that didn't take away the pain I felt as a little girl. I wanted to be with my family. I knew it was impossible, and the only way I could deal with this was to block everyone out with my anger.

Every night I had to wear a cast on each foot so they could get better, but something was wrong with mine, because they hurt every time I put them on. One night I decided to take them off, but a nasty nun was on duty that night. When she came over to my bed, she must have sensed that I was not wearing them. She pulled back the blankets and screamed at me, ordering me to put the casts back on. I yelled back at her and said they were hurting me; but she didn't believe me, and roughly put the casts back on.

She pulled the blankets back up. 'If you take those casts off, you'll be in big trouble tomorrow.'

But I couldn't stand the pain. I waited until she had left the room and took them off again. In the middle of the night, the bitch nun came back into the ward, came over to my bed, and took my blankets off again. This time she didn't say anything. She furiously covered me again with my blanket and left the ward. The next morning the bitch nun, tall, sour-faced, with eyes like the devil, came over to my bed with a bandage.

Next thing I knew she was strapping both casts around my neck. 'You are going to wear these casts around your neck all day, and if you take them off you will be in even bigger trouble.' I cried and begged her not to do this. But she didn't budge. I went to breakfast with my casts around my neck, and the other children laughed. I was mortified and humiliated.

After breakfast we went out to play and Ringo, my sweet friend—he was much older than me, walking with a pronounced limp—came over. 'Why are you wearing your casts around your neck?' Ringo had polio too, but he was about twenty years old. He was our gardener. I was very embarrassed but I told him. He was nice about it, patted my head and said, 'A few more hours and you can take them off.'

I never forgave that witch nun for doing this to me, but she didn't last long in this convent. She was transferred to another one. I was very happy when she left.

After a few years I learned to love the convent. It became my home. I had my best friend Rita, and a few other friends. Music helped me escape from my loneliness, anger and frustration. I loved it when the nuns would put on the San Remo competition for us. They would allow us to watch it on television, this little black and white box, and I made sure I sat at the front all the time.

I loved Rita, and to this day I still think about her. I still think of all the trouble we got into. Out of all the girls, we were the worst. But some of the nuns became used to our naughty behaviour, and the punishments weren't as severe as they had been. Some nuns would tell us off, but they rarely hit us, other than a slap around the head now and then. But we both deserved it. We were really rebellious, but I felt alive when I was like that. I didn't like being nice. Being nice felt like dying on the inside; but when I was naughty I felt alive.

Chapter 4

My mother's visit to the convent—Drama, May 1970.
I was twelve years old.

WHILE WE WERE HAVING BREAKFAST, the nun said out loud, 'And today we will say a special prayer for Lilla's grandfather. He passed away three days ago.' The death of my grandfather exacerbated the situation. I didn't know him very well and saw him only a couple of times; but I was upset. However, I told no one about it. Some of the girls were looking at me with sadness in their eyes and I screamed out, 'Stop looking at me!'

After breakfast, I went back to my favourite spot, where the statue of Mary with little Jesus was, and cried for what seemed like forever. I liked my grandfather, and I remembered the *cento lire* he gave me. Sure, he did look strict, but I didn't care. I still loved him.

I was happy to be back in the convent. I had missed Rita. I missed my three meals a day. And I missed getting into trouble. Going back to the convent was like going back to my real home, where I didn't have to share my bed with anyone.

Many of us adored music. When I went to church and sang, I would feel totally at peace with myself. But one of the best things the nuns

Painting by Lilla Benigno.

did for us was to let us to watch a very important event held in Italy: the Festival di San Remo. When the nuns told us the night before to be good so we could watch the Festival, I became too excited and took a long time to get to sleep. The Festival of San Remo was the biggest event for musicians all over Italy, and still is.

I still remember some singers who became my idols. I loved their songs. Singers such as Adriano Celentano, Gigliola Cinquetti, Patty Pravo, Mina, I Pooh, Romina Power, Mal and Albano... These are some of the singers from over the years, and I loved them dearly. Their songs helped me escape the feelings of loneliness I experienced as a little girl. They helped me to survive the childhood pain and hurt I felt most of the time. Music had become my life.

Life kept going in the convent, and the years were passing by. Still no sign of my family, still no letters, or birthday cards, or presents for my birthdays. But when I was twelve years of age the most beautiful thing happened to all the girls still living in the convent.

The nuns surprised us with a band. We didn't know what kind of band it was, but it was the talk of the whole convent. I was very excited. Our theatre looked and smelled like a church. Suddenly the nun was introducing this band to us. The curtains opened and we were shocked. It was all boys! We had never seen a real live band of boys before, and we screamed with excitement. How wonderful and how happy I was right there and then. I don't even recall what kind of music they were playing. I was too excited to take it all in. My head swung from side to side, bopping away to this crazy music. It became a screaming match. All the girls were screaming, me amongst them. The music was very loud and the drums were incredible.

I was having the best time of my life when I felt a nudge on my shoulder. Sister Maria whispered in my ear. 'Lilla, your mother is in the waiting room and she wants to see you. She has something important to tell you.' I screamed at the nun and told her I didn't want to see her, not now. I was having a good time. I loved the band and didn't want to miss it.

But Sister Maria told me to go and see my mother. I stormed from the theatre. I cursed my mother in my head, and wished she hadn't come to see me.

When I reached the room where she waited I screamed at her. 'Why are you here? What do you want?'

I was very rude to her. I didn't want to hear what she had to say. But then she spoke. 'Lilla, you have to come with us. We are all going to Australia. Your dad is already there, but now it's our turn.'

I screamed at her, 'I don't want to come. You come in here years later and tell me you want me to go with you to Australia? Where in the world is Australia? How far is it?'

My poor mum didn't know either. All she knew was that it was a great country with better opportunities.

I had a big mouth. To everything my mother said, I responded with attacks. I remember most vividly when I screamed at her, 'I am not coming with YOU. I want to stay here. You left me here for years and now you want me to come with you? NO, I won't!'

I couldn't see my mother clearly. She was sitting in a dark corner of the room. I could hear her voice but couldn't see her. The room was very dark. I could see a little bit of her legs but not her face or the rest of her body. Then, suddenly, I saw her, as she stood and walked into the light. She looked so beautiful. Her long black skirt covered her knees, with a jacket to match, black with grey buttons. She wore classy black shoes. Her hair was flicked back, and beautiful red lipstick highlighted her perfect teeth. My mother was slim and slender, and she looked so tall when she stood up. I could see that what I said hurt her. Then she didn't want to argue anymore.

She came closer and said, 'Fine. I can't take you out of here by force. If you want to stay you can stay.'

She gently touched my face and walked out. I watched her walking out of the convent. I could hear her high heel shoes. I couldn't take my eyes off them.

I completely forgot about the band. I didn't go back to listen to it. Instead I felt a brick hit my heart. The way I talked to my mother! It was rude, and I knew now I had lost her forever.

I quickly walked away, feeling so sad inside. I went to my favourite spot, to the statue of Mary. I sat there, outside in the garden, and cried uncontrollably. Rita, my best friend, came to ask what was wrong. I told her to go away. I didn't want to talk to her either. I just wanted to be left alone, away from everyone.

The more I sat there the sadder I became. Then Sister Maria came and sat beside me. She didn't say a word. Finally I said to her, 'I'm never going to see my mother again, am I?' Sister Maria was old and fragile, yet there was something about her that I really liked. I couldn't put my finger on it. I learned to love her as the months and years went by.

'You will see her again. Now, now, wipe away those tears and let's pray.'

I put my head down, held my hands together so tightly, and prayed silently, while Sister Maria prayed out loud.

I felt better. We both stood up. 'You can go and play now,' Sister Maria said. 'Everyone is in the front garden.'

The convent was enormous. I would get lost almost every day. There were so many rooms. But my favourite rooms were the sleeping quarters. Upstairs, there was a long hall on one side and another on the other side. We used the old elevators, with two doors that you had to shut. I used to be scared of the elevator. It was creepy and so small inside. But Rita and I, on a few occasions, went right to the top floor, which the nuns kept telling us was off limits. Rita and I didn't care one bit. We were both so curious and mischievous. I loved that feeling, of been so scared, and yet also feeling so strong and unstoppable.

The sleeping quarters had forty beds on each side, with a long corridor down the centre. In the corner near the front entrance was a tent, in which a nun sometimes slept, especially if some children were sick. During the night three or sometimes four nuns would look after us. Some of these nuns were nasty and vicious.

The beds were made of steel and numbered. Mine was number eighteen. Each had the same type of mattress, pillow, grey blankets and sheets. At the other end of the hall was the bathroom, with three toilets and two basins for cleaning our teeth. Beyond the toilets were two baths and two showers. It was easy to slide my body during the night to go to the toilet. I couldn't walk without my callipers. Without muscles in my legs they were very weak. But I became an expert at sliding my body everywhere, and that's how I got around for the first five years of my life.

Two weeks after my mother's visit, my grandmother Rosella, my father's mother, came to the convent. She told the nuns I had no choice but to go to Australia. Everything happened so fast. I didn't even have time to argue with her. I didn't even say goodbye to all my friends. Not even Rita.

My little suitcase was packed, and off we went to Sicily by train.

I remember looking at my grandmother, and noticing how much gold she was wearing. Some of the gold rings on her fingers were so tight and so big. I was thinking, They would be hard to take off. Grandma Rosella smelt so nice. Her beautiful perfume filled the carriage. I think that perfume was so strong it knocked me out and I went to sleep.

We arrived in Messina, Sicily, late at night. That night I slept at Grandma's place. She had so many stairs, and she gave me a hand to climb them. Her house was beautiful, very clean, with lots of beautiful pictures of her and Grandpa Peppe at their wedding. She had many beautiful things I had never seen before, including a big glass cabinet full of nice glasses and other ornaments.

Grandma brought sheets and blankets, gave me a pillow and made a bed up on the lounge. She gave me one of her nighties. It was big but I didn't care. I was too tired. All I wanted to do was sleep.

The next morning I heard a knock on the door. It was my sister Isabella.

I was so happy to see her. She was so tall and so beautiful, with very attractive, black, shoulder length hair. She wore a mini skirt and a little white top, and had big boobs. Mine were only just beginning to show. She and Grandma immediately started to argue. Grandma told my sister off because her skirt was too short, but my sister spoke back and told her to mind her own business. She turned to me.

'Come on, sis, get up. I want you to come with me to see Mum.'

I was so happy. Isabella knelt down to help me put my callipers on. I think she wanted to hurry up and get out of Grandma's place. There was some tension between them, but I was too young to understand why. I was only happy to see my sister and I wanted to go with her.

After I was dressed I said bye to Grandma and thanked her for letting me stay for the night. I had learned about manners in the convent.

Isabella held my hand as we went down the stairs. She knew it was difficult for me. And she held my hand all the way to see Mum. It wasn't far. Boys whistled at my sister, and I didn't understand why. When one boy yelled out, '*Sei bellissima* [You are beautiful],' I looked at Isabella and giggled, not understanding why he said that.

As soon as we arrived, Mum screamed, 'Why did you bring her here?' She didn't want me to see that awful place and was angry with my sister for bringing me there. It was a very dark, small room.

There were so many children. But Mum still came out to give me a big hug and a kiss.

Then someone picked me up from behind. It was my brother Paolo. He hugged me so tightly and gave me lots of kisses. He was my oldest brother, and I was very close to him when I was little. He had a heart of gold and all the girls in town loved him. He was very good looking. 'Want to come and watch a movie with us, Lilla?'

I had never watched a movie in a real movie theatre before. I became really excited and quickly said, 'Yes, yes, I want to come.'

Then he asked Isabella too and she said yes.

I met Isabella's boyfriend, who was also very handsome. He gave me a long, beautiful necklace to wear, with a big heart made of copper. I loved it. It was the first time a boy ever gave me anything like that. This made my sister jealous, but that only lasted a couple of minutes. My brother and sister both held my hands so we could walk faster. They took me to see a movie starring Toto. He was a funny Italian actor. The smell of the theatre reminded me of the convent, of the band that I had watched a few weeks earlier, and I felt the same excitement.

My brother, my sister and her boyfriend laughed their heads off during the movie, but I sat there without understanding it at all. I was just happy to hold my brother's hand. I missed him so much. And I was happy to see my sister.

We had one more day before we had to leave Messina, and I went to say hello to Auntie Caterina and Uncle Franco, my mother's sister and her husband. All my cousins were still small, but Auntie Caterina was so beautiful and gave me a big hug and kiss. She looked like Mum, same features but a little bit chubby. Uncle Franco was wonderful too, and told me how much I had grown up. They were happy to see me, but sad that we were leaving. I slept at Auntie Caterina's place for one night by myself, while Paolo and Isabella went to their friend's place.

Early the next morning, Isabella again came to pick me up and help me with my callipers. She was always in a hurry, but I loved how she always helped me. Those callipers were a drag sometimes, and it took forever to put them on.

As we prepared to board the ship, I hugged Auntie Caterina and Uncle Franco and said goodbye for the last time. The whole family was ready to go. The children were all dressed, and Mum looked beautiful. Paolo, Arturo, Tom, and Isabella were all older than me. The other children were too young to remember this big day. Isabella held my hand climbing aboard the ship: more steps, small and very narrow. Finally I reached the top and stayed very close to the family, because now we had to settle into a cabin. There were so many other people on board the biggest ship I had ever seen.

Below I saw Auntie Caterina and Uncle Franco waving to us. So many people waving to their families. My mother shouted to Auntie Caterina,

'*Ti scrivo quando arrivo in Australia.* [I will write to you when I arrive in Australia.]'

Then my mother started to cry. I couldn't cry because none of my friends were there. This was going to be a journey into the unknown. I didn't know how long we were going to be aboard this big ship. I didn't know how many weeks or months it would to take to reach Australia. I didn't even know where Australia was or why we were leaving in the first place. I was too young to understand, but I sure felt sorry for my mother.

The ship started moving and we were leaving Messina, Sicily. I never saw Sicily again.

Chapter 5

When we left Sicily to go to Australia, October 1970.
I was twelve years old.

THE TRIP TOOK AT LEAST A MONTH. The ship was called *Galileo Galilei*. It was beautiful and enormous. I became lost a few times, and scared because I didn't know how to get back to my cabin. The whole family was in one cabin. There was me, Mum, Isabella, Paolo, Arturo, Tom, Pippo, Lucia, Adriana, Maria, and Stella. The remaining children, Michela and Anna, were born in Australia a couple of years later.

On the ship there was so much to see. There were nightclubs, and a big room containing baths. I loved the bath and used it quite a lot. I went to the movies. Once there was a singing competition, which Isabella entered. When she stood to sing, everyone loved her. She had such a beautiful voice. When she finished everyone clapped so hard, and some people shouted, '*Brava, Brava*.' She loved it. Sometimes I wish my sister had followed that road and become a singer. She was not only beautiful but her voice was extraordinary. That night Isabella won second prize, and she was happy about that.

The Galileo Galilei, *the ship that brought my family to Australia.*

Isabella was thirteen years old but she looked about eighteen or nineteen. She was tall, skinny, with very long, beautiful legs. She was extremely attractive, with an incredibly funny personality. Years later she still has that.

The meals on the ship were magnificent. Steak every single night. Everything we wanted was given to us. Ice-cream, lollies, chocolates. We had landed in heaven. I didn't want the trip to end. But after a month I started to become nauseous. I felt very sick for a few days, and all I wanted to do was get the hell out of that ship, and touch the ground.

Pippo was my younger brother, smaller than me and so cheeky. But he was so cute.

Sometimes he and I would play on the ship, then he would disappear. I was close to him. He was my brother, after all. The nuns had drummed into us for many years the need to love our parents and our siblings. That was all I knew and I put it into practice. I always felt happy when Mum let me hold Stella. She was little but heavy. A lot smaller then Pippo, and still a baby. But a big baby. I smiled at her and she smiled back. And Mum would smile too.

Isabella was always out with my brothers. They would explore the ship and have lots of fun. They were teenagers, always so happy and curious. I was too young to join them, but I did my own exploring. I often got lost, but somehow I always managed to find my cabin.

My oldest brother Paolo met a beautiful girl, with long, black hair. She was French. Paolo brought her to the cabin to meet my mum. Her name was Chantelle. That name stuck in my mind. It was the best name I had ever heard. I remember thinking that if ever I had a child I would call her Chantelle. My brother and Chantelle made a beautiful couple.

After one month of travelling, in August of 1969 we arrived in Port Melbourne, Australia. Finally our feet touched the ground. My father was so thrilled to see us all, and my mother was so happy to see him. They hugged, then my father picked me up and carried me, while my older brothers and Isabella held the little ones, and Mum held the baby. I was so happy Dad was carrying me, and I hugged him tight and kissed him. Then we saw his little car, and my mother said quickly in Italian, 'But, we can't all fit in there! It's too small.' 'We will fit. Watch.'

And one by one we climbed into this small car, everyone squashed together. Some of the babies started to cry. My father sat me in the front, squashed so tightly against the dashboard that I could hardly breathe. I looked at this man driving the car, at his big moustache, and became scared. So I watched the road instead.

The drive was long, but finally we arrived at our destination: it was Palmerston Grove, Oakleigh. Everyone was relieved to get out of the car and, suddenly, there it was, our new home. We stood next to the car and looked at it for a few minutes.

My father moved first. 'Come on, everyone inside.'

We walked along a little pavement and up three steps. I held the wall while climbing the steps. The rest of the family followed into our new house. I would often lose my balance on those steps and fall over.

I liked it as soon as we walked in. My father showed us around. To the left was a big bedroom for Mum and Dad. To the right, the lounge room, with a divan and even a television. Down the hall was another room, the girls' room, quite big, but with only one double bed. 'Where's the rest of the beds?' I asked my father.

'One is enough for you girls.'

I looked at Isabella and frowned. My sister was scared to talk to Dad. She loved him but was afraid of him. She knew him better than I did. I was in the convent for many years, and I saw my father as an idol, my saviour. But my sister had seen many things I didn't know about.

Next to our bedroom was a bathroom. It was a long hall bathroom with a toilet at the end, and a basin on the left hand side with a mirror. The mirror opened and you could put all the stuff we used for our teeth, or shaving cream and razors, into the cabinet. My father always shaved. His face was always smooth and he used a beautiful aftershave called Pino Silvestre. I loved it. Every time he used it the whole house would smell nice. Sometimes I watched him shaving. It was so new to me. I didn't understand why he did that every morning, but I loved watching him because he did it so quickly. He never cut himself and always looked better afterwards.

On the left hand side near the door was a bath, with a shower that hardly worked. We used to bathe a lot so we could get warm. It was always very cold in this new city that I knew nothing about.

Across from the bathroom was another room, smaller, with another double bed, for my brothers.

Next to this was another little room, like a spare room, with one single bed.

The kitchen was big. I observed everything: the big fridge on the left, benches three metres long, a sink in which to wash the dishes, a stove, and a big table about one metre wide and two metres long. Four chairs at the end of the table were covered with a big, flat piece of wood so that everyone could sit comfortably for dinner or lunch.

Then my father took us outside and showed us another toilet. In the garden he had planted tomatoes, olives, and zucchini. So many vegetables, and my mother admiring it all and being so happy. All this was so new to me, after being stuck in the convent for many years. I suddenly felt so free and ready to embark on this new journey.

We all liked the house, and started living and learning this new way of life. My father went to work every day, while my mother looked after all the children. Meanwhile my mother became pregnant again and Michela was born. Then Anna, the youngest of all. Altogether my mother had fifteen children but three of them died. I was the only one who caught polio.

I had never before been in a place with three bedrooms, sharing my bed with all my sisters. In the small lounge the divan was big enough to seat three or four people. I was so happy to see the black and white TV. It reminded me immediately of the nuns, who once a week let us watch TV. They would let us watch Mr Ed, the talking horse. I loved that show, laughing so much, and amazed that the horse talked.

At first things went smoothly, everyone trying to adjust to this place, Mum and Dad together, and me for the first time with all the family. Together. I loved how Mum and Dad tried to make us comfortable, making the beds, giving us pillows, and cooking beautiful dinners every night.

But something didn't go too well for me at dinner. With the nuns, before and after dinner, lunch and breakfast, I was used to saying a prayer. One night in front of everyone I said, 'Does anyone say prayers before dinner?'

My father gave me a dirty look and said, 'No, we don't!'

I felt a brick hitting my heart. I was thinking, Oh my, this is bad, this is bad. I don't want to be here anymore. I want to go back to the convent. I kept hearing those voices over and over again, but I was immobilised with fear. My father's looks were sometimes evil. Although after a while I grew used to his ugly looks, they used to terrify me.

Everything was new to me. The meals, no prayers, sleeping with six girls in one double bed. Three at the bottom and three at the top, we all fitted nicely. Sometimes some of my sisters would have nightmares. Because Isabella and I were older, we would calm them down, patting their backs until they fell asleep again.

I was scared of this family. I didn't want to be there with them all. I wanted so badly to go back to the convent with the nuns. I kept dreaming I was in the convent, and when I woke up, reality would hit me. I was not in the convent. I was far, far away, in a new land, in a new country, sharing the bed with five siblings, but feeling incredibly scared and alone.

It was many months before I had a good night's sleep. I was also having nightmares every single night. Often my parents argued, and I had never witnessed adults arguing in front of me. Two adults screaming nearly every night, arguing, and then silence. That meant they had gone to bed.

I didn't understand why I couldn't go back to the convent. Whenever I asked Mum she would get angry. Her answer was always, 'You are never going back to that place. Get it out of your head. You have to stay here with us, and don't ever ask me again.'

I would always put my head down, but inside I felt that I was going to explode with anger. A hot rush came to my head and I screamed. Then I went into the girls' room and cried. I cried for a long time.

I was so used to sleeping in my own little bed, having three meals a day; prayer and confession when I did something wrong. But not only didn't these people pray, they didn't go to church. They didn't tell us about God, or their beliefs or morals. They only gave us food, shelter, and a bed in which to sleep. When it came to love, support, understanding, forgiveness, talking, and laughing, these things didn't exist. We had the complete opposite. Don't get me wrong. Now and then the good side would emerge, loving and funny. My parents were children themselves. They had never learned to grow up emotionally and psychologically. They did nearly everything on their own. They hardly socialised with anyone. They had very few friends of their own.

I didn't understand their behaviour. I didn't understand why they were so angry all the time, letting it out in really ugly ways, something I had never witnessed before and which left me scarred for life.

My parents hardly ever showed love and compassion to one another. Only occasionally would I see that side of them, and that was the side I loved. I loved when my father used to chase my mother, calling her, '*Hey Ciccina vieni qui. Ti voglio dare un bacione.*'

'Ciccina' was the nickname my father chose for my mother when he was in a good mood. He would chase after her after eating a big block of garlic. 'Come here, Ciccina. I want to give you a big kiss.' And my mother, laughing and running away because she didn't want a garlic kiss from my father. In the end, Dad always caught her and would kiss her; and all the children would laugh and watch Mum making ugly faces.

There were calm times, too, when we would all sit in the lounge room watching a movie, many of us on the floor. I always made sure I was sitting next to either Isabella or Paolo, and I would hold them. When the movie was finished my father would scream with his controlling and loud voice, '*Tutti a letto* [Everyone in bed].' Just his voice sometimes sent shivers up my spine. It was so authoritarian and abrupt. It was so scary we would all get up quickly and go to bed. And if we talked or laughed, my dad would scream out, 'Shut up now. Go to sleep.' And then we would whisper and make little jokes until we fell asleep.

The first few months were great. Now and then my dad was drunk, but he was often a happy drunk. I loved it when he was happy. But sometimes he would turn violent or crazy.

But things started to change quickly. There were so many arguments between my father and my brothers. It was so hard for everyone, because we didn't know the language. We knew nothing about this new land. Australia was big. I'm sure that my brothers, Isabella and I were all in shock for a long time. My father wanted my brothers to go to work right away, and kept screaming about things I didn't understand.

My father worked a lot but it was not enough to pay the bills. There were too many children. The government in those days didn't help families the way they do today, or we would have all been better off, with more food, more clothes and maybe more outings. But it wasn't like that.

Sometimes, when he didn't like something that Mum cooked, Dad would throw his plate on the floor, screaming at my mother and saying things like, 'What is this shit?' The first time I saw him do that I was petrified.

When my mother cooked pasta with brown beans (*fagioli*), I hated it. I couldn't eat it. But my father would order me to eat it, or else I had to go to bed early without food.

My father became incredibly controlling with us, in such a way that he scared us, especially with his mouth. Some of the things he said were so terrible I remember thinking, Is this my father? How can a father talk to his children like that? He was always angry and we copped a lot of his frustrations. I knew he was trying hard but, instead of drawing us closer to him, fear came in and he was slowly pushing everyone away. Not my mother. She was strong. She could put up with his outbursts. She was the peacemaker. She kept his anger a little bit under control.

In the end I got used to eating pasta with brown beans, but when I grew up I made sure I never cooked it myself. But Mum made the best spaghetti, the best meatballs, and beautiful salads, with crumbed, thin meat. It was beautiful. Or she would cook pasta with lentils. I loved that. I always used to ask for seconds, but sometimes, because there were so many of us, there were no seconds. What you got was it.

Mum tried so hard to stop the arguments between my brothers and my father. She always stood up for her sons, and Isabella too. I was too scared to get into trouble, so I did my best to stay out of everyone's way. The best room in that house was the lounge room, where I would hide and watch television, especially when an argument started within the family. Sometimes I would play with my little sisters, while my mother was either sweeping or washing the floors. I was too young to do any cleaning, so I spent a lot of time with my little brother Pippo and my little sisters.

Sometimes people would come to our door and talk in English. My father was so funny. He would say to them, '*Ma va fan culo* [Go and get lost]. I don't understand what you are saying.' And he would shut the door in their faces.

I knew how to speak Italian well, but I found it extremely difficult to understand my mother and father, because they spoke Sicilian dialect. But I still managed to communicate as well as I could with my mother.

I had spent twelve years in the convent, and here I was with a family I hardly knew or understood.

The same thing that happened to me in Italy began in Australia too, the sexual abuse with this family member started all over again. I remember one night he came into our bedroom, and he started touching me inappropriately. Again the memories of when I was eight years old came back to me, the fear, the terror, the anger. I wanted him to stop. I remember I asked my sister to sleep on my side so he wouldn't touch me again, and he came back into the room, and now he was touching her thinking it was me. She was so scared that she told Mum. I don't know where she got the courage to do that, and Mum fixed the door for us so we could lock it, that was the only way he stopped, and he did.

Again my behaviour was incredibly angry and inconsistent, one minute I was happy and then I would be sad and angry. I never understood about emotions in those days, or how to express them, but somehow I learned to put up masks to protect myself from this sexual abuse. Every time I saw his face I felt sick in my stomach, I felt like vomiting, but instead I kept it all in, because that's what our family was like, something goes wrong, you don't talk about it, you sweep it under the carpet hoping that it goes away. Both my parents were incredibly wonderful people, but when it came to in dealing with traumas, they didn't have a clue.

I remember one night we were eating spaghetti. My brother Arturo, the second oldest, was handsome and very cheeky at times, especially with Dad. He always used to answer back to him. But this time my father became so angry, after a few wines with his meal, he stood up while Arturo was playing his new guitar, grabbed the guitar and smashed it over his head. My poor brother saw red, resulting in the biggest fight I ever witnessed in that home. My brother had a lot of respect for my father, but in the end he couldn't put up with his abuse. My brother chased my father, then my father chased my brother. It was like a mad house. Isabella and I made sure we took the younger children into the girls' room and stayed there until everything went back to normal. This fight between my dad and my brother seemed to go on forever.

Although Arturo was cheeky, he wasn't a bad kid. But my father always picked on him. He never picked on Paolo or Tom, only Arturo, and I never understood why. Today I believe it was because Arturo had the balls to stand up to him. My other two brothers were too smart to get out of line. Furthermore, Paolo had a heart of gold, and Tom was always funny. Arturo was a good brother, but for some reason he rebelled against my father. And he had every right to do that. He was tired of being picked on. About a year later he was the first to leave home. He found a good job as a panel beater, started making his own money, found a girlfriend, and left. I didn't blame him at all. I thought that now Arturo had left, my father would change and become calmer, but that didn't happen.

Now he began arguing either with Tom or Isabella. I never saw Paolo arguing with my father. Like my mother, Paolo was a peacemaker. My mother tried so hard to do everything right for my father and for the children. Instead, things were getting worse.

My father decided to take me to meet Uncle Marco, his sister Rosa's husband. Uncle Marco was incredibly happy to meet us all. He showed me the meaning of Australia money. In those days, fifty cents would buy bread or milk or lots of lollies. I was very interested, because I was curious about everything.

Uncle Marco was talking to my father, and I observed everything around me. Auntie Rosa was incredibly beautiful and classy. She was very tall and wore beautiful clothes, earrings, hats, and stunning shoes to match her outfit. To me she looked like a movie star. Uncle Marco was also very tall, handsome and intelligent. While talking to my father he sat behind his huge desk, two metres wide and one metre long, polished black. On top of his desk were papers, and so many pens, all different colours. There was a picture of Auntie and Uncle at their wedding. My uncle was a lawyer, and my father admired and liked him a lot.

Uncle Marco organised for me to go to a special school, then booked me into the Royal Children's Hospital in Melbourne for an operation on both of my feet, called triple fusion. My callipers were wearing out, so he also arranged for new ones. He was a very kind man, and I looked up to him as a god. I loved Auntie Rosa, and they made a great couple. I loved their house. It was incredibly big, and full of beautiful things I had never seen before. They used to collect African statues, and other things I didn't quite understand, such as swords and other ornaments. They seemed very rich to me.

I only went to see Uncle Marco and Auntie Rosa a couple of times, but I adored them both.

The bills were so high in Palmerstone Grove, Oakleigh, that one night we left that house and moved to Chadstone. Although my father worked every day, the money was not enough to look after us all. There were so many of us, and so many mouths to feed. There was not enough money coming in. This was hard for both of my parents, so new in this country, and trying so hard to make things better for us. But it wasn't working, and my father would get drunk and unleash his frustrations on everyone, in screaming matches with my brothers and my mother. I had landed in hell instead of heaven. I kept believing that one day it would all change for the better. We couldn't go through this drama every single day. But we did. We all suffered a great deal of verbal abuse. My father never hit me; but one day he turned on me too, with words that hurt a lot more than physical abuse.

When my father didn't drink he was the best dad in the world, funny, kind, gentle. He would play his piano accordion, with the children sitting on the floor and watching him play. Sometimes if we knew the song we would sing along with him.

But as soon as my father drank alcohol he became brutal, nasty, and he would give us nothing but fear. This was the side of my father I couldn't handle. I loved him so much, but slowly my love for him was deteriorating, and I turned my love towards my mother instead. I knew how bad it was for her, but my mother loved my father with all her heart. And for her, putting up with his outbursts was better than him leaving her alone with all the children.

I started hating wine, because every time my father drank it he would go crazy. One night I got out of bed, went to the fridge, picked up a big bottle of wine, tipped half of it into the sink and topped it up with water. It still looked the same to me. The next day my father asked my mother, '*Ciccina ma come mai il vino e cosi' leggero? Non sento niente e ho gia' bevuto tre bicchieri ma non sento niente.* [Ciccina, why is this wine not strong? I had three glasses and I still don't feel nothing.]'

I looked at Mum, my heart pounding, hoping they didn't know it was me who tipped the wine out and replaced it with water. But my mother said to my father, '*Ma che ne so, tu hai comprato il vino.* [I don't know. You are the one who bought the wine.]' Inside I was laughing and thinking, I am going to do this again, so he will stop drinking. But of course I didn't. I was too scared of getting caught.

All I wanted was for the fights to end. I wanted a loving family. Now and then I would see that there was love, especially when we sat in the lounge room, watching television together, having a good laugh at my brother Paolo's jokes. He always told great jokes, and we all laughed and laughed, even my father. It was rare to see him laugh, but I did a few times. I loved my mother's laughter, and her laughing made me laugh.

I prayed every fucking single night for this war within my family to end.

Sometimes, while everyone was sleeping, I would go to the fridge and drink a few long sips of that cheap red wine, until my head would spin, and I would go to bed feeling drunk and dizzy, praying to God, and hoping that now that I was drunk he would hear me a lot better. Praying for Him to make all this stop, to make all this rage from my father stop. But again my prayers were never answered. I had landed in hell, and now it was up to me to survive, to come up with a plan to get out.

Moving to Australia was such a cultural shock for us. I couldn't speak the language. I had been raised by the nuns with fairly helpful beliefs, and suddenly there I was living with this big family, in this unknown country, and I was very scared. My parents never knew how to communicate. They were too busy producing children, and being children themselves, hoping that someday the children would make them financially secure.

My father had big problems, but he lacked the ability to express them appropriately. He didn't have a great life himself, and all his anger was misdirected towards the family. He used to take it out on the boys. There were always arguments, punching and screaming.

I couldn't stand this family. I felt I was in hell. I thought I was being punished by the nuns because I was always naughty in the convent. I really believed that I had been sent to hell. Little did I know that this was nothing compared to what was ahead of me. Ahead of me was a world of the unknown. A tough, miserable, disgusting, terrible, horrible, crucifying kind of world. I didn't want to know this world, but in the end I had no choice.

I loved my father for a long time, and in many ways I still do, but I also have so much anger towards him. Nevertheless, this book is not about my father or my mother or my brothers and sisters. It is about my own life experiences. I am not here to blame or point the finger at anyone. I am only stating the facts of my own life.

Regardless of the pain I was going through, I was doing my best to gain my father's approval, but in vain. My father could not accept me for who I was. He wanted me to be someone different. Once we were having lunch, when we were living in Bega Street, Chadstone. My father had drunk a couple of glasses of red wine, and suddenly he was in a good mood, happy, and laughing with Mum and the other children. I went to sit on the lounge when my father suddenly picked me up, callipers and all, and sat me on his lap. I could smell garlic and red wine on his breath. I looked at him with a smile, then he said, '*Letteria allora quando diventi grande cosa vuoi fare?* [So, Letteria, what would you like to be when you grow up?]' (Mum and Dad always called me Letteria. That is my real name, but I changed it to Lilla, because at school I used to get bullied about my name.)

I looked around the room and out of the big window in the lounge room. My sisters were waiting patiently for my answer. '*Non lo so,*' I said. '[I don't know.]'

Suddenly my father said, '*Tu puoi diventare una lawyer.* [You can become a lawyer.]' "*Ma che e' lawyer?*' I said. '[What is a lawyer?]'

My father laughed, then asked me to get up from his knee. My calliper was crushing his leg. They were made of iron and heavy for me to wear, but without them I couldn't walk at all.

And then he said, 'A lawyer, Letteria, is someone who makes a lot of money, and when you grow up you can do that if you want.'

I think my father wanted me to be a lawyer like my uncle Marco. I know my father liked him. They probably had something in common, the disease we dreaded in our home: alcoholism.

I did like the idea of making a lot of money. I was so tired of living in poverty. I suppose we were not really poor, but poor enough not to get what we dreamed of. I wanted new clothes. I wanted to be able to go to the movies. I wanted to have my own money and learn what to do with it. But of course in our family there was no such a thing as going to the movies, or going shopping. They were luxuries we could not afford.

We used to love when my mother received money from Dad. She would get all dolled up to go shopping. I never went with her. I had to stay home and look after the children. But when she came back we all knew we were going to have a nice meal that night. We were like little vultures, but happy because Mum used to buy biscuits and Nutella now and then. We loved Nutella. I still do. When I buy Nutella I eat it all in one day. It brings back great memories.

Mum always did her best with the shopping but, of course, being such a large family the shopping wouldn't last very long, sometimes just three or four days. Then we had to wait until my father was paid to get all those goodies again. But somehow my mother always managed to give us food. I never understood how she did it, but every single day and night we had food on our plates. My father's expectations, not only for me but for the rest of my family, were incredibly high. But, of course, unintentionally we all went our own ways, and did our best to learn new ways, without always encountering pain, pain and more pain.

One day I told my mother that I wanted to go for a walk, just to get out of the house, and I took a blanket with me. I sat at this bus stop, not far from my home, and hid my legs and callipers beneath this blanket. I was so tired I wanted to die. All I was thinking about was how to die with no pain. My thoughts were about killing myself, about not wanting to be disabled, and about wanting a better, loving family, without hate and anger.

The blanket did the trick. Everyone could see me, but not my callipers, and I felt a sense of relief. I could hear car horns beeping, and wondered who they were beeping at. They were beeping at me! I couldn't believe it. So many cars, with gorgeous guys, one after the other. Latest model cars in the 1970s, Chargers and Monaros.

I loved them. They looked so groovy and sounded like trucks. So many cars going by and beeping their horns! So many guys waving and screaming out, 'Hi, beautiful. You're gorgeous. Come with us, party, and party.'

I was loving the attention. It baffled me, because at home no one ever told me I was beautiful. No one ever said I had beautiful eyes, or that I was smart. I was feeling loved and wanted. I felt like a queen. I even had tears of joy in my eyes. I couldn't understand what the fuss was all about.

Men and boys calling me beautiful made me feel a little bit important, and I really liked that feeling. But there was still the little voice in the back of my head. 'You're not beautiful. You're ugly.' Many hours went by but it felt like only ten minutes. I went to that bus stop feeling sad and miserable, but after all that attention I felt happier. Now it was time to go home. When my mother asked where I had been, I just smiled and said, 'Nowhere in particular.'

In the lounge room I kept of thinking of all the boys that day, beeping their horns; and all those beautiful compliments from strangers. Some of the guys had been extremely good looking. I was on cloud nine. But once back home I felt sad again. The high lasted only for a few minutes. I was back in this reality, back in my own prison.

I desperately wanted to go back to the convent. A big part of my life had been ripped apart, and it felt as though no one cared. I was just part of this family and I had to shut up and stay quiet about it. Many times when I fought with my mother I used to say, 'Why didn't you leave me in the convent? I hate this family.' And I did, at the time. Of course I loved all my brothers and sisters and my mother became my angel. But my father became my worst enemy. I was really scared of him.

Once my mother bit my little finger. I had lost it completely with her, and felt a hot blood-rush of rage. I screamed so loudly that Mr Smith, our next door neighbour, heard me. I was scared of him, especially when I found out he had a wooden leg. He lost his leg in World War II. He would take it off, and I always wanted to see it but was too scared to ask. I had been in Mr Smith's home to see Trish, his daughter. She was our new friend, living right next door. Mr Smith heard my screams and called out, 'Leave that poor girl alone or I will call the police.' My mother rushed up to me and that was when she bit my finger. I screamed even more.

I cried so much that day, and all because Isabella had been sitting in the lounge. Mum had told me to start cleaning up the bedroom, and I was doing it, but when I went into the lounge I saw Isabella sitting watching TV. I screamed at Mum in the kitchen, 'Why is Isabella sitting in the lounge? If she doesn't clean, I won't clean either.' And off I stormed into the bedroom.

Next thing my mother came into the bedroom, yelling at me. 'Clean up now.'

I screamed back, '*No va fan culooooo.* [NO! Go and get lost.]' And this is when my mother bit my finger so hard that it bled. And Isabella was laughing, still sitting in the lounge room. But our arguments wouldn't last long. I would come out of my bedroom, after I cleaned it up, and go up to Mum. She would smile as if nothing had happened. I would smile back and we would make up.

When Mum and I made up, or Isabella and I made peace again, it was great. I loved it when I was happy at home. I loved it when my mother laughed and when my father was in a good mood. Paolo sometimes made jokes about my disability. He would say things like, 'Lilla, why don't you put roller blades on and go down the shop for me?' I loved this, because he made me see the funny side of my disability. He never put shit on my disability. He made me see it differently, from the funny side.

Paolo loved to play the trumpet. He also loved to play the organ, like my father, and he still does, although he doesn't play the trumpet anymore. He has an organ in his home, and when I saw him for a holiday in 2013 he played a few songs, and was unbelievably wonderful.

Arturo loved to play the guitar and sing. When he played I thought, How in the world does he do it? I looked up to my brother because I adored music. He sang 'Crocodile Rock', by Elton John, and did it better than Elton. My brother's voice was unreal, and really beautiful. But Arturo didn't pursue music either. He achieved other beautiful things in his life.

Tom loved to play the drums, and Isabella loved singing. She had a beautiful voice. But neither of them pursued musical careers. They moved on to other things. Stella, my younger sister, and Michela also loved singing and had beautiful voices. Later in life I also learned how to play the guitar and wrote a few Italian and English songs. All our family loved music. It was our escape.

At times I felt invisible, as if I didn't belong with this family. It was neither their fault nor mine. I had spent many years in the convent and I didn't know how to get close to them. There were just too many of us.

Sometimes I would become a mother towards my little sisters, who would wake up because of the arguments. Isabella's and my job was to keep them quiet. Sometimes I would sing songs, or invent a little story until they went back to sleep. I was very close to Stella, and always cuddled up to her and Michela.

Emotionally and psychologically I was a mess. I was losing my mind. I was so tired of listening to all those arguments. I had to find a way out. I had to find a way to save my own sanity, but how? I surely didn't know.

I was tired every morning, and sometimes I would skip school to catch up on my sleep. When all the children were going to school, Mum finally found some peace. She always kept the house spotless and got the dinner ready for us. Sometimes she was so tired. She would sit in the lounge, and say, '*Ooo che stanchezza*. [Ooo, I am so tired.]' I would feel sorry for her. She did so much for all the children and for Dad.

Chapter 6

My mother—1971-1974.

MY MOTHER WAS BORN in Messina, Sicily. Her parents, both born in Sicily, had five children. My grandfather died when he was fifty-nine years old and my grandmother died at the age of eighty-three. My grandfather could play the guitar, and my grandmother would sing. They were both very good and loved doing this in their spare time. Grandfather was very strict, but he never hit his children or abused them. But nor did he give them much freedom.

When his first grandson was born, my grandfather felt he was too young to be called grandfather and told his grandson to call him uncle instead. My mother was very close to her own mother, as I became very close to her in later years.

My mother was very beautiful. People stared at her. Her skin was soft and velvety. I loved her skin, and her smell was always pure and clean. I looked up to my mother, but things turned the day I arrived in Australia. I adored her, but over time, as my hopes faded, I became angry towards her.

My mother told me the story of her first encounter with my father. She was carrying two chickens under her arms, and when my father passed

Me and my mother, a painting by Lilla Benigno. RIP, I love you always.

her he whistled. She lost her balance and one of the chickens ran away. My father ran after it and, after a little struggle, returned it to her. Sparks flew and they fell in love.

They were married in their early twenties.

My mother had a beautiful heart, which she needed to look after so many children. She cooked lots of spaghetti, pasta with lentils, pasta with broccoli, *pasta e fagioli* (pasta with potato). She was the only mother in the world to make perfect pasta, no matter what kind it was. Her cooking improved over the years. She taught me several ways of making pasta, and I still cook it today.

I loved my mother's smile. She had perfect teeth, a beautiful mouth, and such a petite nose. She always smelt clean. When my mother used to put on her red lipstick before going out, she would smile, and her teeth sparkled behind that smile. I would look at her in admiration, thinking, Wow, my mother is beautiful.

Now and then I would stay with my sister Isabella when she used to live in the Collingwood flats, and this was when my mother and I would catch up and go out. I was about twenty years old. On our way to bingo, as I was holding my mother's arm, a bird suddenly pooed on my head and I screamed. My mother laughed and laughed, almost to the point of hysteria. I had tears of embarrassment in my eyes. Cars were passing and beeping their horns. I am sure a lot of people saw that big white shit on my head that day. Luckily my mother had a big handkerchief in her bag and wiped the dripping shit off my nose, eyes, and cheeks. Laughing even more, she said it was impossible to get the shit out of my hair. We were running late for our bingo session, and I hated being late. I would feel all eyes on me because of my disability. The fewer people who saw how I walked, the better I felt.

My dear mother turned to me and said, 'You know that bird shit brings you luck? You will win tonight.' She started laughing again.

I looked at her angrily. 'It's not true.'

Laughing like a little girl—and that laughter always made me laugh too—she said, 'You will see.' We finally arrived. Now and then I could smell bird shit, and hoped no one would notice the white patches in my hair. Mum and I went to get our tickets, and when we sat at our table, my sister Isabella came in, bought her ticket, and sat with us.

Mum told Isabella the story of the bird shit, and they both started laughing so hard, until the bingo started. The first to win was my mother, but she shared her prize with another lady. My mother always won. She was very lucky. That night I did not win, and proved to myself that bird shit does not bring good luck. I gave my luck to Mum instead because that night she won not once but twice. She was happy. I was too, although I was mortified by the incident.

Two nights later I went to bingo again with five of my sisters, and I won the jackpot of $1000 dollars. Of course, I shared my winnings with my sisters and mother.

There is another bingo story I remember as if it were yesterday. My mother, Isabella, Carol— a very dear friend of ours—and I all decided to go to bingo. We were late already, and Isabella was looking for Carol everywhere. We finally saw her coming down the alleyway. In those days we lived in the Collingwood Flats, which were all Housing Commission properties. Way too many people lived in those flats, from different races, backgrounds and all walks of life. But we all liked Carol, who had a heart of gold. She had no teeth. She couldn't afford new teeth, and we used to call her *sdentato*, toothless. But we loved her company. She had two children, a couple of cats and a husband who looked like Frankenstein, but we still loved her.

We saw Carol coming and Mum and I screamed at her, 'Hurry up, Carol. Let's go. We're going to be late.'

'Can I quickly change?' she screamed back.

Isabella, who was always impatient, shouted, 'No, no time to change. Let's go now.' I was sitting in the front of Isabella's car, Mum and Carol sat in the back.

Suddenly, Mum says in Italian, '*Ma sento fedo di merda*. [I can smell shit.]' Isabella and I looked at each other and laughed.

We finally arrived at bingo, and I was really happy because the caller was a very handsome man. I had seen him calling bingo before, but tonight I felt like flirting. I was on heat. Every time, one week before my periods, I would have these strong sexual feelings, and the only way for me to act it out was by flirting with good looking guys.

We collected our tickets and sat at our table. Carol sat opposite me, between Mum and Isabella. Again my mother said, '*Ma che e' stu' fedo di merda?* [Why do I smell shit?]'

'Mum, stop it.' I started laughing more and more, but then bingo started.

After a while I looked at Mum and said in Italian, '*Mum, ma ti sei cacata di sopra, sento puzza anche Io.* [Mum, did you shit yourself? I can smell it too.]' Mum laughed so hard, she started missing the numbers. I laughed even harder. People tried to quieten us down, but the more they did, the more we laughed. I had tears in my eyes. I couldn't see the numbers. My mother stopped playing that game.

She couldn't stop laughing. The whole bingo room now stank of shit.

At the start of the next game Isabella said in English, 'I can smell shit. Where is it coming from?' Carol looked at Isabella with those sad eyes, then at Mum, but said nothing. She just sat there looking very sad. During the break I went outside by myself for a cigarette, and next thing I knew the bingo caller came out to say hello. Everything happened so fast. We went behind the wall and kissed passionately for about ten minutes.

He stopped and said, 'You are very beautiful. I love your eyes.'

I smiled and wanted to tell him how great a kisser he was, but instead I said softly, 'Thank you,' and he went back to call the numbers again.

When I returned to the table, my mother looked at me and laughed. 'Two hours to smoke a cigarette?'

I couldn't tell her I had just kissed the bingo caller, so I just said, 'Yep,' and sat down with a smile on my face.

Carol went to the toilet, and my mother said, 'It's her. She smells like shit.'

'I think you're right, Mum,' said Isabella.

'I wonder if something happened to her?' I said.

We had a great night, but back in the car the smell of shit became worse and worse.

The next day, Isabella visited. 'You know why we could smell that shit?' she asked. 'Because Carol got into a fight minutes before we went to bingo, and she didn't have time to change.' At first we felt so sorry for her. Who would want to bash Carol? But then I remembered that Carol did have a big mouth, and she did talk about other people a fair bit. She was not liked by many people. But we didn't care what other people thought.

'I nearly had a heart attack from that smell,' said Mum. 'I was right all along.'

I start laughing, then Mum followed and finally Isabella. We couldn't believe we took Carol's shit with us to bingo. Later, Carol also laughed about this incident.

When they brought out the pokies, my mother and I started playing them instead of bingo. That was more fun. My mother and I won more and more money, but lost lots of it too. I loved dressing up with Mum and heading out to the pokies. We both loved it. Any excuse to leave the house.

Sometimes my mother would say things that really hurt me. I never understood why she belittled me, made jokes about me in front of my siblings. It hurt me so much. I didn't want to be treated like that. I didn't want her to make humiliating jokes about me. When she did, I stood up for myself, and this is where all our arguments began. The more I stood up for myself, the more she would put me down.

I once asked her, 'Mum, am I beautiful?'

She answered abruptly, without looking at me. '*Certo.* [Of course.]'

But I didn't believe her. I felt I was carrying their shame about my disability, both Mum's and Dad's. I felt unworthy of being alive. I wanted and needed so much love that I would go to any length to get it from them, but to no avail. Instead, her humiliating jokes became worse as I grew older. They made me feel worthless and ugly, and my love for my mother slowly faded away over the years, as with my father. I felt I was nothing to them.

One day, at the Spastic School Centre, the teachers decided to let the girls try some make-up. I put a little on and the teachers told me I looked beautiful. They encouraged me to leave it on so I could show my mother. Black eyeliner made my eyes, which are green, look bigger. A little powder, some mascara, and a beautiful light red lipstick, and I felt beautiful. I couldn't wait to show my mother my new look.

George, the bus driver, who became one of my best friends, also said I looked beautiful. When Mum opened the door to me, I said quickly, 'Mum, today the teachers let us wear make-up. Do you like it?'

She became so angry, slapped my face and screamed, 'Go and take that shit off your face before your dad comes home.'

I was mortified. Tears rolled down my face. I went into the bathroom and screamed out in Italian, '*Ti odio.* [I hate you.]' I removed all the make-up and went into the bedroom and cried. I wanted to die. All I had wanted to do was show my mother my new face. It was like a project for me, something new. I had never worn make-up before and I wanted to show her I was pretty, as the teachers had said. Instead I received a big slap that made my ears ring.

That night my mother told my father what had happened with the make-up. He just said, 'And what is wrong with that? She just wanted to try it.' But my mother gave me the dirtiest look. I was happy my father took my side. Many times he did take my side, which is why sometimes I didn't want him to go to work. When he was home I knew my mother wouldn't pick on me. But when he was at work, she would start putting me down, telling me to do things around the house, or to look after the children while she hung out the clean clothes.

I loved my mother very much, but the more she started treating me like shit, the more my love for her began to fade. Slowly, slowly, in place of love I felt anger. There were many questions in my head. Why does she treat me like that? Why doesn't she treat my sisters and brothers like that? Much of the time I felt she didn't want me there with her, and didn't want to look after me. I felt she didn't love me, because if you love someone, you don't put them down. You do everything in your power to make them feel special and wanted. But that was not the case with my mother. I couldn't stand it any longer. My hatred for her was getting out of hand.

My mother had her favourites. She would hug and kiss Stella and my other sisters, showing so much affection towards them. But when I tried to get close to her she would push me away. Sometimes I sat on the lounge next to her, while she was holding either Anna or Michela. For me, just to feel my mum's skin next to mine was enough. I felt happy. I was very naughty all the time at home, but that was because I wanted to be loved. I wanted her to see me like my siblings. But she didn't know or understand how to show that kind of love for me. Because of that, I had no confidence. I had no self esteem and felt incredibly ugly.

Sometimes I would go up to her and tickle her, and when I did that she would laugh. I would even put my hands on her boobs, and she would laugh uncontrollably like a little girl. Then I felt so much love towards her. But on days when she felt down she would turn on me and put me down.

My thirteenth birthday was the worst day of my life. It was my very first birthday with the family, and I said to my mother, 'Mum, today is my birthday.'

She looked at me angrily and said, '*Non ho soldi, non posso fare niente vai via.* [I haven't got any money. Get away from me.]' She pushed me, and I lost my balance and fell on the floor. I didn't hurt myself, but the anger inside was so strong I went into my bedroom and bawled my eyes out. My eyes were sore from crying. All the other children were at school. I know she heard me crying, but she just carried on with her chores.

That night when my father got home he was in a happy mood, but my mother wasn't. I sat at the table and my father immediately asked my mother, '*Che ha la picciridda?* [What's wrong with the little one?]' My eyes were red from crying all day.

'It's her birthday today, but I can't get anything for her. I have no money.'

My father put some wine in my glass and said to everyone at the table, 'Let's sing Happy Birthday to Lilla,' which everyone did. But my mother didn't sing. She was furious. She hated when my father took my side.

'When I get paid,' my father said, 'I will buy you a little present.' But that was a lie. When he was paid a few days later he came home drunk, and there were more dramas and fights with my mother.

Two months went by and it was my sister Stella's birthday. My mother asked me nicely to go next door to borrow some money from our neighbour. When I asked why, her reply was, 'It's your sister's birthday today. We have to get her a cake.'

I couldn't believe it. I went to get money for my sister's cake, but I was furious. That night everyone celebrated, but I got up from the table and screamed out, '*Vi odio a tutti.* [I hate you all.]' I went to the bedroom and I cried again for hours. Then Stella came in with a piece of her cake for me. I kissed her, with tears rolling down my face, then I ate it. It was beautiful.

Stella was growing up a little now, and she could see how Mum was treating me. Isabella could too. But they were closer to Mum because they had lived with her all their lives.

One night, during another of Mum and Dad's arguments, I heard my mother scream out, 'Since she has been here with us we've had nothing but bad luck. She is like the devil.' I knew she was talking about me, and it was then I realized my mother blamed all their problems on me. I was shocked to hear this, and again that night I cried and prayed to God, wishing I could vanish from this house for good. But, of course, I would wake up and nothing had changed.

I was angry with my mother for many, many years. I ran away from home partly because of all her put downs, because of the love I did not receive from her when I needed it most. She must have loved me when I was little, but when we arrived in Australia, as I grew up she distanced herself from me, and I was too young to understand why. Instead I was hurt and many times humiliated. Whenever I joined a conversation, I was instantly put down by her humiliating remarks. It was then I started believing I was stupid and worthless. It was then that I strongly believed I was not part of this family. I was a stranger to them all. I began to hate my disability even more. I believed my mother and some of my siblings didn't love me because of it.

Chapter 7

My father—1971-1974.

I ADORED MY FATHER, especially when I was young. He was a very tall man, handsome, skinny. He walked with a slight limp. Later I learned that he was really sick as a young boy, and after he went to the hospital he was not the same beautiful boy. He was angry and became very rebellious.

He was an amazing musician. He knew how to play so many songs, which he learned by ear. The song he played that I loved the most was 'Blue Moon'.

He loved to play the piano accordion. Every time my father played a tune I would go into a different world. Music has always been one of my biggest escapes, my passion.

During the day he worked as an upholsterer, and some nights he used to play in clubs or pubs for fun and, later in life, for money.

When he was happy, everyone around him was really happy too, but when he was angry, watch out! All hell broke loose. We would hide in our bedroom and stay out of his way until he cooled down.

Painting by Lilla Benigno.

He had a great sense of humour, but in one respect I think he was a very sick man. He had the idea that, although his children were growing up, they had to do what he said all the time, and this could not be so.

I could see his expectations of what a family had to be. Some of his opinions were wonderful and I still follow them today; but many were sick-minded, and some of us ran away from home just to get away from the dramas and clashes.

My father was my idol for many years. I looked up to him more than to Mum in those days. For years I was very angry towards my mother. I remembered when she had left me in the convent.

But somehow I had to keep one parent alive, so I chose my father and made him my saviour. He was my world. I loved him tremendously, more than Mum. I needed a rock to lean on and he was that rock for me.

He had many faults, but I didn't care. I loved him unconditionally. When my father came home from work, always tired after a ten hour shift, I was so happy to hear that doorknob turn. When I saw him I would scream out, '*Ciao, Papa*.'

With a big smile he would ask, '*Ciao Lilla, tutto a posto?*' I would smile, 'Yes, *tutto a posto* [all is good].'

Then he would go to Mum, and sometimes he would give her a kiss or a hug. Then we would get ready for dinner.

Later we would sit in the lounge. I loved spending time like that with my parents. I felt close to them and very safe.

We never understood where my father's anger came from, but when we grew up we realised the sacrifices he had made just to put food on the table and pay all the bills. Not once were we short of anything. We always had what we needed, but not what we wanted deep inside.

I remember one day my mother told my father that I had screamed at her, and while she was passing around plates full of spaghetti, I gave my father the dirtiest look. By now I really hated what he was doing to us. Next thing I knew, he threw his plate full of spaghetti, just missing my face. We were all in shock, and I was terrified. There was pasta all over the floor.

My mother screamed at my father, and my father screamed at me. 'You ever look at me like that again I will hurt you. You are very lucky that the plate didn't hit you. Very lucky.'

I was furious. Mum gave my father another plate of spaghetti and, because there was none left, I went into the bedroom and cried and cried, as usual. That night I went to sleep starving. No food, only terror. I kept seeing that plate passing my eyes, only inches from my face. I couldn't believe what he had done. I had never witnessed violence like this before. I had to find a way to survive, mentally and physically.

But my father never put me down. He never said humiliating things to hurt me, the way my mother did. And because of that, I felt I still loved him, although I didn't like him when he was drunk. My father could not handle alcohol. When he was sober he was a beautiful man, but when he was drunk he would lose his marbles. He would lose the plot completely.

On one occasion my father decided to throw a party. He bought meat for the barbecue, beer, wine, and a bottle of brandy. He really loved his brandy.

We were all excited. A party just for us? What was the occasion? I asked Mum, and she calmly responded, '*Niente*, nothing, he just wants to get to know the neighbours.' I thought, Hmmmm, something is not right here.

The party started, and our next door neighbours, Johnny and Trish, came over. I loved Johnny. I would spy on him through my window while he wasn't watching. Especially when he took off his shirt while fixing his car. I loved his body. He was sexy. But my father hated Johnny, because he had long hair and never wore shoes. My father used to call them bludgers, because they never worked. Well, that's what he thought. No hopers, losers.

Isabella and I were sitting together on the grass, eating our steak with bread, when Johnny came to sit between us. I became aware of my father watching us with evil eyes.

I had only had one beer, but it went straight into my head. Feeling dizzy, I blurted out to Johnny, 'You don't like me because of my legs, true?'

Johnny was shocked. 'Not true. Why do you say that?'

I stood and stuck my finger up to him. 'Fuck off.'

I left him there. With some little effort I made the three steps without falling over and went back inside the house. My head was spinning so much I had to lie down and shut my eyes. My disability made me believe that everyone hated me, even my next door neighbours.

I went into the boys' room and Paolo my older brother was lying in there on the single bed. I could see he'd had a bit too much to drink too. His face was like a ghost. So I flopped on the other single bed and shut my eyes.

Suddenly I heard all this noise, and Isabella was screaming, running from one room to another. My father was chasing her with a belt. They came into the room where Paolo and I were resting, and my father lashed my sister with the belt. I turned away in shock. I wanted to scream. I wanted him to stop. Then Paolo woke up and stopped my dad from hitting my sister.

I felt so sorry for Isabella. She hadn't done anything wrong, other than talk to the young man who lived two doors down from us, Luke. My father saw her talking to him, and that's when he went crazy and started hitting her with the belt.

That party was a disaster. It was then that I realised something was really wrong with our family. But when you are thirteen years old, how can you comprehend this? This was when I learned how to put up masks, so I could protect myself.

The more wrong things I saw, the more I fantasised about leaving home. I believed that if I left home I wouldn't have to go through all these panic attacks, shed all these tears, and be so afraid. I was prepared to go to any lengths to stop these ugly feelings. I wanted love, but not at that price. All I saw was abuse. It was like living with an atomic bomb. You never knew when it might explode. You had to be mentally ready, and sometimes I wasn't. I would cry myself to sleep. Sometimes I would go to the fridge and scull down my father's cheap red wine. I wanted this pain to stop. I wanted all this hate and anger to stop. But I didn't know how to stop it. I could only do my best to stay sane and strong.

Sometimes I would look at Mum and think, How can you do it? How can you stay in this relationship? I couldn't understand why she didn't stand up to him. Later I realised my mother was very co-dependent. She relied completely on Dad. Her biggest fear was to be left alone with the children, in this unknown country.

Sometimes I really felt sorry for her.

One night my father returned from one of his so-called 'down the pub' nights. As soon as he walked in Mum started screaming at him. It was very late. I woke up and opened the door slowly, to see what was happening in the lounge. I saw my mother scratching her face over and over again with her long fingernails. While I was watching in terror, my little sister Stella woke up and wanted to go out into the lounge. I grabbed her and said, 'Go back to bed.' She would have been shocked to see what was going on, and she may even have been hurt if she went out there.

My father was very drunk, but when he saw the blood flowing from my mother's face, he changed quickly and began to be nice to her. I was in tears. I felt so sorry for my mother that night. I didn't know what the argument was about, but I was petrified. I cried and cuddled up next to Stella. Crying silently, I went to sleep.

The next morning we saw my mother's face, covered in scratches. I wanted to hug her. I knew she was in pain. But I helped in other ways, by cleaning my room and the bathroom. Whenever I wanted to do something good for my mum, I would clean for her. I never liked doing the dishes, but when I knew my mother wasn't well, I would do them.

I would sweep and even wash the floor for her, while she was in the lounge room crying. I saw my mother cry once too often. These were the times I would do anything in my power to make her feel better. And she would come up to me and say softly, '*Grazie Letteria.*' There were the times when I wished my father would die and disappear forever, but I kept all this anger inside me. I knew if I stood up for my mother and said something to him, he would get angry and probably lash out towards me. This was the source of my strong panic attacks.

Chapter 8

*August 1971—My encounter with pop singer Johnny Farnham.
I was thirteen years old.*

WHEN I WAS THIRTEEN years old I went to the Children's Hospital in Melbourne for the operation on my feet. I was there for six weeks. The plaster had to stay on my feet for six months. The first question I asked the doctor when I woke up was, 'Can I walk normal now?'

'Well, you will walk a lot better than before, with less pain.'

I cried, because I wanted normal feet. But I felt better when Mum and Dad came for a visit. I gave them a smile. I remember asking Mum, 'Mum, do me a favour. Can you close that gap where my feet are? I can't move.' My legs were raised on a piece of wood and I couldn't even sit up. My mum quickly did that for me, but I was so ashamed because a little boy, a bit younger than me, was pointing at my fanny. I was starting puberty, and this little boy kept looking and laughing at me. My mother quickly fixed the sheet for me and kissed my forehead.

'Am I going to be normal, Mum? Can I run like everyone else?' I watched her anxiously, waiting for the right answer. 'Mum?'

Digital art by Lilla Benigno.

She told me I would walk a lot better, and quickly added that she had two pieces of great news for me. First, Johnny Farnham, a well-known Australian pop singer, was coming to the hospital to visit all the sick children, including my ward. He was a wonderful singer whose career was booming. He was beautiful. I had seen him singing on television. I loved all his songs and wanted to marry him.

The other news was that Mum and Dad had decided to send me to Yooralla, a support centre for people with disabilities, in the suburb of Balwyn, until my casts were removed. Our home didn't have wheelchair access, and I needed that more than anything else at the time. I was happy with both pieces of news, but the best news of all was about Johnny Farnham.

I was really happy when Auntie Rosa, my father's sister, came to visit. She gave me lipstick and a powder for my face. The powder was very white but I didn't know that, because I never wore makeup. I never thought about it. Mum and Dad had their rules, and when I was young I followed them. I thanked Auntie Rosa, and she kissed me on the forehead. I asked Mum and Dad if I could keep these presents, and they said yes. This made me very happy, because I wanted to look beautiful for Johnny, and this make-up was going to help me do that.

By now I had had a few operations in Italy and I knew what the procedures were. They put you to sleep, and when you wake up you have good feet. I always believed that with each operation I was going to walk normally. I was living in denial, especially at that age. And, of course, each operation made no sense to me, because sometimes I would be worse, and sometimes I would be a little better. Every time I had an operation I went in with such high expectations. Especially this time, because I really believed Australian doctors were much better than Italian doctors. I went in believing that I was at last going to walk normally, like my sisters and brothers.

When I had visitors at the hospital, I felt part of the family. I felt that Mum and Dad did love me. I really loved this soft, caring side, and I wished they were like that all the time.

But my mind was on Johnny Farnham. I was anxious to see him. I couldn't wait to put on the powder that Auntie Rosa gave me. I wanted to look beautiful for him.

I didn't sleep well the night before. I tossed and turned, eager for the night to fly away. Then I started getting pains in my feet. I pushed the button and my favourite nurse came quickly to my bed.

'Are you okay?'

I looked at her with sad eyes. 'I can't sleep. I keep thinking about Johnny, and my feet are very sore.'

She laughed. 'I will make you a cup of hot Milo to help you sleep, and will give you a tablet for the pain.'

A few minutes later she returned with hot Milo, and I took my tablet. The pain stopped and the hot Milo was nice. This finally sent me to sleep. At last the big day arrived.

When I woke up I could feel my heart was pounding so quickly, knowing that at last I was going to see my idol. Johnny Farnham was now in the hospital, and he was doing his rounds. I had to do everything in my power to look nice in front of him.

The nurse I liked was still there. She washed me and changed the sheets. I felt clean. Then she gave me my powder and my lipstick.

'You don't need much of this,' she whispered, 'only a little bit.' I smiled. 'Okay.'

A little boy about nine years old, with a cast on his left arm, came over and asked, 'What are you doing?'

I gave him the dirtiest look. 'Get out of here or I will punch you.' I could be nasty sometimes. If I didn't like someone, I would let them know right away. He laughed and off he went.

I opened the face powder. There was a little mirror. With the little round sponge I started putting this powder on my face. Only I couldn't stop. I got carried away. The more powder I put on, the more I looked like a ghost, but I thought that was normal. The nurses were laughing. The whole ward was laughing.

I didn't care. I just kept on putting it on and on and on. And then, my first sneeze. I don't know if I was allergic to it, or if there was just too much. Johnny Farnham was coming any minute, and I was white as a ghost, with no lipstick!

I thought I might look better with the lipstick. So I put that on, and I looked like a clown. But I didn't care. I still liked it. I wanted to make a big impression in front of my idol.

Pale pink lipstick with a ghost face. The nurse I liked came quickly to my bed and whispered,

'Johnny is coming. You've put too much powder on your face. Let me take some off.' But I pushed her hand away. 'Noooo, I like it.'

And suddenly there he was, standing there, looking so tall, so pretty, much better live than on television.

I was angry with the nurse, who was trying to make me take some of the make-up off. 'No way! He is here.'

My heart was beating so quickly I thought it was going to burst out of my chest.

I was sneezing every five minutes, one after the other, and it was rather annoying. I didn't think it was the powder. I thought I was coming down with a cold. I wanted to jump out of bed and into his arms, but I started sweating and sneezing. The damn powder was killing me. Johnny looked around the ward, four beds north and four south.

I was in the south and our eyes met for one second. Then I sneezed again. I couldn't stop sneezing.

He looked so handsome, clean cut with blond hair. He was dressed in black with a white shirt. He looked so clean and perfect. Such a pretty face. I felt both numb and excited. I was so happy to see him, to finally come face to face with my idol, the man who used to sing 'Sadie, the cleaning lady'. This excitement and joy lasted for hours.

While I was looking at him, my face began to itch, so I started scratching the powder off, leaving wild marks on my face.

The cute nurse that I pushed away earlier was still laughing. With my hand I waved for her to come over. She came quickly to my rescue, trying her best to take off some of the powder before Johnny came over to my bed.

Finally he was next to my bed with his crew. I was so happy I wanted to faint.

Then, in a soft voice, he asked 'How are you?' He looked at the head nurse and said, 'I didn't know you had pretty girls in this hospital.' Then he gave me a big smile, and asked, 'How are you?' I thought, He thinks I'm pretty. Yeah! But I was very shy and all I could say back was, 'Good.' Then I put my head down, feeling embarrassed. No words would come out. I was in shock.

Then Johnny took a big doll from a box full of toys, came over to the side of the bed, leaned over and said, 'This doll is pretty, like you. It's yours now. I hope you have a wonderful Christmas.' I thanked him, and became shy again.

I still wonder, many years later, what Johnny really thought about my white ghost make-up. I didn't want him to leave. I wanted to hug him. I wanted to kiss his cheek. I wanted this visit to last forever. But he went to the next child and left me there, with a broken heart, a ghost face, and a lipstick that didn't match. I was a mess.

I was over the moon for days and days and days after that. And the doll? I gave it to another little girl who I left behind in that hospital. At thirteen years old I was too old for dolls. But that had been the best moment of my life.

Johnny Farnham finally left the ward.

'Come on, let's get that off,' said the nurse, referring to my make-up.

It took at least twenty minutes to wash it all off, but it didn't worry me. We all laughed so much that day. It remains a wonderful memory, and I am sure that nurse remembers it too.

I stayed in hospital for six weeks. By the end of my stay I was close to so many children and staff. I knew everyone. I was a social butterfly. I was well liked by the staff and other children. I always did something to make them all laugh.

Sometimes a new bully, either a boy or a girl, would come, and I would put them in their place.

I couldn't stand rough kids picking on little ones. No one would do that in front of me.

After the operation I was sent to Yooralla, in Balwyn, and I stayed there for nearly a year. I loved it there. I met so many children like me. After six months, when my casts came off, I had physio for four months. Then I was sent back home. While I was in Yooralla, I learned what boys were about, I learned how to smoke cigarettes, and I learned more about freedom.

Chapter 9

November 1974—Glen Waverly High School, and why I got expelled.
The party that my older sister Isabella and I went to.
I was fourteen years old.

AFTER YOORALLA my parents decided to send me to Glen Waverly High School. The taxi would come every morning to pick me up and take me to school. The government was paying for that. After school the taxi would be there to pick me up and take me back home.

Finally I was sent by my parents to a normal school. I was so tired of going to all those special schools. I wanted to see and feel what it was like mixing with normal children.

I loved school. I loved everything about it. I loved the teachers. I loved some of the pupils. Some bullied me, but I would brush it off and stick with the older girls. I became very good friends with Toni, a blond-haired girl, taller than me, very attractive and two grades above me. Every lunch break we would go up to the oval so we could smoke cigarettes.

I loved the fact that so many children didn't care how I walked or looked. They just went to their class; and when school was over, there were so many goodbyes to say every day.

I was becoming popular. Many young boys would look at me, but only when I sat down. As soon as I walked they pretended not to see me, and that hurt. I always felt normal, but I didn't look normal. That was very hard for a teenager to understand.

I had been going to Glen Waverly High School for six months and I was very happy there. I felt like a queen. But one day something terrible happened.

This particular day in art class I was feeling very angry inside. I loved art, although I was never really good at it. One girl, a bit taller than me, with black hair and freckles on her cheeky face, said, 'Move over, you crippled wog.'

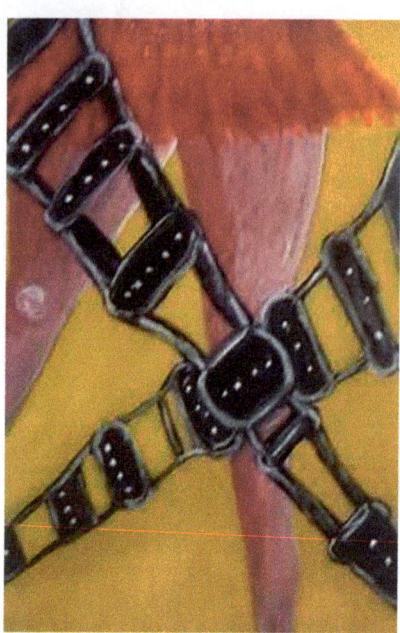

Painting by Lilla Benigno.

'Crippled wog?' I saw red. I felt a hot rush from the bottom of my feet to the top of my head, and I exploded. Before I realised it I had a chair in my hand and brought it down so hard on her head that the chair broke. The blood flowed from the big cut on Julie's head.

An ambulance came to take Julie to the hospital, and I was sent to the principal's office. I realised then that I was in big trouble.

When I walked into the principal's office I was scared that I might go to jail. The principal asked me to sit down. He gave me a piece of paper. All he said was, 'You give this to your parents. You are expelled from this school. We do not tolerate children as angry as you. You are excused. Go home and give this letter to your parents.'

I felt bad for what I had done, but I was also happy. No one calls me a crippled wog, no one. In those days, immigrants, whether Italians, Maltese, Chinese—anyone who was not Australian— would receive a lot of verbal abuse from some Australians. The word 'wog' was an insult. There was no way in the world that I was going to do nothing about it. I knew I hurt Julie, and in a way I felt sorry for her. But I would not tolerate little shitheads like her. I felt good because I had stood up for myself. Sure I wasn't Australian, but she had no right to call me that. I hated the word 'crippled' too, and still do today.

I was also really scared that when I got home I was going to be in trouble with Mum and Dad too.

When I arrived home from school I was very angry. I went up to my mother and screamed, 'Mamma, I'm not going to that school anymore. Everyone calls me bad names. Everyone looks at me as if I'm a freak. And I'm so tired of being bullied by the other girls.'

Mum gave me a long look. 'Okay,' she said. '*Stai a casa, ma se stai a casa tu puoi aiutarmi a pulire okay?* [Okay, don't go to that school anymore; if you want to stay home you can, on one condition, that you help me in the house.]'

I was very surprised and said with a big smile, 'Yes, okay, I will help you.'

When Mum said I could stay home, I went into the toilet, ripped the principal's letter into little pieces and flushed it away. I didn't want to show the letter to my mother. Anyway, she couldn't read or speak English. She wouldn't understand it.

When I left Glen Waverly High School my world turned upside down. This was when I started going downhill, really quickly. I didn't want to help my mother around the house. I didn't want to clean. I hated having baths. I didn't even want to clean myself. My mother once told my father that I hadn't washed for six days. My father put the hot water in the bath and screamed, 'Get your clothes off and go and have a bath.'

I screamed back, 'No, no, no.'

My mother ripped off my clothes and dragged me into the bathroom, with her hands under my arms. I couldn't even fight back.

She put me in the water. 'I will lock this door. I want you to wash yourself properly. Then I will come in and help you to get out.'

I started to cry. I didn't want to wash. I wanted to stay dirty. But with tears in my eyes I washed myself everywhere. Then I called out to Mum to give me a hand, and she did, with a clean pair of undies and a clean nightie. She dried my hair, dressed me in my undies and nightie.

'I want you to have a bath every second day. If you don't I will tell your father, and we will both drag you in here again.' Then she asked, 'Now do you feel better?'

'Yes,' I said quietly. She took my hand and we both sat in the lounge room.

When my father saw me nice and clean he said, 'Now you look much better, *brava, brava*.'

After I left Glen Waverly High School, I began to have panic attacks about water, and I really couldn't understand where they were coming from. My mother and father watched me for a few months, to see if I did wash. They knew something was wrong but didn't know what. Then, after a few months, it went away.

After I left school I was very depressed, always stuck at home, cleaning with my mother, watching her cooking for all of us, always behind her like a little lost soul. I wanted to tell her how bad I was feeling. I wanted to tell her that my legs made me unhappy every single day. I wanted to tell her to send me away to the convent again. But I kept all this inside. Wherever I turned I couldn't see a way out. Now that I was home with my mother twenty-four hours a day, my life was more miserable than ever. I wanted to die. I wanted to disappear. I wanted to chop my legs off and replace them with plastic ones. I wanted so much love, but felt rejection instead. My soul was disappearing. I felt I was no one, alone and incredibly miserable.

I was also very bored. Mum doing her chores, cleaning, washing, cooking, then cleaning, washing, cooking. The same things every single day. I wanted to find out about the world. I wanted to go out. I was curious all the time and wanted to learn.

One day I asked my father if I could go to a party. I lied to him, telling him that no boys would be there, only girls. If I had told him boys would be there, he would never have allowed me to go. So I lied and manipulated

Dad for half an hour. 'Please, Dad. We'll be back at 11 pm. No later than that, I promise. There are no boys, only girls. Please, please.' I was shocked when he said yes, I could go. The big day arrived. At the last minute my father changed his mind. He didn't want me and my sister to go. I guess he was scared. But somehow my mother managed to change his mind and told us we could go.

Isabella and I were really excited. My father gave us money for a taxi there and back. So we called the taxi and off we went.

The party was in an old garage, full of young teenage boys. There were at least fifteen young boys. My sister and I were the only girls. We started drinking shots of tequila, beer and scotch, and talking to all these young boys. Laughing, listening to the same song over and over again: Peter Frampton, 'Show me the way'. I loved that song, and it was the only song we heard all night.

After a couple of hours I was so drunk that I pissed myself, on my black skirt, while I was sitting on an old granny chair. I was too ashamed to get up and walk to the toilet. I didn't want the boys to see me walking. I was too embarrassed about my callipers.

I told my sister what had happened but she was so drunk she laughed it off. Some of the guys started going home. It was after midnight, and we had promised Dad we would be back by 11 pm. We were so drunk we had forgotten about Dad and the time. One of the boys called us both a taxi. We asked the driver to stop at the top of the street. We had to be very quiet. We didn't want to wake Mum and Dad, or we would be in big trouble.

I was so drunk and my callipers made so much noise when I walked. 'How in the world am I going to go down the hill?'

Isabella laughed. 'Lie down on the ground and roll down the hill.'

'Okay. It will be a lot faster too.' And I did. I lay on the ground and rolled. But my callipers were so noisy! I was so sure someone would wake up.

At the house Isabella very quietly opened the back kitchen door. That was the only way we could get in. Suddenly the lights came on, and there he was, my father, in his underwear. I could see one of his balls hanging out, and I started laughing. But my sister was too scared to laugh.

My father screamed at us, waking everyone, my mother, my brother and a couple of my sisters. My mother rushed into the kitchen and screamed at my father, while he screamed at us, calling us bad names in Italian: '*Puttane, disgraziate*'. He was really angry, but finally cooled down a bit and told us both to go to bed. We had to go past him to get to the bedroom, and I received a slap on the back of the head.

He did the same to my sister when she walked past. We were in big, big trouble.

All I wanted to do was go to sleep. I wasn't scared of my father, not while I was drunk. At 6 am he came into our bedroom, woke me and Isabella and said, 'Get up *puttane, e pulite tutta la casa*. [Wake up sluts and clean all the house.]'

Mum was scared of him, but she fetched two buckets of soapy water, and there I was with Isabella, on my knees, without my callipers, washing the fucking floors like a slave. We washed the kitchen floor, but we both were so sick. We had terrible hangovers.

Actually I was still drunk, very drunk.

After that incident, Isabella decided to run away from home. She too had had enough of this madness.

And now I was alone. Without my sister there was no way I could live in that mad house. I had to find a way to escape too. But how? How was I going to run away, and where would I go? The thought of sleeping in the streets didn't enter my mind. I was way too young to think like that. But I had had enough of this physical and psychological abuse from a man who was supposed to be supportive and loving towards his family.

My father was such a beautiful man when sober, but when drunk he would try so hard to hurt everyone feelings. He believed he was saying helpful words, but they weren't. They were very abusive, and sometimes I believed all those bad words.

Before going to sleep I would play back in my mind what he used to say, over and over again, until I started crying. Then I would finally fall asleep.

His words were very damaging spiritually and psychologically to me, so one day I thought: Fuck this. I need freedom. I can't live here anymore. I don't care what happens to me as long as I am out there on my own where I can do what I like and fuck everyone else in this world. I had had enough of living in fear. I'd had enough of worrying about my sisters and my younger brother, about me and my mum. We all were on shaky ground.

Chapter 10

February 1971–1972—My first suicide attempt. I was thirteen years old. My last suicide attempt that landed me in the Glen Waverly Rehabilitation Centre.

I WOULD HAVE LOTS OF NIGHTMARES and now that my sister Isabella and my three older brothers had left home, I was now the oldest of the family. I wanted to die. This was when I became more protective towards my younger siblings. I was also getting closer to my mother. I was learning to respect her and love her more than ever.

I was missing all my friends in Italy, and I was missing my friends from Yooralla, but I couldn't talk to my mother about it. I kept having memories of the sexual abuse in Italy and here in Australia too, sometimes the nightmares would wake me up full of sweat. Every time I mentioned it, she would shrug it off, saying she couldn't do anything about it. I was missing my best friend Rita. I was missing the nuns, my bed, and my three meals a day. I was missing school. I loved school tremendously, and now I was stuck with this family I hardly knew. I cried every single night. I felt so alone and incredibly confused. I had wanted to run away since a few months after we arrived in Australia but, instead, the easy way out was to kill myself. The first time I wanted to die I was thirteen years old.

Painting by Lilla Benigno.

Then, one year later, when I was fourteen, I really meant it.

One morning I woke up and asked my mum if she wanted anything from the shop. Her reply was, 'Yes, I need milk.'

So off I went to the shop. I bought the milk for Mum, but left it on the counter. Then I asked for a packet of Aspro.

I went to the back of the shop, and the little boy who lived in the shop came and sat next to me. 'What are you doing?' he asked.

'I want to kill myself.'

'How?'

This little boy was such a chatterbox, overweight and with red hair. He had freckles on his nose.

'I will take all these tablets,' I said, 'and then I will die.'

'How can you take all those with no drink?'

He was drinking a small bottle of Coke, so I snatched it from him. 'Now I have a drink.' I started taking all these little white headache tablets.

This boy always told me he liked me. I said to him, 'If you tell anyone I will bash you.'

He promised he wouldn't tell anyone, and I was not interested in little fat boys with big mouths. All I wanted to do was disappear forever.

I walked back home, dizzy from all the pills. I told Mum I wasn't feeling well. She told me to go to bed, but I began vomiting up this green stuff. My mother panicked. She wanted to get the doctor but they couldn't afford it, so she made me a nice soup. I heard Dad come home from work, and he asked Mum how I was. For the first time I heard how sad they were because I was sick. I wanted so much to tell Mum what I had done, that I had tried to commit suicide, but I didn't have the heart. I was scared to say such a thing, so I let her look after me until I felt better. I was in bed for three days. I kept vomiting green stuff, but after the third day I started to feel better. Those headache pills were finally coming out of my system. Now I wanted to get better quickly.

The only time I was noticed by Mum and Dad was when I was sick. I loved Mum's caring side, which made me feel alive and part of the family. As soon as I got well again, things went back to normal for a while. Then the arguments would start all over again.

The second time I tried to commit suicide I intended to make sure of it. I wanted to take stronger pills, so I bought another small packet of Aspros, and this time I intended to take them all, not just ten or twenty of them. There were fifty small pills in that pink packet. Again I went to the back of the milk bar. Instead of taking one tablet at a time, I would take five or ten, put them in my mouth and drink my lemonade. I took the whole packet, and now I knew I was going to die. I couldn't wait for it. The pills started to kick in, but I didn't want to be found by anyone, so I started walking. This time I was not going home. I headed in the other direction. I began to feel disorientated and dizzy. I nearly fainted.

As I was walking past a white house with a white fence, I vomited. An old man who was sweeping his veranda rushed to see why I was vomiting.

'Are you all right?'

With a husky voice I replied, 'I want to die. I think I'm dying soon.'

I sat on the front of his veranda and closed my eyes. Everything around me was spinning and blurry.

This old man, who couldn't walk fast, went quickly into his house and called the police and the ambulance. Within minutes both police and ambulance arrived.

I started to drift in and out of consciousness. The only words coming from my mouth were, 'Please don't take me back home. Please.' They reassured me that they wouldn't.

The policewoman kept asking my name, but I didn't want to give it to her for fear that they would take me back home. She promised me that if I told her my name she would take me to a safer place, where lots of children like me were there for the same reason.

'Lilla,' I said. I didn't want to give her my surname.

The police woman kept her promise. First they took me to the hospital. I had tubes everywhere, and they pumped out most of the pills. A few days later I was discharged and taken to Glen Waverly Rehabilitation Centre.

I woke up in a beautiful room, with two single beds. On my right another girl slept. I lifted my head to see where I was and saw the biggest mirror. I had such a fright. I looked like a ghost. The first thing that went through my mind was, Why am I still alive? My second thought was, Where am I? Had I landed in heaven?

A stocky lady walked into the room. She was a nurse, and she told me about this place. I was now an inpatient and had to obey all their rules. I had no choice but to take the pills the doctor in charge ordered for me. They were called 'anti-depressants'.

Slowly I started to get to know this place. I was there for nearly a year. It was run by doctors, but it reminded me so much of the convent. Everything we did was structured by the staff, and we even had a matron. I later discovered I didn't like her one bit, and I was always in her office because I was in trouble.

The rehabilitation centre in Glen Waverly was full of teenagers from all walks of life. Some came from broken families. Some were there because they tried to commit suicide. Others were there because their parents had had enough, dealing with their disability. And some were there because they were completely nuts, crazy, lost souls.

I was learning for the first time in my life how to communicate. I was learning how to speak with people and interact with them, and I was enjoying it. I was put in a classroom where I learned how to type. I had never used a typewriter before and I liked it. Typing classes were the best because they kept my mind occupied. The staff used to run dancing or dressing up competitions. I won once, when I dressed like a gypsy.

I won an old fashion record, a double one, full of piano accordion music. I hated that prize because it reminded me of my father. Whenever I had memories of my father I would have a panic attack. I threw that record in the bin.

After I won that record I escaped. I went to the pub next door, the Graham Greene Hotel. I wanted to get completely drunk, and I did. The security guards of that hotel took me back to the rehabilitation centre. The staff at the rehab put me to bed, and I was warned about seeing the doctor the next day.

I was in trouble.

Sure enough, I was in the doctor's room, being told off by the doctor in charge. He told me that if I kept going the way I was, I would be kicked out.

Three weeks later another incident occurred. I smoked dope in front of many people there, and I was kicked out. My chances at Glen Waverly Rehabilitation Centre had run out.

That night I slept in the streets, in the park, cold, no food, no drinks, just a few sleeping pills and a little grass that someone had given me in the pub.

I stayed on the streets for couple of days, then became scared again, paranoid that someone would kill me or bash me. That was one of my biggest fears. The rest I could handle. I became so scared I decided to go back home to my parents.

Chapter 11

May 1973–1974—My first love John, and my rescuer.
I was nearly fifteen years old.

THE DRAMAS AT HOME hadn't gone away. Dad was becoming worse as time went by, his tantrums of madness now occurring on a regular basis.

This was a really crazy way to live, not only for me, my little sisters and my small brother but for my mother too. I kept thinking how strong she was, how courageous to put up with all this madness.

I would pray and talk to God nearly every day to make all this better.

I was missing my big sister terribly. I wondered what she was up to, and thought how lucky she was to be away from home.

I was getting worse. I started chewing my nails and smoking the big cigarette butts my father left in the toilet. I was a bundle of nerves.

One day I asked Mum if she wanted anything from the shop, and she said she needed bread. I volunteered to get it for her. Poor Mum. I always tricked her, especially when I knew she needed either milk or bread. Pippo, my little brother, was too small to go to the shops, so she would always

'Me', Digital art by Lilla Benigno.

send me. Sometimes I would take my little sisters for a walk, but this time I didn't want to take anyone. I wanted to run away. Every time I left the house I felt a sense of freedom, even if it was only for ten or fifteen minutes. I felt like getting out of the house. My mind was on how I was going to run away.

How could I run? With my legs I wouldn't get far.

I walked to the milk bar and bought the bread. As I was leaving, the same young boy who witnessed me taking the pills approached me and said, 'I know this man that wants to meet you. He likes you a lot, he told me.'

'Really? What's his name?' 'His name is John.'

Suddenly I felt nice inside. It was great to hear that someone liked me. In my house only Paolo, my big brother, made me feel special. But now he had left home. Sometimes my mother made me feel special, but the rest were too little, and my father was losing his marbles from this damn alcohol. I didn't feel the love I needed. When I heard that someone liked me, instead of running away I decided to go back home. I wanted to meet this man. I wanted to see what he looked like.

I asked this little boy, 'Do you think he wants to meet me?'

With the biggest smile he said, 'He does want to meet you. Can he?'

I was so happy now. Finally someone liked me. Finally I had the key to getting away from this insane home. Finally I was going to be married and free from this madness. 'Tell him to come and see me tomorrow at my home. I want to meet him.'

The little boy was so happy and quickly ran away. Then he turned, stopped, and yelled out, 'I am going to see him now and give him the news. He will be so happy to meet you.'

I lowered my eyes but felt so thrilled inside. I felt as though I might explode with happiness. I was going to meet the man of my dreams, and I was so ready for it. I was so tired, living with a family that I simply could not understand.

The next day I was extremely excited. I hadn't even met John yet, but my fantasies took me into another world: marriage, love, passion; a beautiful long wedding dress. I wanted to marry John.

My father was at work. My mother was sitting in the lounge watching something on TV. Dinner was already prepared, and I was in the lounge with Mum. We heard a knock on the door. Not the front door but the back door.

'I'll go and see who it is,' I said.

As I walked all I heard was the clunk of my callipers. They were getting old and rusty. At the door I saw a man, tall, handsome, with a little goatee. He had beautiful, dark brown eyes.

I smiled and said, 'Hello, are you John?'

'Yes, it's me.'

I felt so shy. Suddenly he pulled his hand from behind his back and gave me a gorgeous small bunch of flowers. I was very surprised.

'Are those for me?'

John smiled at me. 'Yes they are. Do you like them?' 'Yes, yes I do, thank you.'

I had never received flowers from anyone before. I was in shock, and now I was in love. When he gave me the flowers he said, 'They are beautiful, just like you.'

My heart was beating so quickly, and I'm sure I went red in the face. I felt a hot rush all over my body.

My mother suddenly walked into the kitchen and screamed out, '*Ma cu' e'?*' in her Sicilian dialect. '[Who is that?]'

I looked at my mother with fear in my eyes. I didn't want her to see John. I quickly said to him, 'Hurry. Get out of here before my mother sees you.'

He gave me a little note. It was his address. With a big smile I said, 'I will come and see you tomorrow.'

But it was too late. My mother saw him and saw the flowers. 'Who was that, Lilla?'

'No one, Mum. Just someone who wanted to give me flowers, that's all.'

When John left, I went into my bedroom and looked at the flowers, and the note with his address, over and over again. I was in love with John. That night I couldn't sleep. I kept thinking of our wedding day. I couldn't think straight. All I had in my mind was the thought, I wonder if John will help me to run away.

I saw John as my way out of this prison. I wanted to run away so badly, and part of me knew that he was the key to my freedom. My thoughts of escape became stronger than ever. I knew deep inside that I couldn't run away on my own. I needed someone to look after me, and he was perfect. He was not the best looking guy, but his charm won my heart, and I was prepared to run away with him, anywhere, as quickly as possible.

The next day I told my mother I wanted to go for a walk, but instead I went to visit John. He lived only two blocks away, with his grandmother. Both his parents had passed away in a terrible car accident, and he lived behind his grandmother's house. It was like a little granny flat, and had everything in it, a double bed, a shower and toilet, a small kitchen. He told me he never cooked. His grandmother did all the cooking and washing for him. He was a loner. He had no friends, but he had a heart of gold, always giving me compliments, always telling me how beautiful I was. And I believed him. He made me feel special and wanted, and that was all I ever wanted. Not being ridiculed, put down by my mother. All I ever wanted was to be loved.

I poured my heart out to John, told him how unhappy I was living at home, told him how strict my parents were, and how they didn't love me as I wanted to be loved. I told him how I had already tried to commit suicide twice. He couldn't believe how I was treated.

The more I saw John, the more I wanted to be with him. He was the first man to like me for who I was. He didn't care about my disability. He kept telling me that. Hearing that someone really didn't care about my legs was new to me. I became very close to him. I really believed I fell in love with him. I asked him once, 'John, I want to run away from home. Can we do it? Soon?'

He was twenty-eight years old and I was fifteen when we met. He was a tall, skinny man. He stank of bad body odour, but because I liked him so much I could put up with it. He was gentle with me, always holding my hand when we walked anywhere, so I wouldn't lose my balance and fall. He had high cheekbones and gorgeous eyes. He had a couple of missing teeth, but I didn't care. He was so good to me, and that's what I loved about him. For once in my life, someone liked me for who I truly was.

After a few months begging him to run away with me, he was ready. He wanted to do it. It was our biggest mission. We planned it all, bit by bit, until one day he felt he was ready, and so was I.

One day John asked me, 'Should we run away to Mildura?'

I was so scared and yet so excited. 'Yes! Yes! Yes!' I jumped on the bed and kissed him on the mouth. I didn't want to stop kissing him, even without his teeth. I was in a different world. I was so much in love with him, and the thought of him loving me in the same way made me more eager than ever to run away from home. I was ready. I wanted to run and run and never look back.

I thought I was deeply in love with him, but I wasn't. I knew deep inside that he would help me get away from this madness I was living in.

It took a couple of days to get organized. I fixed my stuff with Social Security (Centrelink), and John stole money and jewellery from his grandmother. It was a lot of money. I didn't like that idea. I actually felt sorry for her. But the more money we had, the further we could run.

John called a taxi to take us to the train station. We were leaving Melbourne at last, heading for Mildura, to live there forever, away from my family.

When we arrived at the station I was incredibly scared. I was scared that my father would call the police because I was underage. I didn't understand all that stuff about being underage. I didn't understand the repercussions of having sex. My mind was not on sex. John and I never had sex. We only cuddled or kissed now and then. My mind was on how far I could go, so that no one from my family would ever find me.

I remember asking, 'How long is the train trip?'

John smiled. 'It's nine hours long, but when we get there we can go to a motel and to the pub for a meal.'

I thought, Nine hours is a long, long way. So far away that my family will never find me.

We found our seats on the train, and there we were, on our way to Mildura. I put my head on John's shoulder and felt so safe and secure with him. I was free. I felt alive and so happy. At last I was out of that mad house. At last I knew I was going to be looked after and that I was going to be happy. I knew that John would do anything to protect and look after me. I felt so tired emotionally, because I was scared my family would find me. But I was way too excited to sleep.

Chapter 12

June 1973–1974—The trip to Mildura by train. On the run with John.

HOLDING HANDS AND FEELING VERY SECURE with John, I was way too excited to think of anything else. I was so happy to be out of that house. But, for some reason, I kept thinking about Mum.

I felt guilty for leaving Mum with all my siblings. They were too young, but I had to run away for my own sanity. I knew if I didn't, I would have tried to commit suicide again. I really wanted to end my life, but running away with John gave me enough courage to look ahead, instead of being consumed with suicidal thoughts every single day.

My thinking was, I either escape or I will go insane.

We left Melbourne at six in the evening and arrived in Mildura at seven in the morning. The trip took longer than expected because the train kept stopping to let people off, or to let other people on. It was a really hot day when we got out of the train. So much better than Melbourne.

Melbourne's weather can be really daunting and depressing. It is always cold and very unpredictable. But Mildura, a very small town, was beautiful and sunny. Many tourists would go to Mildura to work,

Painting by Lilla Benigno.

picking grapes or tobacco. It was a beautiful little town. I loved it right away. When we got off the train, I asked John what we were going to do next.

'How about we book into a motel, freshen up a bit and then go to the pub for a couple of drinks?' I agreed with him. I held his hand so tightly, afraid of falling over, and we found a nice little motel, not far from the train station. I was very happy, because I didn't have to walk very far. My legs were so sore from having them bent for so many hours. I needed to take my callipers off and leave my legs straight for at least an hour, I felt so much pain.

I didn't tell John that my legs were sore, but he knew something was not right.

When we arrived at the motel, the lady behind the desk kept looking at me. She could see I was a very young girl, but she still gave us the room and one key, and went ahead with her business. She hardly asked any questions. John did all the talking. I only held his hand, so scared, hoping he wouldn't tell her my age. But of course he didn't. This lady looked middle-aged, with a cigarette hanging from her mouth. All I wanted was go to that room and take off my callipers.

When I entered that motel room, I suddenly felt scared. Part of me wanted to go back home. There was no way I would take my clothes off in front of John. This was the very first man I ran away with. I believed I loved him, but I was too young to understand the meaning of love.

I felt safe with John. He made me feel like a human being, not a freak. After we freshened up a bit and I took off my callipers, I stretched out my legs and massaged them. We lay on the bed for a couple of minutes and

John started kissing me. Our kisses became very passionate. I wanted so badly to have sex with him, but I was still a virgin.

I was very shy. I didn't want to take my clothes off in front of John, so I quickly went under the blankets instead.

John kept reassuring me that he would be gentle with me, and that I didn't have to do anything at all if I didn't want to. Then I told John that I was still a virgin and didn't know anything about sex, and that I was scared of it. And John said, 'It's okay. We will go very slowly. Tell me when it hurts and I will stop.'

I had never seen a dick before. It was enormous. I didn't even want to touch it. I didn't like it. It scared me. It made me sick, but I didn't want to tell him that.

It looked like a fat snake. It was hard and I didn't know why. He tried so hard to put it in my vagina, but it was way too big. I was short and petite, and it hurt like hell. The more he tried to put it in, the more pain I felt. In the end I had to tell him to stop. It wasn't working, and I was not in the mood for sex anyway. My idea was to run away, not to have sex with John.

I could feel that John was becoming frustrated. He gave up, and said, 'I have an idea. How about I get a small jar of Vaseline. That way it can be easier for you, especially if it hurts this much.'

'Okay,' I said. 'But what is Vaseline?'

John kindly explained to me that Vaseline was an ointment to use for sex, and that with it sex would be a lot easier and less painful. I was scared. I hadn't thought that a dick could hurt me that much. So John quickly dressed and went to buy this Vaseline. When he came back I read the label. I had never seen Vaseline before.

Again we tried to have sex. We kissed passionately for a while. John kept telling me how beautiful I was, and I loved all the attention he was giving me, more than my family gave me. That was all I ever wanted: someone to love me. Finally I had found someone who loved me for who I was, not a freak, not a cripple.

After trying for a while, my vagina was very sore, so I asked John if we could get something to eat. Afterwards we could try again, now that we had the Vaseline ready. I was really not in the mood to have sex because I was scared of it. I didn't want to go through that pain again.

John thought it was a great idea, and I dressed and put on my callipers. My legs were rested, I felt no pain, and I was starving. I couldn't wait to go somewhere to eat and have a drink.

I found it extremely difficult to walk long distances. After only ten minutes I would get really tired. So John suggested we go across the road to the Mildura Pub, a local hotel. John ordered me a Coke and a beer for himself. Holding hands and looking at each other, we were both really happy. But this happiness didn't last long. A policewoman and a policeman, both very tall, came up to our table.

'I hope you're not drinking alcohol, Lilla,' the policewoman asked. 'After all, you are underage.' I was suddenly really scared. How in the world did they find me so fast?

'No, it's only Coke.'

She nodded. 'Good.'

I panicked and asked her, 'How do you know my name?'

This time the policeman said, 'Your parents are looking for you. And you, John, you are under arrest.'

I was thinking, Under arrest? What does that mean? I was so scared! The policeman put handcuffs on John and started walking out with him.

I cried, but the policewoman was very nice and she comforted me. Then she asked, 'Did John have sex with you?'

I had to tell her the truth. 'We tried, but his dick was too big.'

The policewoman smiled. 'Okay, you need to come to the police station too, to give us your statement.'

Again I was thinking, What is a statement? I started to cry louder now and I didn't want to go with her. I kept telling her, 'I don't want to go. I want to be with John. Where are you taking John?'

The policewoman held my hand. She knew I couldn't walk very well. She opened the back door of the car and gently helped me inside, and off we went to the police station in Mildura. John and I were only in Mildura for two hours before the police caught us.

I couldn't run even if I wanted to. Funny how we were caught so quickly. Was I an easy target to find? Yes I was, because of my disability. My parents were looking for me because I was under age, and it was an offence to have sex with a minor. John was twenty-eight years old. I didn't know it was an offence. I was too young to understand about the law. I was too young to understand that if John had sex with me he could have gone to jail for a long time.

When we arrived at the police station, the policewoman took my statement. She asked over and over again, 'Did you have sex with John?'

I kept screaming at her, 'No, we didn't. If you don't believe me go back to the motel. You will find a jar of Vaseline. It's not even open. His dick was very big.' Again I cried. I just wanted to see John, and asked repeatedly where he was, but the policewoman wouldn't tell me. She was more concerned about whether I had sex with him.

She told me it was an offence for an older man to have sex with me, but I didn't understand. To me John was not old. He was just a man who liked me, who loved me. I didn't want to understand. I wanted to go back with John.

'When can I see John? Please.'

Eventually the policewoman told me that John had been charged, but because he didn't have sex with me the police had finally decided let him go. By the time she had finished with my statement, I could hear John screaming out, 'Bye, Lilla, I will see you soon, I promise.'

I started screaming and crying out his name. 'Don't leave me here. Take me with you'. But John was gone.

The policewoman told me they were going to get my little suitcase from the motel and put me in jail. It was very lucky that the Vaseline John bought earlier wasn't open. That was the best evidence that we didn't have sex, and enough evidence to let him go. The policewoman came back with all my stuff, my little suitcase with hardly anything in it: a couple of pairs of underwear, and two little dresses to change into. That was it.

She then told me that they had let John go, but that I was not allowed to see him anymore. She was going to put me in jail until my brothers came to get me.

I cried and cried. Then, after hours of so many questions, a young man took me into a small room, and I was in jail.

'Why am I going to jail? I want to be with John. Why am I here?'

This policeman was wonderful. He sat next to me on the bed, gave me a cup of hot tea, a sandwich and a couple of cigarettes, and explained why I was there.

'Lilla, you are a minor. Your two older brothers left Melbourne three hours ago. They are coming to pick you up. As soon as they arrive you can go home.' I didn't want my brothers to come and I started to cry.

The policeman continued, 'Now you get some rest. Your family won't be too long.'

He locked the door behind him, and I cried so loud and screamed, 'John! John! Where are you, John? Come and get me out of here.' I screamed and cried until I was out of breath. I had no more tears. Now and then this gorgeous policeman, so much younger than John, would check to see if I was okay, to see if I needed anything. My eyes were so red from crying, and I kept telling him to go away and leave me alone. After more crying I finally went to sleep. I was really exhausted and very scared.

After a few hours I heard a noise. The jail door opened, and the same cute policeman, with a big smile, said, 'Your brothers are here. It's time for you to go home now.'

My brothers Paolo and Arturo signed papers to get me out of that jail. I was happy to be out, but so unhappy to go back home. I was happy to see my brothers, but also scared. I was very ashamed of what I had done, running away from home, and I couldn't even look at my brothers. I knew they were very upset with me, but they were both so tired from driving all the way to Mildura, and then going all the way back to Melbourne. It was a long drive for them, but all I had in mind was to escape again as soon as I arrived in Melbourne. I wanted to be with John.

My brothers talked about me, saying things like, 'She's crazy. Why is she doing this?' But I couldn't tell them how unhappy I was when I was living at home. I felt they wouldn't be able to understand me. So instead I kept quiet. I sat in the back of the car, then lay down. I shut my eyes, hoping that all this mess would end; but this was the beginning of my rebellious behaviour.

I slept nearly all the way. Then, after many hours of driving, we arrived home. Paolo and Arturo got out of the car and went inside.

I was too scared to go in, so instead I walked back to John's place. As soon as I knocked on his door John gave me the biggest hug and a kiss.

John's grandmother was in the lounge and she screamed, 'You watch, Johnny! All her family will be here to grab her real soon.'

John and I went to his bedroom and he began telling me everything that happened in Mildura, how they arrested him and questioned him over and over again about whether he had sex with me. It was madness. In the end he said, 'You know what saved me, Lilla? The Vaseline.' That jar of Vaseline saved him from going to prison.

While we were hugging and kissing, I suddenly heard my brother Arturo screaming outside John's place. He was so loud! 'You'd better let my sister out or else I will have to call the police again.'

I started to cry again. I didn't want to go home, but my brother was so angry with me and John. In the end John said, 'I think you'd better go home. When you get older I will be here for you.'

Crying and so angry, I opened the door and said to my brother, 'Fuck you,' and off I went back home with Arturo. I was really angry that my brother came to pick me up. I hated him for that.

As soon as I entered the house, I knew right away that my father was drunk. It was Christmas Day, and all these ugly Italian bad words came out: '*Tu sei una grande puttana disgraziata brutttaaaaa.*' But the one thing that stayed with me all my life—and even today I find it so disturbing—

was when he said, 'You are ugly, stupid, ignorant and who do you think is going to marry you with your legs like that? No one, no one, no one.'

I was standing next to the cabinet while my father lashed out with all this verbal abuse. I couldn't even look him in the face. I lowered my head and kept thinking, I'm going to run away forever. You watch. I'm going to do it. I hate you, you bastard. You are not my father anymore.

That was the deepest cut into my heart, because I believed him. What my father said that day was the biggest knife entering my heart. It was the day he fell off his pedestal. I hated him with a passion. How dare you say that? How can you say that about your daughter? Not only was I struggling to deal with this disability; this was the worst thing anyone had ever said to me in my entire life. And I believed him.

I ran away for a reason, but no one ever bothered to find out that reason. The reason was because of the sexual abuse, the reason was because I felt I was not loved, the reason was because I couldn't stand my legs, and the list could go and on. Instead they looked down at me and labelled me as crazy, mad, stupid and ugly. Now I felt more strongly than ever the need to run away again. My mind was made up. There was no love for me. I had to run away again to find that love somewhere else. But this time, now that I had tasted real freedom, I felt that I could run away on my own. I knew I couldn't go back and see John ever again, because my family would call the police and the drama would start over again.

My father threw more verbal abuse at me, but I didn't care anymore. I was already planning another runner.

Then suddenly my father said, 'Go into the bedroom. I can't stand looking at you. You make me sick.' And with that I went into the bedroom and lay down. I felt so hurt. I felt so alone. I couldn't even cry. I just put my head on the pillow and curled up, scared that my father would come in and hit me. But he never hit me. He never laid a hand on me. But his verbal abuse was terrible, even though everything he was saying was because he was drunk.

The only person that felt compassion towards me was my mother. I could see that she felt sorry for me. She came into the bedroom to check on me, to see if I was alright; and then she sat on the bed and asked me, 'Why? Why run away with an old ugly man?' I looked at Mum and said, 'Because he loved me, Mum. He was the only one that really loved me.' Mum sat there and couldn't say anything.

Eventually she said, 'I will come back with some bread and some soup. Lie down and rest.'

These were the times I felt a little closer to my mother. I could hear my father screaming in the lounge room and saying things like, 'What in the world possessed her to have sex with an old ugly bastard?' And the bad names kept rolling in.

Then my courage grew, and I went out and screamed at him, 'I did not have sex with him. If I did he would be in jail now, but he isn't.'

I went back to my room, and my father came in, screaming, '*Tu sei una puttana, sei brutta, nessuno ti vuole a te, sei brutta capisci?* [You are a slut. No one wants you, and you are way too ugly, do you understand?]' The more he said that, the more I believed him. Deep inside I knew I had to get away from all this pain and turmoil.

I couldn't stand this anymore. I came out of the room and asked Mum if I could go down to the shop and get her some milk. I promised I would be back before Dad woke up. At first she hesitated, but then she said, 'Yes, okay. Go quickly, but please come back before your father wakes up.' She gave me some money to get the milk.

Instead of going to the milk bar I went to the main road to hitch a ride. A car stopped and picked me up straight away, and this young man told me how beautiful I was, and that he was prepared to take me anywhere I wanted.

I said, 'Take me far away from here. Take me anywhere. St Kilda would be the best place.'

He smiled and said, 'I'm going to get some drugs from St Kilda. I'll take you there and give you some too.'

'No, I don't want any drugs. I just want to be dropped off there.'

103

While we were driving in his flashy car he said, 'Have you ever thought of doing some pictures for Playboy?'

I looked at him with disgust. 'No, I haven't.' When we arrived in St Kilda he gave me a card.

'I am the manager of Playboy. If you ever change your mind, give me a call, okay?'

'Yes, okay.' But as soon as he drove off in his flashy car I ripped the card into little pieces and threw it in the gutter. I thought, Fuck you, you pervert.

I wanted to hide. I wanted to die. But St Kilda was the only place I knew where no one would find me. That's where this young man dropped me off, in Fitzroy Street, St Kilda, and I never saw him again.

This time I didn't care if I slept in the gutter. I didn't care if someone killed me. All I wanted was to get away from my family, as far as I could. And if anyone ever asked me where my family lived, I would say, 'I have no family. I am all alone.' That was always my answer. I said that millions of times when I arrived in St Kilda. Everyone believed me.

I never saw John again. I wanted to go and see him, but now that my brothers knew where he lived I knew they would come back and get me again. John no longer provided a good place to hide. I had to let him go, and that I did.

Chapter 13

The beginning of my hell. My first rape by Rob. I was fifteen years old.

I KNEW BY NOW that the relationship with my family was really bad. I knew my father and my mother were very angry, because they had other children to take care of, and my behaviour was getting crazier every day. I didn't understand why I was behaving that way. I was really nasty with everyone. All I knew was that I wanted to be free, and in my family house I felt I was in a cage. I couldn't breathe or talk. I was living in fear every single day. I hated that feeling. I needed to go far away, so I didn't feel like that anymore.

I felt like an outcast, a young girl with callipers that no one loved. I felt like a monster in my own home. Although my parents tried their best to make me feel part of the family, nothing worked. The damage was done. My head was so screwed up, full of resentment towards everyone: my parents, my brothers and sisters, Australia, God, for not listening to my fucking prayers. I was too angry to think straight anymore. I wanted to be free. I wanted to get away from all this emotional abuse. It was driving me insane. The time had come to think about how I was going to survive in these streets. I didn't care anymore. Living on the streets was quite a challenge. I had to learn their rules really quickly. The most important

Painting by Lilla Benigno.

was keep your mouth shut, no matter what. If you talked to the police about anyone or anything, you would live in hell, and you wouldn't live very long, because no one on the streets would trust you.

I remember once just sitting on a park bench watching everyone walking by, and wondering where in the world all these people were going. Everything was always busy, and the excitement of it became like a magnet.

I felt free. I was scared, yes, very scared, but the feeling of freedom made me feel alive. I loved living on the streets. I saw so many wonderful things; and also so many terrible things. But what I loved the most about living on the streets was feeling free as a bird. I felt so free that I never wanted to go back home, even though life was rough, without food, clothes or even a bed to sleep in some nights. I didn't care. The taste of freedom was more important than worrying about what was going to happen next with my family.

One day I called Mum, while my father was at work, and she was really worried about me. I told her that I was all right, but she gave me my sister Isabella's address. I thanked her and told her I would keep in touch with her as much as I could.

I was travelling on foot and it was incredibly hard. Sometimes I would sit for hours, with nothing to eat or drink, hoping that someone would feel sorry for me and give me a bottle of water or a sandwich. My legs were always sore because my callipers were broken, and I didn't want to go to the hospital in case the doctors called my parents. I persisted despite the pain. The last thing I wanted was to go back home. My panic attacks were now becoming regular, and sometimes I felt I was going to die.

Many men took advantage of me because I was very young and beautiful. They did give me food and water but they wanted sex too. I would come up with an excuse and tell them I was very sick, and they would leave me alone. But one day I was not so lucky, and all hell broke loose.

Finally, after days of searching, I found where my sister Isabella lived. She was not pleased to see me at all. She was really angry with me and told me to go back home. I screamed at her. 'NO! I'm never going back home.' Then she told me that the guy she was living with was a bastard. He was crazy. But when I met him I found him quite charming.

I thought she said that just to push me away, to scare me so I would go back home. Then finally I met Rob when he came home from work. We bought a pizza for dinner, and we were all drinking red wine. Then he gave me and my sister two tablets each. I had taken pills before, when I wanted to commit suicide, and I thought these may be the same. I thought, This will be harmless. They won't kill me. I had taken pills before and not died. But those pills were only headache tablets. Now I understand why I never died from them.

The tablets we took that night were called mandies, heavy pills. I blacked out. I remember crawling on the floor like an animal, and then I blacked out. When I woke up the next morning, my sister gave me the bad news that I had been raped. She saw bits and pieces of it, then she blacked out too.

I didn't understand what rape was. I didn't understand that my virginity had been taken away from me. I felt no pain because I was unconscious, but my sister explained what had happened and showed me my underwear. There was blood on it. I felt a rush of anger. I felt dirty and disgusted. I also felt it was all my fault because I ran away from home; but I misdirected my anger towards Isabella, my sister, because I felt she didn't protect me. When my sister explained what rape was, and that I was not a virgin anymore, I stuck my finger up to her and said, 'Fuck you! I'm leaving this house.' I blamed her, and with that I ran away from her and Rob too.

I felt so ugly. I felt so unclean. I thought, Now who is going to marry me? The news that I had lost my virginity made me sadder than ever, and

I was incredibly angry. The words of my father came back into my head: You are too ugly and stupid. Who in the world is going to marry you with your legs like that?

I knew my father was drunk when he said that, but it was coming true. That made me more determined to stay away from my family, and to learn to live life on my own. Not that I was doing a good job! But I didn't care anymore. The excitement and the fear gave me so much strength to explore new ways of life, to explore the good and bad, and to do my best to survive, one day at a time. My thinking was always that I had no past and I had no future, so I should just live in the present. And this made me wiser later in life.

Now I was living in the streets with nowhere to go, sleeping at bus stops, begging for food and warm clothes. I experienced many cold nights and sometimes, to keep myself warm, I would piss on myself; and then I would freeze even more. No blankets, just a jacket full of holes. The jeans I had been wearing now for weeks were falling apart. I smelt of urine. I smelt dirty. I wanted to die. I wanted to disappear. But despite it all I had a strong urge to carry on.

I slept on park benches, freezing cold. I slept with alcoholics and other street kids. Now and then I would sleep in a comfortable bed in a hotel with a stranger I had met. I was always drinking. I was always going from street to street, trying to find some comfort in this new life. I witnessed so many people getting bashed because they owed money to drug dealers. I saw people scavenging food from bins, and I started doing the same thing.

Once, when I was really starving and had no money, I saw half a hamburger in a rubbish bin. The hamburger was covered with maggots, and one by one I took them off and ate the burger. I nearly vomited, but I was starving. I needed food so badly, and it did the trick. It stopped the hunger for a little while. When I was thirsty I would go into a hotel and sit and wait for men to buy me drinks. That always happened. Men always bought me lots of drinks. Sometimes I would be so drunk that I would go and sleep it off with other alcoholics who were living on the streets.

I blamed myself because I ran away from home. I felt a strong sense of shame, and I felt so dirty inside. I didn't know what a virgin was, but

I knew that not being one was a bad thing. If you wanted to get married you had to be a virgin. If you weren't you would be labelled a slut or a whore. So I tucked this knowledge away in the back of my mind and never talk about it to anyone. It was my sister's and my secret.

I beat up on myself for taking those drugs. If I hadn't taken those pills I might have had control and perhaps been able to stop the rape. But I was drugged so heavily, and even today I have no recollection of the rape itself. Being so young, it was easy to brush it off and keep quiet about it. It was easy to sweep it under the carpet. But emotionally I was a mess, because I knew now that no one would want to marry me. I knew now that my life was over.

My anger now became rage, and all I wanted to do was hurt every man in this world, as I had been hurt. The shame and guilt were unbearable. When I was living in Italy with the nuns, they taught me that if you fell in love with a man, you had to be a virgin. Now I was not a virgin, and that disgusted me. It made me sick inside. I wasn't pure anymore. I wasn't marriage material anymore. I was a reject and disabled.

I would go into pubs and sit there until men bought me drinks. Men loved my face and my eyes, and this was an advantage for me. My eyes were my weapon, and I used them to get what I wanted.

But sometimes I wanted to be on my own, even if it meant sleeping at the bus stop, or under a big tree; anywhere, as long as I was not back home.

Disabled, broken and lost, my life was not mine anymore. Now it belonged to the streets. I didn't care if I was cold. I didn't care if someone hurt me. I didn't care about anything anymore. All I knew deep inside was that I never wanted to be treated like dirt by anyone ever again. My family had made me feel as if I was dead anyway, so why stay in an environment where there was not love, but only war?

Living on the streets was very scary, but I was free. I felt alive. No more abuse, no more put downs, no more telling me what to do. Living on the streets meant no more spastic schools, no more feelings of rejection, no more hate and no more suicidal thoughts. Now I had something bigger to do. I was learning how to survive, learning about the predators and how to stay away from them; learning to shut my mouth and learn all the streets rules; learning how to survive from one day to the next.

In those days I used to wear runners with my callipers, and it was just as well. The cold weather made my legs and feet itchy and I used to get sores. I had been living on the streets now for seven months, sleeping anywhere: at bus stops, on the grass in the park, curled up like a big turtle, trying so hard to keep myself warm. One night I found a bus stop with no light. It was dark, and I thought, Perfect. I don't want anyone to see me here.

I was freezing. One car went by, but for some reason it came back to the bus stop. I didn't know who it was, but a man wound his window down and asked me, 'Why are you there alone? Haven't you got a home to go to?'

I was always rude to everyone, but to this man I was nice. 'No I haven't. I'm all alone.' I said this with a sad face, freezing my arse off.

He opened the door and asked me to get in, and I did. He saw me walking and asked what had happened to my legs.

'I had a motorbike accident,' I lied, and left it at that. He looked so handsome and the car was beautiful.

'You can stay at my place for tonight,' he said, 'and then tomorrow I will see if I can organize for you to be in a better place. You can't live on the streets.'

I thought, I hope he doesn't ask me to sleep with him. I don't want to. That fear crept up on me, but I was very cold, so I said, 'Yes, okay.'

After about thirty minutes we arrived at his house. He stepped out of the car and came around to my side and opened the door for me. He gently gave me a hand to get out of the car. There were a few steps up to his house and, seeing I couldn't go up the stairs, he held out his hand. I grabbed it and pulled myself up the three steps. He opened the door and turned on the lights. I thought, Wow, what a beautiful house. The kitchen was really big and so clean. Then I turned around and saw the most gorgeous leather lounge, big and black. It sure looked comfortable. This kind man asked if I was hungry.

Very shyly I said, 'Yes I am.'

'Okay. Go and lie down on the lounge. I will get you a couple of blankets and a pillow. You can sleep on the lounge tonight. It's very comfortable. I slept there a few times.'

I smiled and said, 'Thank you.'

He went upstairs for the blankets and the pillow, then he made my bed for me and told me to lie down.

I took my off callipers while he was making me a sandwich. I was ashamed to show anyone my callipers, so I did this quickly, then put the callipers under his lounge. I slid under the blankets. I felt warm and comfortable.

He gave me a glass of hot milk and made me a ham and cheese sandwich. I was really hungry and ate it very quickly.

When I had finished, he kindly asked me, 'Would you like me to make you another sandwich?'

'No, thank you.'

He took the glass and the plate into the kitchen and said, 'Goodnight.' I didn't respond. I just watched him go upstairs and switch all the lights off.

I had the best sleep that night. Then, in the morning, I heard these people coming down the stairs. When I saw the whole family coming down the stairs, I was in shock. There was a very pretty lady and two children, who must have been seven or eight years old, dressed in school uniforms and ready for school. They ate breakfast very quietly. I think they didn't want to wake me, but I was already awake. Then the man who helped me the night before came down the stairs, dressed like a policeman.

I panicked, got up quickly, put my callipers back on, and wanted to run away.

His wife had long blond hair, was very pretty, and wore a suit, a skirt and a beautiful jacket. She wore beautiful earrings, and her hair was styled like a model. She was incredibly beautiful and classy. Nicely, she asked me if I wanted any breakfast.

'No thank you.' I never ate breakfast.

I couldn't believe I had slept in a policeman's house. But he was very nice. He told me that he and I were going to Centrelink (then it was called 'Social Security') so he could find someone to help me. I didn't want anyone to help me. I wanted to be left alone. But I still went for the ride. We went in an elevator to a large empty room, full of computers and desks, but no one was there. The policeman picked me up, sat me on a big stool and ordered me not to move. He was going to get help for me. But as soon as he left I managed to step down and make a run for it. Next thing I was back in the street, and trying to hitch a ride. An old woman stopped and asked me to jump in.

She asked where I wanted to go, and the only place I knew and felt comfortable in was St Kilda, and that is where she dropped me off. I was back on the streets. I didn't want to be helped by anyone. I wanted to be free. I didn't want to be pitied, I just wanted to run, run, run, where no one could find me, especially my family.

I thought of the policeman. I couldn't believe he was kind enough to help me that night. And I was so surprised when I saw all his family. He was a good man. And even today, now and then I think of the wonderful act he did for me. He helped me without any expectations. He gave me food and a beautiful lounge to sleep on. This policeman and his family are still in my heart, even though I never saw him again.

Chapter 14

December 1974—My second love Frankie. I was sixteen years old.

I HAD BEEN LIVING ON THE STREETS for over a year. It was as though I was partying every night, from one nightclub to the next. Living on the streets was really bad, but I found strength deep within me to carry on. Fear or not, I was not going to let anyone ill treat me again. I was learning quickly where the hot spots were for sleeping, especially when it was really cold; and sometimes in Melbourne the weather was incredibly cold and miserable.

As I curled up in a bus stop, trying so hard to keep warm, a car pulled up right in front of the bus stop, and a young girl, about my age with blond hair, got out of the car. She wore black pants and a red, classy jacket, but when she saw me looking at her she screamed out, 'What the fuck are you looking at?'

I retaliated quickly and screamed out, 'Fuck you!'

Her eyes were black from the running mascara, and I could see that she had been crying. As soon as she slammed the car door, the car zoomed off, and she stood there crying by herself.

Lilla Benigno at sixteen.

She sat on the bench where I was trying to get comfortable and warm. She asked me, 'Haven't you got a home to go to?'

I felt sorry for her. I didn't like when people cried. It reminded me of my own tears, my own pain.

I answered softly, 'No, I haven't got a home. This is my home tonight.'

'Hi, I'm Lia, and that's my house just up the road. I live with my father. Do you want to come and stay with me until you find a place to stay?'

I was so happy! 'Yes, I would love to.'

I talked rough. Every second word was fuck. It was a new language, a tough language that gave me a sense of control, a sense of toughness. But inside I was paralysed with fear of the unknown.

I had forgotten about my polio and, when I stood up, Lia noticed my limp. 'What happened to you? Why do you walk like that?'

I was too shy to tell her the truth. I was full of shame about being disabled. I told her the same lie I told everyone. 'I had a motorbike accident.'

Whenever I walked I had to look at the ground, afraid that I would fall. But Lia didn't care how I walked. All she was worried about was that she didn't want me to sleep in the bus stop. She felt sorry for me. Bus stops became my motels. I felt safe sleeping there. I experienced everything: strong winds, stars, and quietness. I used to be so scared, but inside I felt free and alive.

I remember the first time I entered Lia's place I loved it. It looked like a mansion. Lia asked her father if I could stay there for a little while, until I found a place of my own. Her father was really nice and said yes, I could.

That night I was fed. I even had a bath. I hadn't washed in weeks. Lia gave me a pair of pyjamas and showed me my bed. The room was perfect, with two single beds, one along each wall. There were two lamp shades, one at the side of each bed. I had a pillow and blankets. I had landed in heaven. That night I slept really well.

Next morning I could smell coffee and toast. I quickly got up, and breakfast was prepared for me by Lia. I told her I never ate in the mornings, but that morning I was starving and ate all my breakfast. Lia was a little taller than me. I am five feet two, while Lia was five feet five.

Lia and I become friends, very close friends. Everything she did, I did; everything I did, she did. She was blonde and I was a brunette. She was extremely attractive, with dimples when she smiled, beautiful blue eyes, and curly, long blond hair. She had a petite body, like mine. We were both thin, and we were both still growing. Our breasts were perky and out, and sometimes young boys would blow us kisses from their cars, or if they were walking by.

I loved being a teenager. I never had any time to think about my next meal, or worry about what was going to happen at home, or worry about where I was going to stay. I was strongly attracted to freedom. Feeling free gave me strength and perseverance to keep going ahead and never look back. I wanted to experience everything. I watched people and learned. I was very rebellious but so curious about everything. I was learning new ways of keeping myself safe, even if it meant lying or manipulating people so I could stay alive.

Lia was always happy, with such a vibrant personality, a lot of cheekiness, yet so much warmth and compassion. She loved animals. At the time, I didn't. I was scared of every animal. Every time I saw a dog, I panicked. If I saw a spider I panicked. Even if I saw a cricket or a moth, I would start screaming.

If ever I saw a black cat, I knew I would have many years bad luck.

Finally I felt safe. Everything she did I copied, such as brushing my teeth and washing my hair. I didn't like wearing make-up in those days. I had terrible hygiene. It wasn't as important as surviving.

One day Lia, out of nowhere, suggested we go to the city of Melbourne, just to get a cup of coffee. I loved the city. I was always drawn to the high-rise buildings. Some of them were so high that every time I tried to look at them, I felt dizzy. So tall, and I felt so small.

Lia and I found a small coffee shop right in the middle of the city, near Flinders Street Station. It was very small, with a long hallway, and tables that looked like desks, and seats secured to the floor. We found a nice table close to the main entrance. I sat so I could watch people walking by, and Lia sat in front of me, and we ordered our coffee.

Sometimes I would see women stare at me, or old men, or people in suits. They would turn and stare, and I would think, Why are they looking at me?

There was a little jukebox on the wall, and if I pressed a number music would come out, so Lia put twenty cents in and we started listening to music that we loved. We both liked Peter Frampton, or the band Deep Purple. They were the kind of songs we listened to over and over again.

I saw two young men looking at me and Lia, and one of them shouted out to me, 'Hello beautiful. What are you girls up to tonight? Want to come to a party tonight?'

When I saw him I liked him immediately. I thought he was very cute, and cheeky. He reminded me of James Dean, pacing up and down, looking down at the floor, and then looking at me again. He looked wild, yet so attractive. His eyes were incredibly blue; and he had curly black hair, shoulder length. He was skinny, yet dressed cleanly and properly.

I suddenly felt shy. I was scared to talk to guys, so Lia looked at me, winked, and made a sign to tell me that she liked his friend. His friend was standing next to him. So I nodded to her and she turned around and said, 'Yes we want to come. Where is the party?'

The young man kept looking at me. 'It's in Altona. Do you know where that is?'

We did. We had been there a few weeks back for another party. In those days, Altona was a great place to have parties. First, it was far away from the city; and second, the police were miles away if we ever got into trouble. The further away from people and the police, the better chance for us to have a great time.

'My name is Frankie. What's yours?'

He was looking at me, and I knew I was going red. I felt shyer than ever and my heart was beating fast. He was incredibly handsome, and I always felt stuck for words, especially with good looking guys. Unless I was drunk or off my face with some other drug. But this particular day I was straight. Lia and I at the time weren't into heavy drugs. Sure, we were both experimenting with small amounts of dope or alcohol, but we weren't into heavy drugs such as heroin or speed. That came into my life much later.

I noticed how much of a rebel Frankie was and I was even more attracted to him.

'Lilla,' I shouted.

'Lilla. What a beautiful name. You are gorgeous. I hope you can both come to the party.'

My heart was beating so fast. I had never felt like this towards anyone. I wanted to see him again, and I couldn't wait to go to the party. Lia and I looked at each other and knew we wanted to go. We started giggling. We were both really happy.

Frankie was with a friend called Tim. He had blond hair, was a lot taller than Frankie, and a lot quieter too. He had blue eyes, a skinny physique and was incredibly good looking.

Frankie was the negotiator. Lia liked Tim, and Frankie liked me. He was saying, over and over again, sounding like a parrot, 'Make sure you come, okay? Please, I want you to be at this party.' I smiled at him, loving all the attention, and reassuring him that I would be there for sure. Lia got the address from Frankie.

When the boys finally left, Lia and I were stunned. We kept talking about these two boys. I liked Frankie the first time I laid eyes on him. But there was something wrong here. Frankie didn't know I had a disability.

He didn't see me walking, because when we met at the coffee shop I was sitting down. I didn't get up to get the address from him. Lia did that.

I told Lia after the boys left, 'I'm scared. Frankie doesn't know how I walk. What if he doesn't like me?'

Lia was beautiful. She always had a great, supportive response. 'Lilla, being disabled is nothing. You are beautiful, and you can be really funny. I know Frankie wouldn't care, and you shouldn't either.' That put my heart at ease and I couldn't wait to go to the party.

After our coffee, we walked from pub to pub in the city. There were so many beautiful shops full of gorgeous clothes, but we loved to go into the hotels, searching for nothing, really. We were both very curious. I had finally met a friend I was comfortable with. All these wonderful emotions, without taking drugs, and without having this fear of being left alone.

Lia had the address, and that night the taxi stopped right in front of a big garage door.

'Well, lovely girls,' said the taxi driver, 'this is where you get off. This is the address you gave me.'

Lia and I exchanged looks, then Lia said, 'This is not right. It doesn't look like a party is going on here.'

'Let's go in,' I said. 'Maybe we're early.' In fact, we were about an hour early.

We let the taxi go, and Lia opened the brown, rusted garage door. Inside was only a single bed, with a very dirty blanket. That blanket quickly become my security blanket. It was a big hall, with nothing in it except empty beer cans on the floor, this small, single, dirty bed, and two broken chairs. It had a concrete floor and a high ceiling, and was incredibly dark inside. Lia became frightened, and so did I, but we didn't want to leave just in case it was the right place. So we waited for the boys.

We had a few cans of beer and made ourselves comfortable on this single bed. I put the blankets over my legs. I didn't want Frankie to know I was disabled.

We drank two beers between us and had four more to go. We were getting a bit drunk, and started talking about the guys we had met earlier that day. We were happy and high, when we heard a noise at the door, and it slowly opened. There they were, Frankie and Tim. They looked so clean and so gorgeous. We knew we were going to have a great time.

I was very young and nervous. I could feel my heart beating so loudly. I liked Frankie. I loved the way he talked. He was so confident and sure of himself. His self-assurance was what attracted me to him. I loved his cheeky, rebellious behaviour, which made him very sexy. When he talked to me I was really shy. He could hardly get a word out of me. Whenever I liked a boy I felt so lost. I didn't know how to talk. I didn't know what to say or what to do.

I felt that so many boys left me because they didn't understand why I walked like a zombie. They didn't understand why I limped when I walked. I didn't want Frankie to run away from me like the other boys, so I covered my legs.

I was on my third beer now and had more confidence. I asked Frankie, 'Where is everyone? I thought this was going to be a big party.'

Frankie smiled at me. 'We are the party, me, you, Lia and Tim.'

I lowered my eyes, as usual. I felt shy, even though I also felt a bit dizzy from the alcohol. It was because I really liked him. Every time I looked at his eyes, I felt butterflies in my stomach. I didn't want him to know that I liked him. Just in case he didn't like my legs.

I always heard demon voices in my head, telling me I was no good, I was ugly, I should be dead, I was a waste of life, I had no right to be here, why was I here? But when I drank alcohol or smoked dope, those thoughts would stop, and I would be in the present, enjoying pleasurable moments.

Frankie was eighteen years old and I was sixteen, nearly seventeen years old. Lia was the same age as me, sixteen, and Tim was older than all of us, nineteen years old. We sure were two cute couples.

We were having fun, talking away, now that I was on my fourth beer, and suddenly Frankie rose from the big chair that was facing me and sat on the single bed where I was sitting, with my legs covered by a blanket.

Lia and Tim were laughing and talking among themselves, and Frankie sat beside me and started talking to me. I didn't feel like talking. I wanted to kiss him. But Frankie was talking away. He loved talking. He was a real chatterbox. Did he talk that much because he was nervous too, or was he just born like that?

Frankie said, 'You don't talk very much do you?' I looked at him, and he said, 'Your eyes are the most beautiful eyes I've ever seen.'

I never said thank you to anyone when they paid me a compliment, because inside it would make me sick. Sometimes I felt like vomiting. My hatred towards my disability never let me feel beautiful, and the words of my father were always in my mind like a tape recorder. I was ugly, and I believed him.

But that night, when Frankie gave me this beautiful compliment, my heart melted. I looked at him and he looked into my eyes; and as I was just about to kiss his cheek he quickly turned his face and kissed my lips. All time stopped.

I went into a world of bliss. It felt as though I had died and gone into a different world. I felt that my body was going to explode. My heart was beating so fast, but I didn't care if he felt my heart beating. I wanted him to feel what I was feeling, and he did. We kissed and kissed and kissed for a long time; one position, just kissing.

Then he said, 'I'm cold. Let me get under the blanket with you.'

I froze. I screamed out, 'Nooo!'

Frankie looked at me, surprised and curious. 'Why not?'

I didn't know what to say. I was lost for words, even though I was a bit drunk. I didn't want him to feel my callipers. I was scared but, because by now I was drunk, I changed my mood and had more confidence. 'Okay, but wait just a second.'

We began to kiss again. He kept telling me, while he was kissing me, 'You're a beautiful kisser. Let's kiss forever.'

I wouldn't respond to his comments. I just kept kissing him. I loved kissing him. He was a magical kisser. I didn't want it to end. But it was very cold. I was freezing. Then Frankie suggested that we go under the blanket, but I didn't want to share my blanket with him. I didn't want him to find out about my callipers. They were made of iron and they were very cold. Every time the callipers touched my legs, I felt I was getting shock treatment.

But Frankie always went for what he wanted. He had such a cheeky personality, and I knew he wasn't going to be like the other guys.

He looked more curious than ever. Then, slowly, I moved so I could give him space to lie down next to me, and he did. I was trying so hard not to make a noise with my callipers, but suddenly there was a loud noise, and I felt I was going to die. As he went under the blanket he put his leg on top of mine and suddenly screamed out,

'Wow, what was that? Why is your leg so cold and hard? It felt like steel. Have you got a false leg?' His face made me laugh, and I started laughing so hard; and then he started laughing too; and, finally, I came out with the same lie I told everyone.

'I had a motorbike accident couple of years ago and I'm wearing callipers, but doctors say I will get better soon. I have to wear these for a little while.'

I was stunned, surprised, and relieved at the same time. This gorgeous, funny, unpredictable young man was going to stay with me all night, and I did not complain, because I wanted the same thing. To be held and kissed forever. We kissed for hours and hours. Now and then we would stop, sip our beers, and then kiss and kiss, until the early hours of the morning. He didn't touch me anywhere. We only kissed passionately for what felt like eternity. I didn't want it to stop. But then we fell asleep in each other's arms. Both of his legs were on my legs, and that made me feel that he and I had become one soul, one person. I fell in love, deeply in love, with Frankie.

One year went by, and Frankie and I began to get very serious. We were so much in love. He would hold my hand, always helping me to walk and watching the floor for me, just in case I tripped. Frankie became my walking angel, and this helped me to go to parties and have fun. That was all we did, had lots of fun and laughter, smoked dope, and drank lots of alcohol. Life was one big party.

But one night, after consuming a lot of alcohol, I was drunk again; but considerably awake and very functional, a happy drunk. Frankie was the same, laughing with all his friends, holding me in his arms, and kissing the back of my head, while talking to his mates.

And then he whispered in my ear, 'Let's do it tonight.'

I knew right away what he wanted. Sex. Frank wanted sex. I was a very happy drunk that night so I whispered back in his ear, 'Yes, let's do it.'

We said good night to everyone and went to bed. We started kissing passionately as we always did, and then Frankie said, 'Hang on. I need to get a condom.' I didn't know what that was. Last time I'd had sex was when I was raped, and I had completely forgotten about that night.

Frankie put his condom on and started to kiss me again. I responded lovingly and full of passion; and then Frankie was ready to go in and he did, slowly, but his dick was too big, and it was hard and it hurt me. He tried a couple of times again slowly, and then… Success! It went in, and he went for it, started screwing so hard, and I had my eyes open in terror. He was drunk and I was drunk. He kept on going faster and faster, and the pain had stopped now. But his dick was so big and I wished he would come quickly and get off me. Suddenly I heard this big roar, and he scared me. I had never seen a man having an orgasm before. We had only kissed for the whole year and this was our first sexual encounter.

Suddenly he came, and I felt his body trembling and hardening; and I felt his heart beating so fast. Then suddenly he got off and said, 'You fucking slut. You're a fucking cunt whore.'

He put his jeans on and left his bedroom. He went downstairs and screamed out to his friends, 'That whore made me believe for one fucking year that she was a virgin. She was not a virgin. She is a slut.' And he kept going on and on and on, while I was trembling in his bed. I couldn't believe what he was saying. He changed, all because he found out I was not a virgin.

I did tell him that I was a virgin, because I had completely forgotten about the rape two years earlier. I had swept it under the carpet, hoping it would go away. But that night the demon came out of the closet and let itself loose, out of control.

Frankie came back into the bedroom and started screaming at me while he was sitting on his bed. He didn't even give me a chance to explain to him. I didn't understand what the big deal was. When I was raped I felt no pain. I was drugged. I was blacked out. How could I explain this to him? Now it was too late. For him now I was a slut and a whore, and there was nothing I could do to calm him down.

'Tomorrow,' he said, 'I want you to clean all the house, and I want you to cook for everyone in here. Do you understand? Do you understand?'

I could not get a word out. He kept calling me all these bad names. Then, after two hours of cursing me, he lay down and went to sleep.

Next morning, as soon as he woke up he said, 'Wake up, bitch. You have a lot of work to do. Get up, slut. You will never sleep with me again. Go straight into the kitchen and wash the mess we made. Your mess too.'

I dressed. 'Fuck you,' I said.

All his friends were in the lounge room. There were at least twenty-five people, all Frankie's mates.

I sat on the last steps and Frankie started talking. 'Everyone, this slut had been leading me on for one fucking year. I believed she was a virgin, until last night I found out that she was not a virgin.' To me he said, 'That's fucked, Lilla, really fucked. So today you are staying here. Go into the kitchen and wash all the dishes. Also, I want you to change the fucking sheets on the bed. No way do I want to sleep in those dirty sheets. Then vacuum the whole house. And when you've finished, I want you to go, and I never want to see you again.'

He humiliated me in front of his friends. Then I stood up and said, 'Fuck you. I'm not your fucking slave. Do your own fucking work.' And as he was just about to hit me, two of his friends stopped him.

Then everyone left.

I was mortified. I was dying inside. I could not believe what was happening. One minute we were in love, talking about children and living in a nice little house, and suddenly this love was gone, and gone completely. I had never seen Frankie angry before. He felt so betrayed by me, because he really believed that I had set him up by telling him that I was a virgin. I started to cry.

When eventually I got up, wanting to get out of that house forever, I heard a voice.

'Wait, don't go yet. Wait until everyone goes, and then we can make a run for it.' One guy had stayed behind. He felt sorry for me.

'Will you help me to run away? I'm not cleaning anything. I'm not washing his fucking dishes. He can get fucked.'

When we knew that Frankie was gone, we left the house, and I never saw Frankie again. I felt so hurt. Again I wanted to die. But this guy with blond hair, and so good looking, asked me to go with him. We were going to run away together.

While we were walking away as fast as we could, he held my hand and helped me to walk faster. His name was Alan. He had long, blond, curly hair past his shoulders, and a beautiful body. He had really white, soft skin, and he was eighteen. He wore a Bob Dylan T-shirt and a pair of tight, sexy jeans. While he was holding my hand he kept telling me how beautiful I was, and how he wanted to spend time with me to give me lots of pleasure. I liked his face, his lips, his eyes, and his presence made me forget Frankie really quickly.

We arrived at a destination Alan obviously knew well. He had keys for the front door. He opened it and let me in. He turned to me, and I nearly lost my balance, but he grabbed me in time and kissed me really slowly, and I loved it. I didn't want him to stop.

He kissed me more and more, and I was in heaven. He was such a beautiful kisser. His kisses were so tender and passionate, loving, not like Frankie's. In the end, Frankie's kissing became a bit rough. I guess all he wanted was sex from the beginning, but because I kept on putting it off, his kisses became rough and sometimes ugly.

While we kissed, Alan picked me up and gently lay me on an enormous double bed, with white sheets. It looked like a bed from heaven.

He took my jeans off and, with his soft hands, gently removed my callipers. He took off my socks and looked at my legs. He stroked them, then began to kiss them gently, one small kiss, and another small kiss; then touching and caressing my legs up and down.

He looked into my eyes and said, 'You are beautiful. Your eyes mesmerise me. I want to be with you for the rest of my life. You're too beautiful to be treated so bad, the way Frankie did. I will be here for you forever.'

We started kissing, more passionate than ever, twisting our bodies to the rhythm of love and passion, mixed together, blending, touching, kissing, and feeling only his heartbeat and my heartbeat.

Alan and I made love for three days. We only stopped for the toilet, water, and food. And the rest? Sex, sex, lots and lots of beautiful sex.

On the third day, after making love for possibly the thirtieth time, the front door smashed open, and two ladies came into the bedroom. I was shocked. I quickly pulled the white sheet over me so they couldn't see me. Then the younger woman screamed, 'We are engaged to be married, Alan. What the fuck you are doing?'

I looked at him with terror in my eyes. I didn't know he had a girlfriend and was engaged. I quickly put on my callipers and clothes and started walking out. Then I turned around and said, 'Alan, are you coming with me?'

This beautiful woman, with long black hair, wearing classy clothes and black high heels, came up to me and said, 'You'd better fuck off. I won't hit you because you're disabled, but if you weren't I would have slapped you so hard! Now, get the fuck out and I never want to see you again.'

I had tears in my eyes. I didn't want to let Alan go. We had talked of so many things. We were going to be together. He loved my legs. He loved me.

The next day, while I was struggling in the streets of Fitzroy, I saw Alan and his girlfriend walking into the restaurant I loved to go to. I tried to walk in, but the owner wouldn't let me in because he knew I never had any money. He had helped me in the past with food, because he knew I was a runaway, a lost cause.

When I saw Alan I started screaming, 'Alan, come away with me like you said. Let's go away from everyone. I know you're not happy with her. Come with me. I miss you, Alan. I love you.' I started crying and made a big scene in front of everyone in the restaurant.

The boss of the restaurant, a big, fat man without hair, came towards me.

'Fuck off. You'd better go before I get the police. Now scram. We don't want any trouble, understand?'

I stuck my finger up at him. 'Fuck you. Leave me alone.' And with tears pouring, I left.

I knew Alan wouldn't come out. He was controlled by those two women. He wasn't happy with her, but I knew he wouldn't leave her either. I could see she had a lot of money. I was poor, living on the streets alone, surviving, and begging for food and sometimes shelter. When I met Alan, he made me forget those terrible moments, living on the streets.

My heart was broken, not once but twice. I knew now that my doors were shutting down on this thing called love. In a matter of a week I lost Frankie, with whom I had a relationship for one year, and Alan, the tender young boy who I had sex with for three days.

Now I was back on the streets, learning more survival skills and living life one day at a time. I was devastated. After spending three days with Alan, and feeling so much love towards him, I knew it was time to move on again. Now what? What was I going to do? Where was I going to go? I surely didn't know. Wherever the callipers took me I went, like a lost soul, confused, scared and plagued by panic attacks. Again, death came to mind. I was nothing to anyone. I was all alone again. I had lost Lia's friendship, lost Frankie's love, and now I had lost Alan too. Lia and I went our separate ways. After I finished with Frankie I never saw her again.

Chapter 15

*December 1975—The first pimp I met, Pete.
I was seventeen years old.*

I WAS BACK IN ST KILDA, back in hell. I was begging for money on the streets. St Kilda in the seventies was the city of homeless people: prostitutes, drug addicts and alcoholics were everywhere.

One day I went into a coffee shop and this was where I met my first pimp, a Greek guy named Pete. He was a short, stocky guy, full of himself, yet very polite and good looking. He came over to my table as I was sipping my coffee in peace and started talking to me.

After about ten minutes I asked him for some money, and he gave me $20, but he also told me he wanted it back as soon as possible. I told him I couldn't work. I lied to him about my disability, telling him I'd had a motorbike accident.

After that coffee I left and didn't see Pete until one night in St Kilda. Again I asked him for more money, but he asked me, 'Do you want lots of money, Lilla?'

'Yes I do.'

Painting by Lilla Benigno.

He smiled and asked me, 'Do you want to work for me?'

'Doing what?'

'I will show you.'

Next thing I knew Pete was with me all the time. We had sex a few times, but it was rushed. Then one day he said, 'I have a surprise for you. Come with me.' He took me into a little, very pretty terrace house. 'This is where we're going to make lots of money.'

'Doing what? How?'

'Wait and see. When I finish this room I will ask some of my friends to come and see you.'

This little house had one room with a single bed and white towels. In the corner was a small table with a candle on it. The room smelled like roses. It was dark. There were no windows. I still didn't know what I was supposed to be doing. But I liked Pete, and part of me trusted him. I was so tired of begging for money from people I didn't even know. I had to do something, and I believed this was going to be my biggest break.

I was only seventeen years old, very naïve and trusted Pete. He was a lot older than me. Pete and I become very close. I didn't understand why we were having sex. I felt nothing when I had sex with him. He never held me close. He never kissed me, and he never told me I was beautiful. But having sex with him made me think that he did like me.

The big day came. After many weeks spent preparing this new place, one day Pete said, 'Tomorrow we can start working.'

It was a couple of days before Christmas. I was so excited, because I knew I would have money for Christmas. I could buy lots of presents for my family, especially my mum. I always thought of my mother. By now God was my enemy, and my mother had become my angel. She was always on my mind. I knew she was struggling with food, and with Dad, and with looking after all the children.

The next day we were ready for whatever was going to happen. I was still very naïve. I couldn't understand what Pete wanted me to do. He put both his hands on my face gently and asked me, 'Are you ready for this?'

Scared, confused, not knowing what was going to happen next, I said, 'Yes, I'm ready.' I lied. I was terrified. I had been tricked into something new, and I still didn't know what.

In front of the door, Pete had installed a red light. He switched it on. 'Go and put this on. It's very sexy, and men will like you more that way.'

I did what he said. Within half an hour, the doorbell rang. I wore a black, laced, gorgeous long dress. You couldn't see my callipers. My hair was very long. I wore no make-up. Pete said I looked beautiful and very ready. I was nervous but ready, although I was thinking, Ready for what? That is how naïve I was.

He didn't say anything about sex to me, so obviously he thought I knew what I needed to do, but I didn't. I had never worked in a massage parlour before and didn't know what to do.

The front bell rang again, and Pete said, 'Well? Go and open the door, quickly.'

When I opened it a stocky, ugly looking man came in and asked me, 'How much for sex?'

I felt disgusted. 'I don't do sex, I just do massages.'

After this man left, I went into the lounge room and said to Pete, 'He didn't want a massage, and he said he wanted sex. I'm not doing that.'

Pete came up to me and slapped my face so hard, and started calling me all these bad names. 'You stupid bitch, slut, spastic retard.' Every name he called me reminded me of my father.

I wanted to please Pete and I didn't want to be hit again, so the next time the doorbell rang I was ready. I knew by now that Pete wanted me to have sex with these men. That was how I was going to get rich, by having sex. I didn't want to do it, but it was too late. I felt like a prisoner. I couldn't escape. I was put there to become a sex slave. Sex, sex, money, money, more sex and money. I was descending into a world of despair, ugliness and disgust.

I didn't know what I was doing, but I was learning quickly. Old men would knock on the door and I would welcome them in. Sometimes there were five men, or ten men; and because everyone knew I was a newcomer and young and pretty, suddenly the lounge was full of men waiting to have sex with me. I felt repulsed by them and sick inside, but I was not scared anymore. I told Pete that doing this was making me sick, and I was scared I would vomit on someone. So Pete gave me a shot of heroin. Just a small dose, and this made me work faster. I had to pretend that I knew what I was doing or else I would really get into trouble with Pete. I didn't want that to happen. I wanted to please him. I wanted him to love me.

These men were so ugly. Some were short, with a big stomach and white hair. I thought they were the same age as my father. Many of them came so fast and left. Others went back to Pete and asked for their money back, because they saw my callipers. They would say things like, 'I don't want to fuck a spastic whore. Where are the normal sluts?' Some of them wanted their money back; but some of the men gave me money for nothing. And this was when I realised I was becoming a prostitute. This was when I realised and understood that I was selling my body to men who made me sick.

So many complimented my looks, told me how beautiful I was. Yet so many were repulsed to see me with my callipers on my legs, and they would run out the door, without asking Pete for their money back. It was a nightmare. That first night I had sex with about fifteen men, and Pete made lots of money. I had never seen so much money since I lived on the streets. I hated doing this, but the idea of having money made me relax a little.

I remember getting all this money and going into the lounge. I opened the door and chucked the money into the air and said to Pete, 'Here, catch.' Now that I was stoned on heroin, this job became like a game for me. I would go into the room where a client was waiting, feeling disgusted and hoping I wouldn't vomit on him; but the idea of seeing that much money made me determined to get more and more.

Time flew and word of mouth spread quickly. By now I was going through fifteen or twenty men a day. Some wanted sex, some only wanted a massage, and some just wanted to talk about their problems. They would pay me extra time for it. I never understood what they were talking about, because my mentality was way too young. My mind was only on how I was going to get this money, and what drugs I could buy with it.

The very first day I worked there I made $850. Well, I'm sure I made more than that, but Pete took most of it. He gave me only $200. I remember this clearly because the next day I went out and bought Christmas presents for all my family. I remember this beautiful, gold, antique phone I bought for $40 for my mother and my father. For my sisters I bought shoes, clothes and jewellery. I had so much fun buying all those presents.

I had all the presents wrapped up nicely that night, while I was staying at the massage parlour. I couldn't wait to go and see my family the next morning to give them all these new presents.

The next day, when I knew my father was at work, I caught a taxi to Chadstone to drop off all the presents.

My mother was in shock when she saw this big bag full of presents, and with a big smile I said, 'Merry Christmas, Mumma. These presents are for you all.'

She asked, '*Ma dove li hai presi tutti questi soldi?* [Where did you get all this money from?]'

I couldn't look her in the eyes. I said quietly, 'Never mind, Mum, *non ti preoccupare* [don't worry].'

I smiled at her, left them to enjoy their presents and went back onto the streets. I felt too ashamed and scared to tell my mother where the money came from. If she knew, I'm sure she would have had a heart attack.

I didn't receive anything, no presents, no Christmas cards, from anyone. But that didn't worry me because I knew my family was happy.

I went back to that awful place and spent Christmas on my own, crying and wishing so hard to have a different life, wishing I was back home with my family. I didn't want to be a prostitute. It made me feel so sick and dirty. I was wearing so many masks, trying so hard to block this disgusted feeling inside. I felt so ugly and sickening. Several times I had to go to the toilet to vomit, disgusted with what I was doing.

I closed within myself more and more. I was switching off from the real world and going into a darker and terrifying world, a world where death became my best friend.

I felt as though I was in prison. Pete would take more money from me and I was always broke. I worked man after man, and he took more and more money, leaving me helpless and hopeless. He would only give me $50 or $100, and only if he was in a good mood.

But whenever he gave me money, the first person I would think of helping was my mother. I would call her, asking if she needed money, and if she said yes I would go and give it to her. This was the only pleasure I had, helping my mother and my younger sisters.

Pete and I were arguing way too much. I did like him, although he didn't treat me well. I felt protected by him. But our arguments, when I was very jealous of him, were really getting out of hand.

I couldn't stand him looking at another woman, especially when we'd had sex quite a few times. I honestly believed that we were a couple, but that wasn't the case. He was using me as a sex slave, and he made lots of money off me, and I was too naïve to understand what he was doing and why he was doing it.

One night after work I decided to follow him, because I felt we were becoming distant from one another. He didn't even want to have sex with me anymore. He didn't want to talk to me. He would leave me alone in the massage parlour for hours and hours. Now and then he would send someone in to check up on me and to pick up his money, and then I wouldn't hear from him for days.

But this particular night I thought, No, I want to see where he goes. I followed him and I saw him going into Clare's house.

Clare was a girl we had met earlier in the week. She was Italian, like me, with black hair, nice eyes, a big nose and thin lips. She was skinny and had no boobs or arse.

Pete knocked on the door, and Clare opened the door, kissed him on the lips and put her arms around him. I saw red and screamed out, 'You are a fucking bitch, Clare. You pretend you are my friend and you fuck Pete? You fucking slut. How dare you.'

I screamed so loud that many people came out of their houses to witness this drama. I could see Clare was really embarrassed, and she and Pete quickly went inside.

I kept screaming out, 'You fucking whore. You slut big nose, slut ugly bitch.'

I went on and on until I had no more breath, and went back to the massage parlour. That was my home now. It had been my home for a few days. I didn't want to sleep on the streets anymore, and my money was going on pills, alcohol and heroin.

Chapter 16

Three days after Christmas 1975—I was gang-raped by many men in one night. I was seventeen years old.

WHEN I ARRIVED AT THE MASSAGE PARLOUR, I went straight into the lounge room. There was a small bed near the wall, so I lay down there and started to cry. I was so hurt that Pete was with Clare. Anyone else yes, but why her? I couldn't understand how he could love her nose. It was too big and I hated her. More tears and more tears, until I fell asleep. I was sure Clare's reputation was fucked, and that was my intention. You hurt me, and I will hurt you back, you bitch. That was my mentality.

While I was sleeping I heard someone opening the front door. The only person who had keys at the time was Pete, so I sat up in bed and screamed out, 'Pete, is that you?'

I heard so many footsteps, and they all came into the little room where I was lying in bed.

Someone shone a torch in my face. 'Shut up or I will fucking hurt you.'

I trembled with fear. My eyes opened so wide. I couldn't breathe, I was so scared. He pulled his pants down and ripped the blankets off me.

'Rape', a painting by Lilla Benigno.

He put one hand on my breast, and then I felt his fucking dick penetrating me so hard. He was big, so I started screaming. He slapped my face and put his hand over my mouth. I remember his eyes clearly. I remember the eyes of everyone that raped me that night.

He screamed out, 'Shut up, you cripple whore,' and kept hurting me, up and down with this dick so big it felt like the biggest knife in me. Suddenly he came. I started to cry and pushed him off, but when I pushed him off, another man jumped on me, and another and another. This went on forever.

I believe today that there were at least twenty men in that room, and I was raped by twelve of them. The rest watched as I struggled and tried to push them away. But they were all really big men. I shook my head from side to side, trying so hard to push them off me. But they kept on doing it, one after the other, and the pain was indescribable.

I could smell their sweat. Sometimes I could see their eyes. Sometimes I could get their dick out of me, but they were all too strong, and they put it back again. This particular man was so big, and because I tried to push him off he punched me in the face. I saw stars. My right eye and my jaw were really sore from that punch, and my mouth was sore from the hands they used to stop my screams. I couldn't stop any of them. They were all too strong for me.

Then I stopped screaming and went into shock. I didn't move for several minutes while these ugly men raped me. Then I started screaming and pushing again, doing my best to pull their hair or push their ugly bodies away from me.

I was crying uncontrollably. I couldn't believe what was happening.

From time to time I would see their faces, but for only a few seconds, because of the torch that one of the men was carrying. Otherwise it was pitch black. Their eyes are still so fresh in my mind. They were all evil. There was no humanity, no conscience in any of them, until I heard a young man's voice from the background screaming, 'No more! Leave her alone. Enough! Let's go.' One of the bastards who was watching must have felt sorry for me. And for some reason they decided to leave.

One of them grabbed my face and held it so hard, saying, 'You tell this to anyone, you're dead.'

I was so scared and so hurt that I said nothing. I just shook my head meaning, 'No, I won't tell anyone.' I was left in shock and full of fear, and the pain I felt within was indescribable. I was terrified that they would come back and do it all over again.

Suddenly my mind went to Clare. She was the one who did this. She was the one who planned this. There was no other explanation, or unless Pete wanted me out of his life. He could have given the keys to his friends so they could all rape me.

Either way, that was the lowest act that anyone could do to anyone in this life, especially to someone who was disabled. How in the world could I have run away from such an attack? Even a normal woman with normal legs couldn't have run away, not with so many of them. I never pursued legal charges against any of these men, from fear that they would kill me. But what they did will stay on their conscience for the rest of their lives. Raping a young disabled girl. What chance did I have to escape? None whatsoever.

I was in so much pain after what had happened. I curled up into a ball. I couldn't move because of the pain I was feeling inside, and the terror I went through. I was in that position for what seemed like hours. I simply couldn't move. My body felt broken all over, and my vagina was incredibly sore. When I touched my vagina I saw blood. I couldn't move. I couldn't even cry anymore. I had no more tears and no more voice from screaming. Yet somehow, slowly, I still managed to get dressed and run away from that massage parlour. I left the keys on a small table and walked out of there. No way in the world was I going to stay there and work for Pete ever again, not after that traumatic night.

It was really cold that night, but the pain was worse than the cold. I went back to Fitzroy Street in St Kilda. I went to Topolino's Pizza place, to find my friend with the biggest moustache ever. When he saw me, he knew something was very wrong. My face looked like a ghost, he told me.

'What happened?'

But as soon as I looked at him I started to cry. I put my head on his fat belly and sobbed for at least fifteen minutes.

'Come in and sit down.'

He brought me two pieces of pizza and a soft drink. He knew something terrible had happened, but I couldn't open my mouth. I was too sore and too scared. Joe felt so sorry for me. He tried his best to get it out of me but I couldn't talk. I just kept crying uncontrollably. I pushed the food away. I didn't even want to eat or drink. All I wanted was to be held, and Joe held me so tightly, until a customer came in.

'I will be back soon, okay,' he said. 'Don't move.'

I was too upset and very sore. I couldn't go to the police. I was too scared. I kept remembering the words of one of the rapists. 'You tell anyone, you are dead.' These words rang in my head over and over. But Joe was not stupid. He knew something terrible had happened. He came over after the customer left and kindly pulled $20 from his pocket.

'Go into a motel,' he said gently. 'Have a bath and a good sleep. Come and see me tomorrow, okay?'

I took his advice and did just that, but first I scored some smack. I had an extra $50 on me, and while I was heading to the motel, not far from where Joe worked, I saw a friend of mine who was a dealer and scored myself $50 worth of heroin. Then I booked into a motel.

That night I got really stoned. The pain of the rapes went away a little bit, but I could still see their faces, their eyes, smell their sweat, and feel their excitement while they were raping me, over and over again. My vagina was extremely sore, but somehow, after I took that shot of heroin, I managed to get some sleep. The pain in my vagina was worse when I walked, because I was wearing callipers. I walk with my hips, and when I moved my hips all I felt was pain.

I didn't go to the hospital. I was too scared that someone would call the police or my family. The next day I wandered the streets for hours and hours, scared to go back to work, scared to do anything anymore.

I was defeated. The aches and pains of the rape left me scarred emotionally and physically. I wanted to die. I hadn't realised that humans could be so cruel, especially to a person with a disability. I didn't realise they could be so heartless, with no empathy for someone who could not run. To them I was trash, I was a prostitute, I was like dead meat.

It took months and even years to stop the pain I felt that night. I still remember one of them, and his eyes. He was the first to rape me, the ugliest man I have ever seen. I remember his eyes because they were cold, with no feeling in them.

He was a monster. He was a bastard.

I was losing my mind. I had cried so much that I had no more tears left. I booked into another motel, with more heroin, and this time I wanted to die. I wanted to take it all. Everything was building up until, one day, I took the biggest dose of heroin. The cleaner of the motel found me half dead, so she called the ambulance. Again I was back in St Vincent's Hospital in Melbourne.

When I woke up two weeks later, doctors told me what had happened, and when I was fit enough to leave the intensive care unit, they thought I qualified to be locked up in Ward Six. This is the ward for mentally ill patients. I was there for two weeks.

I become very manipulative with the doctors. I tricked them all, telling them I would never try to commit suicide again, and I discharged myself. But, of course, I went back onto the streets of Saint Kilda again. These awful streets became my home.

I was happy to get away from Pete, but I was scared too. I had no money. I had no place to stay. I didn't want to go back home because of all the hatred and disgust I felt about myself, working as a prostitute.

Topolino's Pizza became my home. I felt safe every time I walked in. Whenever I saw Joe I would smile, because if I felt hungry, tired or lonely I knew Joe would look out for me. If anyone gave me a hard time he would kick them out. Joe was like a father figure for me.

But I was living in hell and I stayed there for a long time. I became incredibly dysfunctional. Everything I did was wrong. Every word from my mouth was vulgar. I was the rudest person alive. If you knew me when I was a teenager, you either loved me or hated me. Women were usually the ones who didn't like me. I didn't like myself either. I never felt close to a woman. But some men didn't care how bad and vulgar I was. They stayed, more out of pity than anything else.

That rape destroyed my soul. I died that night. I died inside. That was the night I really began to hate all men, and I wanted to do everything in my power to hurt them as they had hurt me.

I felt like scum and dirty. I felt so much shame and anger for letting this happen to me. I couldn't understand why all these bad things were happening. I felt so much pity for myself. I wanted to run again, but wherever I went, I took my troubles with me. I wanted to be a nice person. I wanted to be happy. Instead I was attracting so much wrongdoing.

Chapter 17

April 1976—My motorbike accident. I was eighteen years old.

I WAS NEARLY EIGHTEEN YEARS OLD and still on the run from my parents. The further I went from them, the better I felt. I wanted to keep my freedom, mentally and psychologically. I was on a mission. I was always living in fear of the police. They did take me back home a few times. I was the worst runaway ever. And, of course, my disability made me very visible to the police. I was caught a few times, but in the end my parents gave up, and so did the police. Nothing was going to stop me now because I was nearly legal age. I knew my family wasn't looking for me anymore. When I passed a police station, not even the police cared if I was alive or dead. Now I was fully qualified to live on the streets. I could go anywhere, anytime. But deep inside I had only one person on my mind: my mother.

I loved her so much, and I carried all this guilt about her looking after all the children. If things hadn't been the way they were, I would have stayed at home and helped her. But I knew that that was impossible. Having a taste of freedom was more important than going back to that lifestyle, which gave me so many panic attacks. I was there to witness real life on the streets. Of course, I was paying a big price for my freedom.

Lilla Benigno on her friend Tim's Harley.

I went to hell and stayed there for ten years, unable to get out, unable to move or speak.

Nevertheless, I didn't care about that too much. Somehow, I knew that one day all this would all fall into place. My mother was always on my mind. It was as though she was my guardian angel. I had given up on this fucking God that I had prayed to for years and years. I replaced him with my mother. Whenever I thought of her I would become calm. Some of my fears would go away for a time.

My freedom was more important than my sanity. I was always scared, but that fear turned me into a tiger. I knew bad things were going to happen, but I also knew that I was going to get through them. I was so happy when I was not living at home. I was sick and tired of living in fear, sick and tired of my family fighting and arguing. Sometimes those arguments would go on and on. My fear would increase and, in the end, all I could think about was that I had to leave before it killed me. And that I did.

I ran and ran and ran, and all my running took me from one experience to another. My life became completely chaotic, all in the name of freedom. I wanted to be so far away from everyone. I wanted to be left alone. There were no more negotiations in my head. I had to disappear from my family, and I did.

Lucy was quite the opposite. She was a gorgeous girl. Her eyes gave away her emotions. She was confined in a wheelchair. I never found out what kind of disability Lucy had. We never discussed it, and it was never an issue for her either. We never asked each other the big question, because we didn't compare each other. As far as we were concerned we were all normal, but for others out there, we were like a curse. The stares, the gossip; children screaming at us; parents trying to explain to their children why we were like this, and projecting their own fears onto their children.

The three of us, all disabled, and a boy called Michael, in a wheelchair, all decided to rent a beautiful house in Brunswick. It had three bedrooms. Lucy and I shared a room, while Anna and Michael had their own rooms.

Lucy was the sweet one. Everyone loved Lucy, including me. She was smart too. We helped each other cook the meals. We shared the rent, and we lived quite well. This became our little nest. We listened to lots of music. Michael had a stereo on which we could play records, and listen to all the music we liked. I was living in heaven. I have loved music since I was born. My father had music in his blood, and gladly passed it on to me. Bob Dylan was his favourite, and he became my favourite too. I loved Rod Stewart, an awesome singer; and, of course, Johnny Farnham. I was also really into Deep Purple, head banging music. I used to go crazy.

We all loved Rodriguez, playing his music nearly every day. We would listen to it while we were cleaning. We all got along quite well and never argued. If something was wrong, we talked about it and fixed it quietly. Then party again. We partied so much in that house.

Lucy was the peacemaker, and I was the troublemaker. Anna was the loudest one, and Michael was the quiet achiever. Yet, we all got along quite well. I had met Anna and Lucy in Yooralla, Balwyn, and now and then we had kept in touch and gone out together.

One day, out of the blue, without much thought, I suggested to everyone that maybe it was time we all went to Luna Park, in St Kilda. It was a venue full of wonderful games and rides, such as the ghost train, the big dipper, and dodgem cars.

They all stared at each other, then Anna said, 'I'm in. Why not?'

But Michael said no. He had other plans. He had a lot of friends and was well liked by everyone. We loved him, and made sure that when dinner was ready, he always received more than us. We girls believed that men needed to eat a lot to keep up their strength, so we fed Michael big dinners and he loved us for it. Michael was a very straightforward person who loved to smoke pot at the time. He was a paraplegic. He could move his arms, but was paralysed from the waist down. I never asked him why he was in that wheelchair. He was happy and didn't care at all. I didn't smoke pot because it gave me panic attacks. I was into the big drugs, such as trips pills. These would give me hallucinations. I only took them three times, and then stopped.

It was a gorgeous day. The sun was out and it was warm. By lunch time it would be a lot warmer. Before we went to Luna Park, we decided to go to the pizza shop in Fitzroy Street, St Kilda, for a bite to eat and couple of glasses of wine. After lunch I pushed Lucy's wheelchair and Anna held my arm for support. We headed off to Luna Park.

We were all a bit tipsy. I had had three glasses of red wine. I went on the big dipper with Anna and screamed so loud. It was scary but so much fun. I wanted to go on more and more rides, and we did. Then I talked to Lucy, to see if there was a way we could put her in a ride. This gorgeous man, about six feet tall with blue eyes and blond hair—his name was Christian—volunteered to take Lucy for a ride on the big wheel, and she loved it. We stayed there approximately four hours, after which we were tired and decided to go home.

The taxi arrived at the front of Luna Park. We were all exhausted yet very happy. I sat next to the window and Lucy was in the middle, chirping away as usual and saying how beautiful the day was. And me, I was thinking, Yeah, yeah, boring. I wanted more excitement. I always wanted excitement. I couldn't stand being still.

As we approached the lights in Fitzroy Street, a gorgeous guy on a Harley stopped next to our taxi. He turned and smiled at me. I wound the window down and screamed, 'Can I get a ride home with you?'

He smiled at me and said, 'Sure, jump on.'

Lucy and Anna screamed at me, 'No, don't go, Lilla, please don't go.'

'I'll be fine. It will be fun. You go home and I'll meet you there.'

They were really upset with me. I got out of the taxi, and slowly climbed on the back of his Harley. He gave me a long scarf and told me to put it around my neck. He said it was going to be a little cold. He gave me his spare helmet, and off we went. The taxi went first and this guy I didn't even know followed.

I was enjoying the ride so much, holding this man so tight. I didn't care if anything bad happened. I was just so happy to sit on the back of a Harley. My biggest dream was finally achieved. I was in heaven, a little tipsy from all the wine I had drunk. I'd had fun in Luna Park with the girls, and now I was sitting on the back of this Harley, with the longest Carlton Football Club scarf around my neck.

I felt so free and happy. I wanted to scream and shout out my happiness to everyone. But this guy was going a bit fast, and I was beginning to get scared, holding him tighter and tighter, afraid that I was going to fall off.

Then, as we approached a T-junction and turned right, my scarf became caught in the back wheel. Suddenly I was in the air. I hit the ground, but the guy rode on for a while, because he didn't know I had fallen off. Then he saw me, rolling on the road with the scarf still around my neck, and stopped. I nearly choked to death. A couple more seconds and I would have died.

I blacked out. When I woke up I could hear someone saying, 'Can you hear me? I'm a priest. If you want to say anything you can talk to me now.'

I slowly raised my head, looked at the priest and said, 'Fuck off. I'm not going to die. Fucking leave me alone.' The priest moved away.

Then a lady said, 'Hi, I'm a nurse. I've called the ambulance. They'll be here any second now. What's your name?'

I couldn't move, my head was so sore. Slowly I said to her, 'My name is Lilla.'

The ambulance was there within minutes. I had a swollen face and my front tooth had come through my upper lip. I got five stitches, which left a scar on my top lip. I had a broken collar bone and was in St Vincent's Hospital for two weeks.

My mum and dad came to the hospital and walked past my bed without recognising me. When they finally saw me they were shocked. I had a splint on my arm, my collar bone was broken, half my face was swollen and black and blue, and I could only see with one eye. When I had the accident I hit the right side of my face on the ground and half my tooth came through my lip. I wasn't recognisable.

When I saw them walking past me I screamed out, 'Mum, I'm here.' My father and mother turned around and looked at me in complete shock.

My mother began to cry, and my father was gentle. 'As soon as you get a bit well,' he said, 'we will look after you.'

Two weeks later I was discharged from the hospital and I was back living with my parents. My father told me that I was going to get a lot of money from that accident, but when I found out that the person who was riding that Harley didn't have a licence, there was no way I would go to court. I didn't want him to go to prison. I felt it was my fault, getting on that Harley in the first place. So when I was well, I ran away from home again. I didn't want to get him into trouble and I didn't care about the money. I wanted my freedom back.

After the accident I didn't want to live with Lucy, Anna and Michael anymore. I wanted to be free. I didn't want to pay bills, or buy food or even be responsible. I wanted to be wild and alive. I didn't want to settle down with anyone, so I ran away from that house in Brunswick. I never saw Lucy, Anna or Michael again.

Instead I went back to living on the streets. I went back to St Kilda, the only place where people didn't pity me for who I was. Street kids accepted me as I was, and some drag queens became my best friends. Living in Saint Kilda gave me freedom again.

Chapter 18

Living in the streets and pregnant.
The birth of my daughter Chantelle, January 21, 1976.
I was eighteen years old.

I WAS HOMELESS, but I felt so free. Now and then I would find a man, and he would pay me for quick sex. This is how I survived for drugs and sometimes a hot meal.

Now and then I would get tired of living like a scavenger, and begging for food and a bed. But whenever I called my mother to let her know how things were, I always lied to her, because I didn't want to hurt her. I didn't want her to feel the pain I was feeling, and I didn't want her to know about the humiliation I felt at being disabled.

I went to see my older sister, Isabella. I heard she had settled in a nice little unit, one bedroom, big enough for her and her newborn baby girl. She said I could stay with her and give her a hand with the baby.

I loved little Paola. She was so little and so pretty. She was only four weeks old when I met her. All I wanted to do was kiss her and hold her. I was happy with that arrangement. I didn't mind looking after little Paola while Isabella went out.

'Desperate', digital art by Lilla.

One night, my sister came home from a night out with about six guys. They came back to smoke dope, laughing and talking.

In those days I was very shy. I was always scared to open my mouth. Many times when I did put my opinion across, I was put down. I felt my opinion was never important. But this particular night, one of the guys Isabella brought home kept looking at me, but never said a word. I sat observing everyone. Now and then I looked at this man. He was very handsome. He had the most gorgeous eyes I had ever seen. That night I didn't want to drink or smoke dope, just in case little Paola woke up. I felt as though I took the mother role. I wanted Paola to be safe.

My sister was going through a hard time. She was deeply in love with Paola's dad, but circumstances kept them apart. It was sad to see.

Isabella was taller than me, almost six feet tall. Her shoulder length hair was naturally light brown, but she dyed it blond and it really suited her. She was there for me many times when I lived on the streets, and I have always been very grateful towards her.

I slept in the lounge room. There was only one small bedroom, a tiny bathroom, a very small lounge room, and a tiny kitchen. The apartment was only meant for one person. I took off my clothes and callipers, tucked myself in and was ready to settle for the night.

Suddenly I heard a knock on the door. 'Who is it?'

From the other side a man's voice replied, 'It's me, Dominic.'

I remembered his voice but didn't know his name. This man, tall, dark and handsome, with beautiful, big brown eyes, a small petite nose and a smile that suited his beautiful face; slender, but with big muscles. It was the guy who had been staring at me all night. I really don't understand why I did this, but I opened the door and let him in. No words were spoken. He started kissing me, and we fell on the bed, kissing passionately for what seemed forever.

Nothing was said. We looked in each other's eyes for a long time. He kissed my eyes, my lips and my face, and we made passionate love. Then I went to sleep.

I was starving for affection. I wanted to be loved, and sometimes I didn't think of the consequences. I went ahead and made lots of mistakes. In my mind, the love I was receiving from him made me feel like a woman, made me feel out of this world. The all sex encounter was unbelievably beautiful.

He lay next to me, still kissing my eyes and telling me, 'You have the most gorgeous eyes I have ever seen.' Then, after lying there with me for about an hour, he said he had to go back out to his friends. I didn't mind. I felt satisfied with him. I felt a lot of love and affection.

When he dressed and walked out, I kept thinking how beautiful the sex had been, and how close we had felt. That was the last time I saw him.

One morning about three weeks later, I woke up with sores from my chin to my upper lip, and these sores had pus in them. I was shocked. I didn't know what was going on. First it was a rash, which the next day became big pimples full of pus. I was too scared to go out, but my sister insisted I go and see a doctor.

The doctor told me I had an infection. He took blood and urine for tests. Then the doctor came back with the news. 'You are pregnant.'

I was eighteen years old. The only person I'd had sex with recently was that Greek guy, Dominic, who came back when everyone went out that night. I had so many questions running through my mind. Me, pregnant? How? But I had not used a condom. I was not responsible at all with my body.

I was devastated. I was young and homeless. I was living with my sister at the time, but we argued so much I had already decided to run away. But I had to find the right moment, and this was it.

I didn't want to leave little Paola. I was very attached to her. I was scared. Isabella and I got into the biggest argument when I told her I was pregnant.

'What the fuck are you going to do?' Isabella screamed.

I surely didn't know. I was so irresponsible.

I hated when Isabella screamed, but I remember looking at her and saying nothing. I felt numb, paralysed with fear. I turned around, opened the front door and walked out. That was the last time I saw Isabella for many years. I lost contact with her. I was too busy bailing myself out of the ugly situations I got myself into.

I went back to Fitzroy Street, St Kilda. I went to see my best friend with the biggest moustache, at Topolino's Pizza. I was so happy he was on. That meant I was going to get free food. I was so lucky sometimes. Men, out of nowhere, would take me to restaurants and nightclubs. I was living a life of action, full of adventures. There were some nightmares, but I would be rescued, fed and clothed by strangers, either little old ladies, or rich men who loved my face. I always ran away from those guys. They used to be so annoying. Rich people think they can buy your love with money. I found out the hard way.

One night, before I ran away from Isabella, she and I went to a nightclub. A baby sitter was looking after little Paola. We met two very good looking guys. They were rough looking, but they booked a motel for me and my sister, so we could have a good time. My sister told me to go with the darker guy to fetch some pizzas, and I said, 'Okay. Sure, why not.'

This man, extremely good looking, instead of driving to the pizza shop drove to a dark area near the airport.

'What are you doing? Where are we going?'

'Shut up. I will show you.'

He parked the car far away from the traffic and I was terrified. He opened his door and sat on the back seat, then grabbed me by my hair.

I started screaming. 'Don't do this. Stop it. What are you doing?'

He put his hand around my throat, dragged me onto the back seat, pulled his pants down and said, 'Suck on this, you stupid fucking crippled slut.'

While I was trembling with fear, fear of being killed, I started giving him oral sex whilst bawling my eyes out. He pulled my hair. 'Harder! Do it harder, you slut.'

So I did it harder, until he came inside my mouth. I spewed it all out, it made me so sick. I was scared he would kill me.

Then he opened the door and pushed me out. 'Go back and sit in the front, you whore.' Then he sat in the front seat, turned on the radio, and made a U-turn, heading to the pizza shop.

I was shaking and crying in the car while he was getting those pizzas. I couldn't wait to get to the motel to tell my sister what had happened. When he returned he screamed at me, 'You ever tell your sister what I did to you, I will fucking kill you, slut. You are beautiful, yes, but you're a fucking cripple and I hate cripples.'

I sat there in shock, tears rolling from my eyes. I just wanted to get back to that motel.

As soon as we arrived at the motel, which was in Brunswick, I took my sister to the toilet and told her what had happened; but she was too stoned and said to me, 'Don't worry about it. Let's have some pizza.'

I looked at her, then at him and the other guy. 'Fuck you all. I'm not fucking staying here. You are all bastards.' And I was looking at my sister, too, when I said that. As soon as I was outside, I put my finger out to hitch a ride. A car picked me up to take me back to St Kilda.

I could still taste that horrible stuff in my mouth, so I asked the driver if he wanted to come with me for a few drinks at the pub. He was an older man and he didn't say no, so we went to the Graham Hotel. That night I got blind drunk, and slept at this old man's place, on a single bed. He didn't want to have sex with me, thank God, but I felt shaken and still in shock. I always hated doing oral on men for that reason. I couldn't stand the look of them, the feel of them, and the taste of them. Again I didn't go to the police because

I was very naïve and very scared. It took me a long time to get over that incident. I never forgot the way he treated me and what he called me: crippled slut and whore. Part of me thought he was going to kill me too. Thank God he didn't. Thank God he took me back to the motel.

After that incident, I left the old man's place while he was still sleeping and went back to Fitzroy Street, St Kilda.

So here I was, pregnant from a man I really didn't know. All I knew was that his first name was Dominic. I didn't have the money for an abortion. I didn't really understand what an abortion was. I was too naïve to seek help; plus by now I was about twelve weeks pregnant. I had no choice but to go through with the pregnancy. My legs were always in pain, my callipers were falling apart, and my body was getting weaker because I hardly ate good meals. I was a scavenger, always searching for food and a place to stay. One question that kept haunting me over and over again was, 'What if my baby gets polio, like me?' This was my biggest nightmare.

Homeless people, some of whom became my friends, let me stay with them, shared their food and their plonk with me. One old lady who kept stealing food from rubbish bins, and materials that were like gold to her but garbage to me, asked me one day, 'Limpy, what you going to do with the baby? Are you keeping it or are you going to give it to a family who can look after it?'

I looked at her. I was so scared. 'I don't know. I think tomorrow I'm going to see Mum. I will ask her.'

One morning I went to Bega Street, in Chadstone, where my parents lived at the time. I knew my father was at work. He always worked.

'Mum. Help me. Can I come back home? I got nowhere to go.'

I was starting to show. I was about seven months pregnant. My mother was horrified. My father was working so she let me in for a while. She didn't know what to do. She and Dad were settled now that I was not living at home, and Mum also had the other children to think about.

'You can't stay here,' she said. 'You have to go; and don't let your father see you in that condition. Here's fifty dollars. Go and stay somewhere else, but you can't stay here.'

Many times my mother was there for me. She used to give me money behind Dad's back, just enough to get something to eat. Or sometimes, late at night, I would meet her outside and she would give me spaghetti. I would eat it quickly, then hitch a ride back to the streets. But this time I knew that Mum could not help me, not because she didn't want to, but because she was scared. I was very scared too. I hugged her.

'I will find a way, Mum, don't worry. I'll let you know what I'm going to do.'

Mum had tears in her eyes. She knew I felt helpless and confused, but I knew she had other smaller children to look after. If my father had seen me in that condition, God only knows what would have happened. I didn't want my mother to get into trouble, so I decided to leave.

I left my mother's house, and never went back to see my family. I knew now that I was really alone. I had to find a way through this on my own.

I knew I wouldn't survive if I stayed on the streets pregnant, but one day I saw a friend of mine, Trish. She reminded me so much of Liza Minnelli: buck teeth, the same big eyes, and a gorgeous smile. Her personality was bubbly, likeable. But she was such a people pleaser. People would walk all over her, but not when I was around. I used to stand up for her, and show her that people didn't have the right to talk to her like that. That was why we became friends.

Trish was gentle and kind, and one day when I saw her in the streets, she approached me and asked me, 'Have you got anywhere to stay when the baby arrives?'

I responded quickly, 'No I don't, but I will be fine. I will find a place soon.'

Trish said, 'Nonsense! You can come and stay with me and my family until you have the baby.'

I was so happy. I accepted the offer and we went back to her place. Trish lived just outside the city of Melbourne, near Altona.

I loved the little house where I was going to stay for the rest of my pregnancy. I had a small bed in Trish's room. We shared a room, and it was great. Trish and I became a lot closer. I loved her parents. They were both old people in their seventies, but gentle and tender, just like Trish. I felt safe and I didn't want to leave. I wanted to live there forever, but I knew that was not possible, especially when the baby was born.

While I lived at Trish's place I stopped taking drugs and stopped drinking. Everything I took made me sick. But I ate good food every night and I had a bed to sleep in like normal people. The months were going fast, and my belly was getting bigger. I was not close to this baby inside me. I felt nothing. It was nothing but a burden, and all I wanted to do was give birth and run away again. I knew I was not a fit person to look after this baby. My brain was fucked with the drugs and all the negative thinking. I was scared of the unknown.

I went to the hospital for my regular check-ups, and it was Trish who took me everywhere in her car. One day when I went to the hospital I found myself in the social worker's office. She told me I had no choice but to give up the baby because I was disabled and because I was a drug addict.

I said, 'You can't tell me what to do. I'm over eighteen now and you can't have this baby. I will make the fucking decision, not you. Fuck you!'

The social worker said, 'Family Services won't let you keep the baby because of the conditions you're living in. You live on the streets. You've got no home, no clothes ready for the baby. You haven't got a safe place for the baby. Think of the baby instead of yourself, and stop swearing at me. I'm here to help you.'

I stuck my finger up to her. 'Fuck you.' I went back and sat next to Trish. It was time for me to see the doctor. He checked me out and told me that I still had a long way to go, but the baby was fine.

Two months went by and, one day, as I was having my shower, my waters broke, and I was rushed to the hospital. This time Trish couldn't come with me because she used to work in a massage parlour, and it was her night on. She had a lot of clients, and that's how she made her money. There were lots of regulars who loved her, so she was never broke. She always had lots of money.

Every time I went to the hospital for my regular check-up, there was the social worker, and I always saw her before I saw the doctor. She kept pushing me to give up the baby, to put it up for adoption, and I would fight with her. I would say things like, 'What? Because I'm disabled you really believe I can't look after my baby? Why are you using my disability for everything? I'm not mad. I'm not crazy. Sure I live on the streets, but maybe if you did your job right you could find someone who could help me raise my child.'

But this social worker always told me that it was not right for me to raise this child, not in my condition. First, I didn't have a home; second, I had no family to support me; and third, I was a drug addict. She always reminded me of that. And I used to hate her.

The time arrived. I was ready to give birth to my new baby. I was at the hospital on my own. They gave me a bed. A nurse came over and gave me a white gown, then shaved my private parts. Within two hours I was in labour. Strong pains. Pains that felt like I wanted to do the biggest crap. Very painful.

Suddenly all the nurses and doctors went to the window. Something was happening, and I was left alone. I wondered what they were looking at. It turned out that an accident had happened just outside the hospital, and all the staff were looking at the accident, forgetting that I was on that fucking table, feeling scared, cold and in so much pain.

I was eighteen years old and incredibly scared. I didn't know what was going to happen next. I screamed out, 'Hey you all, what about me? My baby is coming. I am in pain. Can someone help me?'

I was left all alone. I shivered. Underneath me there was no blanket, only a steel table. I started to panic. I could feel the pressure of the baby. I wanted to push and push, but I stopped myself and screamed out to everyone, 'The baby is coming!' I screamed so loud that the two nurses, the midwife and a male doctor turned and rushed over to help me with this delivery.

They made me feel terrible. This was the first time I had given birth and I was alone with these crazy people who did a wonderful job of looking down on me, and treating me as if I was a piece of shit, a freak. I wanted it to be over so I could cover myself and feel warm. My feet were icy, and my legs were up on each side, strapped, so I could push the baby out.

One hour it took. I remember the two biggest pains. It felt as though my vagina was ripped apart; and then, as soon as the head was out, the rest was nothing. I felt the doctor stitching me, but it wasn't as painful as giving birth.

The baby was born just after midnight. The nurses told me that everything went great, and asked me if I wanted to breastfeed. I quickly said no. When the nurses finished cleaning the baby, one of the nurses brought her into my ward. I still didn't know what to do. I still didn't know if I was going to give my baby up for adoption. I was incredibly confused and so alone. I knew it was my decision, but I was not ready to sign any fucking papers.

My daughter was born on January 26, 1976, just after midnight. I could hear the nurses talking to one another.

'This baby is very beautiful isn't it?' And the other nurse replied, 'Yes. I have never seen such a beautiful baby.' That made me feel so proud and excited.

The nurse was tall and skinny, with her hair pulled back into a nice, tidy bun. She had big brown eyes, a petite nose and a curvy, tender smile. Some of her teeth were crooked, but very white. After she cleaned the baby, she said, 'Would you like to hold your new baby girl?'

I looked at her big brown eyes. 'Yes I would.'

The nurse picked up the baby, who weighed six pounds. She was a bit small, but she was so beautiful. When she placed this beautiful baby in my arms, I melted. I looked at her for a long time, at the shape of her eyes, her tiny little nose, her lips. Then I saw a small mole on the side of her chin, and I have that too. I kept holding the baby, then the nurse asked me, 'What name are you going to give her?'

I looked up at her, then at the baby. Suddenly a name came to my mind and I replied, 'I will call her Chantelle.'

'Chantelle. What a beautiful name.'

'Yes. My brother used to go out with a girl on the ship, and that was her name. She was absolutely beautiful. I like Chantelle.'

In those days people with a disability were treated like second class citizens. We were ridiculed, criticised and judged. In those days, if you were young, homeless, and disabled, staff would do anything in their power to push you towards adopting the baby out.

Throughout history, people with disabilities have been ignored, hidden and cursed. When made visible, they have been subjects of exhibitions and objects of ridicule. Society has 'dealt' with the 'problem' of people with disabilities by placing them in institutions or prisons, and by sterilising women and girls as an acceptable treatment.

Up until the late 1970s, the views of persons with disabilities were mainly filtered through the voices of disability service providers, professionals working in the area of disability, and family members. This was also occurring at the international level. At the time, the key international disability organisation, Rehabilitation International, had a policy that while people with a disability could attend its periodic international conference as observers, they were not permitted to speak. People with disabilities strongly protested against this policy at the 1980 conference of Rehabilitation International, held in Winnipeg, Canada, where a decision was made to establish a new international organisation of and for people with disability. The organisation founded was Disabled Peoples International, which now has members in over 160 countries throughout the world.

I didn't want to put my baby up for adoption. I wanted to see if there was a way I could look after her by myself; but my social worker, a young woman who went to college to get her degree in social work, pushed me over and over again to adopt my baby out.

'You can't look after your baby,' she would say. 'You have polio, you're on drugs, your family doesn't want you, and you're homeless. How can you look after this baby?'

I hated her when she talked like that, but she was right. I was in denial. I had this fantasy in my head that I could look after my baby, but in fact I couldn't. That was my reality.

I looked around the room, hoping she could come up with a better idea. I was tired of hearing of teenage girls being treated as if they were monsters, just because they became pregnant. I remember one day, sitting in the front foyer of the hospital, waiting to see the doctor. I was about eight months pregnant.

When I sat down, an older woman shouted to me, 'Shame on you.'

I became so angry and screamed at her. 'Fuck you.' I stuck my finger up at her, then moved away. If I'd had to look at her any longer I would have smacked her in the mouth. My anger always got me in trouble. I couldn't keep it inside. I always blew up.

Now, with tears in my eyes, I was observing everything about this little angel. Her eyes opened the moment I picked her up. They were the same colour as mine. Her tiny nose, so beautiful, and her little lips, hands and feet. I looked again at the little mole on her chin, like mine, and started to cry.

I was overjoyed. My emotions were all over the place. All I wanted to do was hold my daughter. I didn't want to let her go. Doctors kept asking me what I was going to do, and I kept screaming at them to leave me alone. I wasn't ready to make that decision.

My social worker came to see what I wanted to do, and pushed me more and more towards adoption. I wasn't free. I had so many people pushing me, because everyone was interested more in the child than me. I was too young to understand any of this. I wished I was normal, so I could run away with my new baby. I knew this was not possible. I knew I couldn't keep Chantelle, not in my position. But I was too naïve to think responsibly. I just wanted to run away from everything. I wanted to keep my baby so badly but, deep inside, I knew it was impossible.

Three days went by, and the doctors were getting more and more impatient with me. They kept asking what I was going to do. They so badly wanted me to sign the adoption papers. But I kept putting it off, hoping for a miracle.

I looked after Chantelle for ten days. I was losing my mind. I would pick her up in the middle of the night while she was sleeping and cry, and talk to her as if she was an adult. I remember one night, while she was in my arms, I was crying and talking to my baby, saying things like, 'I will look after you. I will get a good little place for you and me. I'm not going to leave you. I am your mummy.' I kept saying this over and over again, and softly crying my eyes out. I felt so alone. I felt so confused and lost.

One night I crocheted eight little white hats, one for each baby in my ward and, in the morning, when all the new mothers woke up and saw the little hats, they all thanked me. They put the little white hats, with little pom-poms, on their babies' heads, so they could stay warm. It looked so beautiful, to see all the babies wearing my little hats. The new mothers knew I was going to give my baby up for adoption, yet they all took a liking to me. Some offered to let me stay with them. But deep inside I knew I was not capable of looking after the baby.

I ran out of time. On the tenth day, a woman doctor, tall, slim, wearing prescription glasses, and holding a big file, came over to my bed. 'It's time, Lilla. It's time to sign the papers. As soon as you do that, you can leave the hospital. You will be discharged.'

Just like that, sign and be discharged. I panicked. All that went through my mind was, I can't leave this baby here. I can't do it.

Finally I signed the papers. The thought of my baby going to an Italian family, with Italian beliefs, put my heart at ease a little, but not for long. I was broken. I was devastated. What my parents had done with me when I was small, I now did to my baby. I abandoned her. I left her in the hospital. I signed the papers, and when I did it felt as though the staff were going to throw me out.

Saying goodbye to my baby was the hardest thing I've ever done. I sobbed, and there was no one there to help me, no counsellors, no doctors, and no nurses. Everyone was more concerned about the baby than me. There was no one there to help me to deal with this devastation, to deal with the biggest decision; no one was there to tell me, 'I will help you with your grieving. I can help you.' No one. Being disabled, I felt I had no more rights. I was too devastated to think about anything. I wanted to die.

I remember the last time I kissed Chantelle, so beautiful, so precious, and so little. I didn't want to leave her. I wanted to run away with her, but I couldn't.

After I said my goodbyes I went down the stairs of the hospital, instead of taking the lift. I was hoping I would fall and die, but I reached the bottom and I was back on the streets. Back on the streets, alone, walking with my callipers. They were hurting me. I needed to change them. But my whole world was falling apart.

I sobbed, thinking over and over again, What have I done? I want my baby back. More sobbing, walking into the night. Alone, grieving, and praying for some kind of a solution, to no avail. I had no way out but to kill myself. Now I really wanted to do it. Now I was ready to die.

Chapter 19

The pain of adopting out my daughter sent me back to heroin and back living in the streets. I was nineteen years old.

AFTER MY DAUGHTER WAS GIVEN UP FOR ADOPTION, my life was finished. My thoughts were about how I could kill myself, and never be rescued again. Why was it so hard for me to commit suicide and why was I coming back into this mad world? I felt so guilty leaving my new baby at that hospital. I felt I was the worse mother in the world. I kept seeing her little face. I wanted to go back and get her.

Living on the streets or not, I wanted my baby back. I couldn't leave her there all alone.

Leaving my baby at the hospital was sending me insane. I kept crying. I walked from suburb to suburb wondering how I was going to get her back. I went back twice to the hospital, trying to get her back. I still had two days left. The doctors and nurses told me I had thirty days to change my mind, to get my baby back, but when I went back she was gone.

Part of me died instantly. I screamed and screamed at all the nurses and all the doctors there, at the Royal Woman's Hospital in Melbourne, Victoria. I became hysterical, tears rolling down my face, begging, and

'Suffering', painting/digital art by Lilla Benigno.

cursing everyone. My behaviour was out of control, and the staff decided to call the security guards. Two big men—they looked like policemen to me—grabbed me and threw me out of the hospital. I lost my mind completely. I realised I had no hope whatsoever of getting her back. That killed my soul. I wanted to die, right there and then, but I knew going under a truck or bus would have been very painful. So I went back to St Kilda. I had an idea.

Now I was ready to kill myself, but I had to do it properly, because I didn't want to come back. It was too painful to stay alive. I had done the most terrible thing. I had left my little baby and now she was gone. I approached a tall man. I had scored heroin from him before. I always paid him, but this time I had no money. His face was covered with pimples. He had dark eyes, and you could see from miles away that he took heroin himself, as well as dealing. I looked a bit like him, very skinny with dark eyes. I begged him for drugs.

He pushed me to the ground and threw me a small packet of white powder. He warned me, 'Don't take too much. That's pure heroin. Next time you pay, okay?'

I was scared of him. I was shaking because he pushed me to the ground. I wasn't hurt physically, but my fear was worse than the push.

I slowly struggled to my feet. Sometimes when I fell it would take me forever to get up, and this time it was no different. I went to my hiding place, where I used to take heroin years earlier with Sue, a young girl who was a full-on junkie. It was an abandoned block of units, five storeys high. There were hardly any windows left. Most were smashed. The place was really run down, but it was the best hideaway for junkies.

When I walked in I found a needle on the floor. There was still dry blood on it from the last shot someone else had. I went into the empty apartment and found a small, dirty, smelly bathroom. There was lots of graffiti on the wall. Some of the art was beautiful, but there were also swear words, or people's names and dates. The sink was black, but in places around the tap it was white. I thought, 'Once upon a time this sink used to be white and clean. But now it was black and had blood stains on it.'

Walking into that place was dangerous. Many junkies would rob other junkies or bash them, so they could take their drugs. For some reason, this never happened to me. I was lucky.

I got some dirty water from the tap and put it in a little teaspoon that I carried with me. I took some of the white powder from the little plastic bag and put it into the spoon. I lit my lighter to mix the heroin and dissolve it in the water. Then I took a small piece of filter from my cigarette and put it into the tea spoon. With the syringe I slowly sucked all the liquid in.

I remembered the dealer's words, 'Be careful. It's pure.' Everyone, including myself, was scared to use pure heroin for fear of overdosing on it. I looked at this syringe and everything came back. My daughter, all alone in that big, big hospital. I had left her, abandoned her. I wanted to die. I wanted to disappear forever. I was so tired of feeling all these terrible emotions. I couldn't stand it anymore. I cried so many tears, hoping someone would get me out of this hell. While looking at the syringe I remember thinking, If this is not strong enough I will take all of it.

Then I heard a noise. I hid the syringe behind my back. I saw a man's figure and heard a voice.

'Hey, Limpy, is that you?' It was my friend Steve. Steve and I met on the streets, and whenever we bumped into each other we would spend many hours together, sometimes days.

Steve believed he was a rocker. Well, he dressed like one, with high black shoes and his hair flicked back. He told me oil always did the trick, so his hair was always oily and greasy. He was quite attractive, but had four front teeth missing. His eyes were between grey and blue. I loved his eyes.

Steve was much taller than me, with hardly any fat on his body. He loved to wear a black belt with studs on it. He also wore a black band on his left wrist, also with studs. He showed this macho side by dressing tough. He did look rough, but he had a heart of gold. Steve and I slept together like brother and sister. He never made any advances on me. That was why I respected him and saw him as a great friend. He had seen me walking into this ugly apartment and came to see what I was doing.

I called out, 'Yes, it's me. Come here, Steve.'

He walked in, all rugged up in a big black jacket, made of thick wool, and a pair of black jeans and black shoes. I knew his walk. I saw his smiling face in a beam of light, coming through the window of this ugly, dirty room.

'What are you doing?' he asked. 'What happened with the baby?'

I hadn't seen him for a few months, because I had been living with my friend Trish, away from everyone, and away from the streets.

I looked at him and began to cry uncontrollably. 'They took the baby away from me, Steve. I can't stop crying. It hurts too much. Please, can you do this for me? Can you shoot me up? I will give you some of this stuff if you do it. Please, Steve, I beg you.'

Steve knew I hated to shoot up myself. I always missed my veins, mainly because I would be overexcited and scared.

Steve took the syringe from me and asked how strong it was.

'Pure,' I said.

Steve then pulled back and said, 'I can't do it, Limpy. If it's pure I'm scared to do it for you.'

'I haven't got my daughter,' I screamed with tears in my eyes. 'They took her away from me. Fucking shoot this up, now.'

Steve got his rubber band, put it around the top of my arm, and told me to shut and open my hand a few times. The lighting in the bathroom was very poor. The only light was from a street light that shone in a thin line.

'I can't find your vein. I can't see too well.'

I remembered my lighter. I lit it and held it very close to the vein. Steve nervously put the needle in the vein, getting it first time.

I looked at him. 'Do it.'

Steve put all the heroin into my blood stream. As he took the rubber band off my arm I felt the rush. At first it was mild, then it became so strong, and I was out of it. I lost consciousness.

I woke up in Saint Vincent's Hospital, in Ward Six. I was a regular there. Everyone knew me. I had overdosed on heroin many times, but this was the worst. I woke after four days, with tubes in my arm. The nurse came over and said very cheerfully, 'Ha, you're awake. Great to see.'

This nurse, a petite woman with long blond hair and a beautiful smile, leaned over to fix my blankets. She helped me to sit up so she could fluff up my pillow.

'What happened?' I asked. 'I don't remember.'

The nurse answered politely, 'Doctor is coming over to see you now that you're awake. He will tell you.'

I had overdosed again. Damn, I was so angry! Why couldn't I die in peace? I was locked in the mental institution. I was horrified. I had wanted to kill myself and had shot pure heroin. But the doctors, hearing that I had left the baby in the hospital to be adopted, knew that I was trying to end my life. They knew I wanted to commit suicide again.

I didn't know that yet. All I knew was that I had wanted to die. I was so angry that I was still alive. When I couldn't see doctors and nurses around, I ran away in my white gown, down the back stairs. I came out of the back of the hospital. It was night time. I crossed the road and entered a backyard to take a pair of jeans, a small black top and a big jacket off the line. Then I hitched a ride back to Saint Kilda.

One night, while I was off my face on heroin, sitting down and drinking orange juice with a friend, I saw my second oldest brother, Arturo. He came into Topolino's Pizza shop, where I was. He screamed at me, 'You are coming home with me right now.'

'Fuck off and leave me alone,' I screamed back at him.

The owner, my sweet friend, came over to me and asked, 'Is this man bothering you?'

'No, this is my brother.'

Arturo grabbed my arm and dragged me to his car. He opened the back door and pushed me in. He pulled out a big knife. 'I'm going to kill you if you ever come back to this hole. You need to get off heroin, do you understand?'

'What, are going to kill me now? Do it, do it, do it!' I was screaming at him. My sister-in-law, with quick thinking, grabbed the knife from Arturo and threw it out the window.

My brother was screaming and cursing. All he wanted was to get me off heroin. He was there to help me, not to kill me. When we arrived at his place, he took me to a little bedroom and locked me in, so I wouldn't escape again. But he didn't realise there was an unlocked window. I quietly opened it and, with lots of difficulty, managed to climb out and run away. I didn't want to stop taking heroin. I wanted to take it until I died. All I wanted to do was die.

My life was fucked, but I never forgot that he was the only brother to come after me. He tried very hard to get me off the streets. That was not the only time. He always took me back home, but I just kept running away, in such a sleazy way. Everyone thought I had lost the plot completely and, at the time, I had. I was mad. I was angry. I was furious, and all I wanted to do was die.

My brother didn't know that I recently let my daughter be adopted. He didn't know I wanted to die. He didn't know anything, and I was too scared to tell him.

What I had done was the worst thing any mother could do, and the guilt was ripping me apart. The voices in my head were screaming at me, 'Go and get the baby back.' But other voices would say, 'You're a bad mother. Leave the baby there. You are disabled and can't look after the baby.' I was dying.

I was totally losing my mind. I was already crazy, but I was reaching a point beyond crazy. I wanted out. I had no one to turn to, alone in this world, grieving for my baby, and wanting so desperately to end my life.

Bit by bit I was killing myself. While living on the streets for the past nine months, I had already been in St Vincent's Hospital twice, overdosed on pills or heroin. The second time, the doctors thought it was best to put me on the sixth floor and keep me there for a long time. They made sure I was watched twenty-four hours a day. The insane ward, where all the mad people were. I looked insane, too. Black eyes, drawn and tired, skinny. I looked about sixty years old and I was only nineteen. I was so out of control. Nothing I did was exciting anymore. My life was about how I could die without these damn doctors bringing me back to life over and over again. How could I do it?

Living on the streets was so damn hard. I didn't trust anyone anymore, and the more I didn't trust people, the more I got myself into trouble. The incident I am about describe scared the hell out of me, but somehow I managed to escape.

One night I met this guy, John, in Fitzroy Street, St Kilda. He was short like me, but very good looking, very charming, and we started to talk. We became a team. I was having sex with him, but one night I saw him take out his false teeth and put them in a jar. That made me so sick, so in the middle of the night, while he was sleeping quietly, I put on my callipers and ran away from him back to St Kilda. Somehow he found me again. He always had these pills that I was very addicted to at the time. They were called 'chewnals'. When I took one I would be off my face for hours. If I took two or more I would blackout, not remembering what I had done. They were in a capsule, half light blue and half dark blue, the strongest pills I have ever taken in my life.

When John finally found me again in St Kilda, he was angry with me because I ran away. I couldn't tell him I ran away because he had false teeth, so I made an excuse and told him I wanted to be free. I didn't want a boyfriend. He gave me two chewnals. I took them right in front of him, and next thing I knew I had been kidnapped.

He took me to a house, and every time I woke up, I was either doing sexual acts with other women or other women were doing sexual acts with me. I would wake up to see John wanking himself while watching us girls having sex with each other. He quickly gave us two more chewnals each. I blacked out again, with no food and no water. Just sex with other girls.

I was there for about two weeks or more. One day I realised that this man was really insane. As soon as I woke up from the blackouts, he would give me a piece of bread to eat, and then two more chewnals, so I could be off my face again. But this time I only pretended to swallow them. As soon as he left, I woke up properly from this nightmare.

I saw so many other young girls, all having sex with each other. I wanted to rescue them all. There must have been at least ten or fifteen other girls, all young, and some of them very pretty. I had to find a way out of there really quickly. The little sanity I had left gave me the courage to look for my callipers. They were under the bed. I put them on quickly, scared he would come back. One of the other young girls was also awake, and I asked if she wanted to run away with me. She quickly said yes, but couldn't find her clothes, so we stole clothes from the other girls. They were too far off their heads to run away. Even if I had wanted to help them I couldn't. Those chewnals were really heavy pills that would knock you out for hours and hours. I was scared that John would come back, hit us, and keep us there for good. We had become his sex slaves.

The other girl, who was so skinny and covered with pimples, ran away with me. When we opened the front door, the light outside nearly blinded me. I hadn't seen the sun for what felt like months. She started running and she left me behind. I became scared then, because I couldn't run. Luckily there were many cars around, so I put my finger out to hitch a ride. A car stopped, and I quickly jumped in.

'Quick,' I said. 'Go, go! I was kidnapped by this man, and if he comes back he will take me back into that mad house.'

The driver, an older man, believed me and asked the name of the man, but I only knew his first name. 'His name is John,' I said, 'but I don't know his surname.'

He asked if I wanted to go to the police, but I was always scared of the police, so I told him no. All I wanted to do was go back to St Kilda. I started to cry in the car because I was happy, finally, to be free of this madman. Finally no more chewnals. Finally no more sexual acts with other women.

At last I was free.

A few years later I heard from a friend who lived on the streets, like me, that John was caught and sent to jail for a long time. All the girls who were there gave evidence. That girl and I, who ran away, didn't give any evidence because we didn't know he had been caught; but the idea of him now being jailed for what he did made me feel so happy. That bastard got what he deserved.

One day I was upstairs playing pool with a friend when a young girl rushed in, screaming, 'Who wants to take these chewnals off me? The police are after me. Please.'

'I will,' I said. 'Give them to me.'

'Swallow them real fast, before the police arrive.'

The police were already coming up the stairs. She put the pills in my hand, and I swallowed them, without thinking of the consequences. I didn't even see how many I took, but I knew it was a lot. The police took her away, and she screamed that she didn't have anything on her. I kept playing pool. I knew those pills were very bad for me. I had swallowed them to help her, without thinking.

Next thing I knew, I woke up in St Vincent's Hospital again. I had nearly died. I didn't even remember collapsing in the pool room. The nurse told the doctors I was awake. The doctor came to see me and told me I had wanted to kill myself. I wasn't able to respond. I had tubes everywhere, down my throat, up my nose, and in my arm. I wanted to tell the doctor that I didn't want to kill myself, but no words came out. I had no voice and I felt so sick. I was told I was out for two weeks, and they didn't think I would make it. But, again, I did make it. I was still fucking alive, although I didn't want to be alive at all.

Finally, after so many stupid counselling sessions that I didn't understand, and so many talks to my doctor, they decided to discharge me. It didn't take me long to find my way back to St Kilda. Perhaps an hour or so. I hitched a ride, as always. That was the only way I could get around. I went to Topolino's Pizza, where my best friend was happy to see me.

The first thing Joe asked was, 'Where have you been? I haven't seen you in weeks. Are you all right?'

I could see he was concerned but I kept my head down and said nothing. I didn't want to tell him what I was going through. I couldn't. I felt so lost and numb. I felt like a dead soul.

Joe was happy to see me, and I ordered the usual hamburger with a juice. I sat at a table. In this shop I loved sitting on the stools, but I always needed a hand. This time I was in a bad mood and didn't want to ask anyone for help.

Chapter 20

Gang-raped by many bikers, 1977. I was nineteen years old.

I WAS LIVING ON THE STREETS AGAIN. Now and then I would find shelter from old men and sometimes old ladies. Many people tried to get me off the streets, but the more they tried the more I would run. I wanted to be left alone. I couldn't stand myself, and my self-hate sometimes led me into bigger problems.

I met this guy with a Harley while I was having a coffee. He looked harmless, although I was thinking, How long since you have had a bath? I didn't dare to ask him.

In those days, a lot of bikers were evil, always on the news, bashing each other or shooting one another over things I felt could have been negotiated. I met so many incredibly good looking bikers, but I was scared to be around them because some of them looked and were very tough. I always had to be drunk to be around bikers.

He came and sat at my table and introduced himself. 'Hi, my name is Animal. Want to come for a ride on my Harley?'

I thought, 'Not only are you ugly but you have an ugly name too.'

I loved Harleys and without thinking I said, 'Yes, I would love to, but I have a problem.'

This biker, Animal, who stank like hell, asked me, 'What's the problem?'

I went into a long story about how I hurt my legs in a motorbike accident. He looked under the table and saw my callipers. They were falling apart. Some straps didn't stay on the wire of the callipers. Sometimes I used sticky tape to keep them together. Little by little they were falling apart, and I was too busy surviving in the streets to think about getting a new pair.

'Raped and Desperate',
Painting by Lilla Benigno.

'I don't care about your legs,' he said. 'Your face is astonishing. I could look at your eyes forever. I promise I won't ride fast.'

I limped my way out, following him to his Harley.

Sitting on the seat I looked a bit taller than him. The back seat was a few inches higher. He put a helmet on my head and smiled, showing his crooked yellow teeth. I didn't like anything about this man, but there I was on his Harley, with a helmet on and ready to go for a ride.

'Animal, don't go too fast. I'm still scared about the accident I had a few years ago.'

He reassured me that he wasn't going to go fast, and he kept his promise.

Off we went, and, oh my God, I felt so free. I was in heaven. With one arm I held Animal around his waist, incredibly tightly. My other hand was on my right leg. The wind kept throwing off my leg, and I was scared it was going to get stuck in the back wheel. My right leg doesn't have much muscle.

I was enjoying the ride. It felt like as though we went everywhere, all over Melbourne. I loved when he took me to the city: all the tall buildings, the city lights, so many people. At these times I loved Melbourne. I thought it was the most beautiful city in the world.

Animal and I were always together, but I never let him have sex with me. Sometimes he made me sick, especially when he was around his friends. He changed. He wanted to be like them: arrogant, rude, loud mouths, putting down women and me, saying disgusting things. If I were male I would have punched them all. He always had friends over, and they always came with booze and drugs. I didn't mind about the booze, because in those days alcohol was my favourite drug of choice if I didn't have heroin or pills. Without alcohol I wouldn't have survived. My big mouth, being tough and disgusting like them, pulled me through. But one night, my stupid mouth got me into the worse nightmare you could wish on a young teenager.

One night about thirty bikers showed up to celebrate the birthday of one their mates. I was the only female there. I had known Animal now for nearly six months, and felt that I could trust him a little.

Everyone was having fun. I was drinking, sitting on the floor and holding Animal's leg. Now and then I smiled at him. There were a few bikers that spewed inside their helmets and started drinking their own spew, and that made me sick.

I turned to Animal and said, 'Can I be a biker too?'

I wanted to become a biker and get a bike for myself. I was tired of those callipers. I wanted to ride on my own, with no men, just me and my bike, and move away from everyone and everything. Now that I had a taste of what it was like to be on the back of a Harley, I wanted one too. I wanted a trike, because I knew I had to have balance to hold a two wheeler Harley up. There was no way I could. I was too weak to hold myself up, so how in the world could I hold a Harley?

Suddenly the mood changed and one biker—he was simply disgusting—screamed out, 'Yeah, really? You want to find out what it's like to be a biker? Go in the fucking room, and we will all show you.'

I whispered to Animal, 'What is he saying? The bedroom?'

Animal slapped my face. 'You stupid bitch. Do you think I like a crippled girl like you? You don't want to have sex with me. You probably can't have sex. And why did you open your mouth? Why did you say that? Go to the fucking room.'

Now I was scared. Of course, I couldn't run. If I screamed they would kill me. I got up and slowly went into the bedroom. It was a big room, dark, with a small light at the right side, a stained mattress and a dirty blanket. I walked slowly towards the mattress and carefully sat down, while my heart was pounding. Then the door opened abruptly.

A tall biker, with a vest covered with different signs, came in, jumped on top of me and ripped off my undies. He pushed in his tiny dick and went for it. Thank God he had a small dick. He came very quickly, but as soon as he was done another biker, and another… It went on and on forever, while I cried and tried to push off the bikers who'd had a lot to drink and simply couldn't come.

And then I snapped. I started screaming so loudly. After so many had sex with me I was crying, and moving my head from side to side. I felt so much pain, again, like the last time I was raped by so many men. The same thing was happening all over again. Not knowing how to stop this nightmare, I begged each one to stop but no one listened. Some of them were very rough. They pulled my hair or hurt my breasts. One of them bit my arm because I was trying to get his big dick out of me. I was now feeling more pain than the last time. There were so many of them, one after another, and I couldn't escape. I was stuck in that bed full of pain and terror. It was worse than last time.

Then this one guy with the eyes of an angel was gentle, not rough. After he came he said, 'No one will come in again, I promise you that.'

With tears in my eyes I looked into his. They were so beautiful. 'Please keep this promise, please.'

He kept his promise. No one came back into the room. My vagina felt as though it had been ripped apart, by one dick after another. I was in so much pain.

Thirty or more bikers gang raped me that night. I was devastated. The memories from the other gang rape in the massage parlour came back to me, and there I was in the same situation, gang raped again. No one would stop until this last guy. He told me he was the leader of this biker gang. That didn't make any difference to me. Leader or no leader, again I was raped, again I felt the same pain, the same trauma. I had to get away from them, but how? How was I going to do it?

After that trauma I was too sore and too exhausted from fighting everyone off. I cried way too much. I even slapped my own face, saying things like, 'Fuck you, Lilla! Why do you let this happen to you? Why?'

Finally, alone in that ugly, awful room, I went to sleep. I was exhausted. I was too scared to go and wash. I was too scared to get up. But when I woke up I knew I needed to run away. I needed to leave these bikers and this lifestyle behind. It wasn't for me. Maybe all the women did that, just to become bikers. I would never know, because that morning, quietly, I left. No way was I going to stay with Animal. I was angry with him too, for calling me bad names in front of his friends, belittling me. When we were together, just him and me, he was sweet as pie.

When I shut the door behind me, I knew I wanted to kill myself more than ever. I did it by going into so many nightclubs. I did it by getting absolutely drunk off my face, having blackouts, waking up in the dirt, with rats and cockroaches, and sometimes dead dogs or dead cats. I would wake up in my own vomit. I would take heroin, or speed or pills, to block out all this pain. But nothing worked. I was easy prey because I was good looking; and I was disabled and very naïve about life and men.

Every time I shut my eyes, I saw all those scenes, over and over. All the ugly and heavy guys that raped me that night. I was losing my mind. I wished I lived closer to Mum so I could see her. Every time I went through something really bad, my first thoughts were of my Mum. And I think now I understand why I am still alive today. I had my own little rock to hold onto, and that rock was my mother.

I was treated like dirt by the bikers, and because of that I never wanted to join them, ever. And I kept that promise. I still love Harleys. But I don't like the way I was treated because of my disability. They saw me as less than a woman. They saw me as scum, with a beautiful face.

Again I blamed myself for this rape. I loathed myself. I felt sick. I blamed my disability, preventing me from running away. I blamed myself, for being good looking. I didn't want to be good looking. I was hoping always to be ugly. I didn't want to be raped anymore. I was still terrified to go to the police. I was afraid of them, and I was afraid of what the bikers who raped me would do. If I had gone to the police, they would have killed me. No doubt.

Chapter 21

Hashish party where I nearly died, 1978. I was twenty years old.

THE ONLY WAY I COULD COPE with this turmoil inside was by going to lots of parties. The more parties the better. I was meeting so many people, especially guys. One day Frank, a tall, dark and handsome young man, asked if I wanted to go to a hashish party. I said yes, although I didn't know exactly what hashish was. It was a drug I'd never had before. But my curiosity took its toll. I wanted to see what this party was all about. It was not far from St Kilda.

When we arrived I was shocked by how beautiful the house was. The host was a millionaire. His house was full of great decorations. My eyes fell on a big painting in the lounge room, a portrait of his mother. I don't know who did the portrait but I am sure he must have been an incredible artist. She was incredibly beautiful and looked like a movie star. We were all excited.

I was looking at everything in this room. There was a big table around which you could fit at least twenty people, and on this table were at least twenty big white plates. In the middle of each plate was a block of black hash, 3 cm wide and 4 cm thick.

'My Vision of Death',
photo/digital art by Lilla Benigno.

Frank told us each to take a seat and wait until lunch was ready. As I sat down I became incredibly excited. I looked at this little black block on the plate. I picked it up without thinking and said out loud, 'What is this?'

As I said it, I decided to put it in my mouth and swallow it. All of it. I didn't chew it. I didn't even taste it. I just took this piece of hashish and swallowed it.

Everyone stopped and looked at me. Frank screamed at me. 'Nooo, Lilla, what have you done?'

Suddenly I became really scared, because I felt this had not been the right thing to do. I was naïve, in a way I was happy that I did it because now I knew I could die in peace, I knew it was a heavy drug but didn't care anymore. I didn't know what this drug could do. I panicked. Was I going to die now?

People around the table started telling me what 'hashish' was, and what it did. It was a great drug, they said, but to take so much of it… They didn't know what to do and neither did I. We waited patiently for the effect to appear.

And it did, fifteen minutes later. I began to feel really hot and my head was spinning. I felt as though I was entering a different world. I could hear people talking but I couldn't make any sense of it. I was really off my face. I felt numb. I begged people to take me to the hospital, but Frank was so nice. He picked me up and put me on the lounge, telling me that everyone was going to look after me, and that I wasn't going to die.

I started to cry, and I was screaming, 'I want my mum! Where's my mum? Mum!' I slept, then woke up full of terror, feeling out of control. I felt nothing but fear. I was going out of my mind. I didn't know how long this drug would stay in my system, but everyone took good care of me, until the drug wore off.

Hours later, the madness finally stopped and that was the last time I had anything to do with 'hashish'. That big block of 'hashish' opened my eyes into a world of the unknown, such a lonely world; and that world was called madness. I nearly died because of that experience. It left me scarred for life.

I thank God I had the right people to look after me that night. Now and then I would wake up, and I saw a young girl put a wet cloth on my forehead, telling me I was going to be fine. I could see, now and then, a guy come up and check on me.

'I hope she doesn't die on us,' he said to the others.

But in my mind I was thinking, 'Yes! Yes! I want to die. Let me die in peace.'

But that didn't happen. I was off my face for many hours, but the next morning, when I woke up, no one was around. So I opened the front door and slipped away. I didn't even know where I was, but I managed to find the biggest road and hitch a ride back to St Kilda. The black hole.

Chapter 22

My third love José, 1979. I was twenty-one years old.

NOT ONLY WAS I COMPLETELY LOST, especially now that I didn't have my baby with me, but I was wandering from street to street, begging for food and shelter. The men who helped me always wanted sex in return, and I gave them sex so I could survive. I was going through a very bad time, sleeping on benches, not having a shower in days, feeling dirty, hungry and thirsty.

But one night I grew very tired of this, and I ended up in Fitzroy near a Spanish coffee shop. I looked through a big window and watched people drinking coffee and eating biscuits while they were playing cards. I could hear beautiful Spanish music.

I was hungry and tired. Suddenly someone pushed me, and I fell on the floor. A girl bent down, giving me her hand to help me up. She was so apologetic and I instantly liked her. Her name was Paquita.

She was taller than me, very attractive, with big brown eyes, a petite figure, and beautiful gypsy clothes. Her black, curly hair was very long, past her bum. Paquita was Spanish.

*'Third Time in Love',
painting by Lilla Benigno.*

She plucked me out of the street and gave me a place to stay in her house. I was sleeping in the lounge room on a single mattress on the floor. She made up the bed for me with clean sheets and a clean pillow.

She asked if I was hungry and, full of shyness, I said, 'Yes, I am.' She made me the biggest sandwich, with a hot cup of Milo. I was eating so quickly that I nearly choked.

'Easy, easy,' she said. 'There's more food if you are still hungry.'

I looked at her with my mouth full of sandwich and smiled. Oh my God, she is so beautiful. She must have read my thoughts, because she suddenly said to me, 'You are very beautiful. Why are you living on the streets?'

I didn't answer her immediately. I was too busy eating my sandwich. But when I had finished I said to her, 'Because I want to.'

She left it at that.

'I have made up a bed for you,' she said. 'Get a good night's sleep. Goodnight. I am going to bed.' I smiled. 'Goodnight, and thank you.' She smiled back.

When Paquita left the room, I drank my hot chocolate and I went to bed too. That night I went to sleep very quickly. I was exhausted, mentally and physically. That was my best night's sleep in years.

Next morning I had breakfast with Paquita. She told me that breakfast was the most important meal of the day, and asked why I hated eating breakfast. But that morning I had two pieces of toast, with orange juice.

Paquita took me under her wing. She became my friend. I loved everything about her, the way she talked, how intelligent she was. And when she danced, her Spanish style, clapping her hands, she looked like a goddess.

Paquita took me to her favourite coffee shop in Fitzroy. She loved music and so did I, but she liked Spanish music, and I was Italian. I loved Italian music. When we walked in, all the old men wanted Paquita to dance for them. She went over to the jukebox, put on her favourite Spanish song, and started to dance. I admired her more and more. But a few guys there warned me to be very careful. They told me she was a little bit crazy.

Paquita was a lot older than me. I was in my twenties and she was in her thirties. But I didn't care what people thought of her. She kept dancing and having a great time, and I loved her because she was kind enough to give me a bed.

I wasn't getting any money from the government in those days. I was a street kid, and I didn't know how to go about getting money from the government. I did my best to survive with no money. Whilst living with Paquita, I was quickly learning new things, such as making my bed, brushing my teeth, and having a shower. Paquita let me borrow a lot of her clothes, and for once in my life I looked a little bit decent.

I met José at Paquita's place. He was short and handsome, with a big nose and very loud voice. I liked him because he was always happy, and he always made me laugh. He also made my heart beat fast.

One night, when I got drunk on tequila with Paquita, I found the courage to go to José's bedroom. I asked if I could sleep with him and he said yes. We made love that night, and the next day I knew that he and I were going to be girlfriend and boyfriend.

We became a couple. We even moved out of Paquita's place and started living on our own, in a cute little house.

Every morning, when José woke up, we had to get ready and go down to the pub. Being young and naïve I didn't understand why he wanted to go to the pub that early, but I realised later that José was a chronic alcoholic. He drank every single day, from morning until night, talking shit to all his other alcoholic mates. He dragged me from pub to pub, because of all the arguments he would start when he was really drunk.

But I felt very protected and safe with José. I knew that I loved him, but I couldn't understand why. He reminded me a lot of my father. He was twenty years older than me.

We went together for nearly a year until, one day, in one of his drunken states, he shit in the bed. On another occasion he set the house on fire while he was sleeping. We both nearly died that night. By then I had had enough, and I left him. I went back to living on the streets. I was tired of seeing him drunk and hopeless.

One day I did the unthinkable. I cheated on José right in front of his eyes. I went to a motel with one of his friends.

'Now, give me a blow job,' he said.

'Fuck off! I'm not here to give you a blow job.' He was handsome, always well dressed and well spoken, but a lot older than me.

'Why in the fucking world did you ask me to come here with you?' he screamed.

'I wanted to have sex only. I hate blow jobs.'

'Do you think I am going to have sex with a cripple like you? You must be crazy.'

I picked up a cup and threw it at him. I missed him, but it broke the mirror behind him.

'Keep this fucking room. You're not getting any sex from me.'

I stayed there all night, drank all the liquor in the fridge, and had a good sleep. Then I left, still thinking about that blow job. I hated doing that to guys. It always made me sick inside. It always reminded me of the episode of that guy who took me into the bush years earlier and forced me to give him a head job, and ever since then I swore if anyone ever asked that again I would say no or I would cut their dicks off.

I didn't like José drinking every single day. He didn't work, and I couldn't understand where he got all his money. Then I discovered that he would borrow money from his friends. He thought that was cool, but little by little he lost all his friends, because he never paid them back.

I didn't want to live with an alcoholic. It was bad enough with my father. Now I was repeating this, living with an alcoholic that I called my boyfriend. I found out later that José's friends all left him. He was ashamed, and when I left him, he disappeared. No one ever saw him again.

Now I was living on the streets again. How was I going to protect myself from being raped again?

Now and then I would catch up with my sisters. I never dared to tell them what I did in the streets. First, they wouldn't believe me, and second, they would put me down the way Mum used to. So I kept my mouth shut and tried to be a sister to them, even though I still felt out of place.

By now some of my sisters were old enough to go to nightclubs, and one night I decided to go with them. This was while I was living with my sister Isabella, in Altona. We all got changed and looked beautiful. This was the first time I had gone out with them all.

That night we went to Chasers, a beautiful nightclub in Toorak. At that time it was the best nightclub in Melbourne. When we arrived I walked in among my sisters. I was too shy to show the boys my legs. But soon all my sisters left me, and there I was on my own, in the middle of this nightclub. I had to find a chair quickly. I tried not to walk too much, so no one could see how I walked. One of my sisters asked me what I wanted to drink.

'Scotch and Coke, and make it a double, please.'

While I was sitting there, all these young guys came to my table and started to flirt. I was straight, but when my sister came back with the drink I sculled it down, and started flirting back. Soon all my sisters joined me and we were having a great time. So many compliments were poured on me and my sisters, and we were meeting more gorgeous guys every minute. I decided to go to the bar to get myself another scotch and Coke. I would always have a double. It would give me the strength to do whatever I wanted. When I was drunk I didn't care about my disability. All I wanted was to pick up a man and have sex with him, that's all.

A big guy, a security guard, came and sat next to me, telling me how beautiful I was. 'When my shift is finished here, want to go to your place so we can spend some time together?'

He was incredibly good looking, very tall, with big shoulders and lots of muscles. His hair was short and black, but he had gorgeous eyes; and his lips looked so beautiful, with a lovely smile.

'Let's go now,' I said.

He was very surprised. 'Hang on. I want to see if someone can cover my shift.'

I completely forgot about my sisters. They were all having fun. They were also meeting lots of good looking young men. I was really drunk by then. This was my fourth double scotch and Coke.

The security guard came back and said, 'We can go now if you want.'

'You have to carry me out. I can't walk. I'm too drunk.'

He picked me up and I waved goodbye to my sisters. They were shocked, seeing me carried out by a big, handsome man. We were going to have sex, and I was really looking forward to it.

We arrived at my sister's place. The door was unlocked and he carried me up the stairs and gently put me on the bed. I took off my clothes and he did too. We kissed passionately, hugging each other and kissing some more. I loved to kiss when I was drunk. I loved it more than sex. My hand moved down to grab his dick but I couldn't find it.

'Where is it? Where's your dick?'

He became really offended. I started laughing my head off, because I couldn't believe what was happening. I was incredibly drunk and I wanted to have sex, but this guy didn't have a dick. Or rather, it was so small that even with two fingers I couldn't get it. He had lots of muscles, because he used to take steroids, but no dick there, nothing.

He dressed quickly. 'You are a total bitch.' And with that he left the unit. I was left there in shock, wondering, What just happened here? He got angry with me because he didn't have a dick?

It didn't take me very long to go to sleep. I was way too drunk to get dressed again and meet up with my sisters, but it wasn't long before everyone came back. They talked about all the guys they'd met, and all the phone numbers they'd been given, but I was too ashamed to tell my sisters what had happened with that security guard. So I let them talk until the early hours of the morning, and then I went to sleep.

The next morning my sister Isabella said, 'Wow, you sure were quick to get a guy last night.'

'Yeah, sis, but one big problem. He didn't have a dick, so I didn't have sex. We only kissed and then he ran out the door.'

Isabella laughed and laughed and so did I. That was the very first time I had met someone without a dick. Such a gorgeous guy, with no dick. When my other sisters found out, they all laughed too. They all thought it was very funny, and in the end so did I.

After that I went away again. I was always leaving. I never felt comfortable around my family. I always found an excuse to get away from them all. The pain inside was too strong, and I didn't want to talk to any of them about what I was going through. The only place I felt I belonged was St Kilda. At the time my sister was living in this beautiful place in Altona. It had lots of stairs, but I used my bum to go up and down.

But, again, I did a runner. I ran away from Isabella again, not because we were fighting, but because I had so much pain inside; and St Kilda always made me forget it all. I met so many people, but getting away from everyone became a habit for me. I became a loner. Even living with my sister didn't help my grieving for my daughter. She was always on my mind, and I was dead inside. I didn't know how to talk to anyone anymore. Any trust I had towards everyone was gone. I knew now I was alone. But I loved running away. Without telling my sister where I was going, one morning I opened the door and disappeared. I went back to that fucking hole again, St Kilda.

I loved all my sisters, but I was scared to tell them what was happening to me, scared that they would not believe me, and scared of them abandoning me again. Fear of abandonment was my strongest fear. And the one thing that kept me alive was the love of my sisters and a couple of my brothers.

I never told my sister Isabella about the rapes. I never told any of my sisters. I didn't want to shock them. I also had a strong feeling of disgust. I kept thinking, If they knew what I am going through they would probably freak out. So it was better to run away from everyone, especially my family. I ran and ran, always believing that maybe one day all this would stop. But it didn't.

Chapter 23

Selling my disabled body for heroin to stop the pain and turmoil I was going through.

I FELT ALONE, wandering the streets of Melbourne, having nowhere to stay, and always searching for my next meal or my next drug. Sometimes luck was on my side. People always commented on my looks. 'You're beautiful, very beautiful.' But I never believed their words. Plus I was disabled, and this made many people feel sorry for me. So I started to play on this. It became my biggest game for survival.

I was desperate, and always very scared about everything and everyone. I didn't trust anyone, not even myself, yet I had a strong determination to survive. Although part of me really wanted to die. I was prepared to try new things, as long as my family never found out. Melbourne was a big place, and it was easy to hide. I hardly talked to anyone. I was so afraid to voice my opinion. If anyone tried to have a conversation with me, I would quickly run away from them. I was not fit to communicate with anyone. I was only existing and learning how to survive. The only time I would get a black eye was when I drank a lot and mouthed off to everyone. Then someone, either a man or woman, would punch my face, and in the morning I would have one or two black eyes.

'Selling my Disabled Body', painting by Lilla Benigno.

By now I was a full-on drug addict. I had to find a way to get money, and this was the only way I knew how. I went to work in many massage parlours. I would only do sex. The rest I would call other girls to do, because I didn't want to vomit on the clients.

I needed money to survive and the only thing I learned by now was how to work in those terrible places. Back in the massage parlours.

Altogether I worked in about five massage parlours. I remember one guy clearly. Steven owned at least twenty parlours. He was a good and fair pimp. I used to work long hours, and I would have lots of money for drugs, and for helping my mother. I never told my mother what I was doing. I was incredibly ashamed. I'm sure if she knew where the money was coming from, she would not have accepted it. Instead I told her once that I was working at an Italian coffee shop, and that all the men who played cards would give me tips if they won. My dear mother believed me. No way in the world could I tell her how disgusted I felt, every single day, working in those terrible places.

I was taking lots of heroin to block out the guilt, the shame and the disgusting feelings of despair. I wanted to die every single day, but somehow I had an inner strength that helped me to move on.

I started to make lots of money. Many guys kept on coming back for me. They became my regulars. They only wanted sex, and no other weird stuff.

One night I made over $700. I felt so rich! All the men I did that night were rich, and loved good looking women. They didn't care about my disability. They just wanted to have sex. I was too stoned to knock anyone back; and if I did that, if I refused to see anyone for no apparent reason, I would get fired, on the spot; or I would get hit by the pimp, or bashed.

Being a working girl was not a good job. I met so many lonely men, men that only paid to talk, men that only sat there and looked at my eyes, men that only wanted to rescue me. They knew they couldn't, so they would give me more money on the side, so I would fall in love with them.

I received so much money from men who felt sorry for me. Some men who paid only for sex, instead, once they were in the room, wanted to find out why I was working there. Why didn't I have a normal job? Or, better still, the most popular question: 'Where is your family?'

My answer was always, 'I don't know.'

It didn't matter how lost I was in this dark world. My thoughts were always towards my family. I didn't want to hurt anyone, but my lack of intelligence led me into a dark world, and I didn't want my family to know about it. Fear of rejection, and fear of abandonment.

Sometimes when I made lots of money, I would call Mum to find out if Dad was around. If he wasn't, I would go and see Mum and give her some money. At the time Mum was looking after the children and they were small. I knew my father was struggling with his work, and Mum too. So behind his back I would give her money to buy food, to buy the things she needed for the children. It took me ten years to find the courage to tell her where the money came from. She told me she knew all along, but didn't want to say anything.

Once a week I would call my mother and ask her, '*Ti servono soldi mamma?* [Mum, do you need some money?]'

She would quietly say, 'Yes, Lilla.'

I would catch a taxi all the way to Chadstone and knock on the back door. Mum would open it in her pink dressing gown, and I would give her $100 or sometimes $200, and she would thank me, and off I would go, back to St Kilda to get my heroin, and sit in my favourite shop, Topolino's, feeling happy that once again I had helped Mum.

One time, after making lots of money, I went back home, and this time I gave my mother $250. But I said something before I gave her the money. 'I want you to give me a kiss first, and then I will give you this money.'

And my mother did. She gave me a kiss on my cheek, and I gave her $250. I knew this was going to help her feed the children that were still at home, and also enable her to have some fun, buying things she needed. But of course, my mother always put the children first. I was like that with her: first my mother, then me. That was the first time I felt I bought love off my mother. That kiss for me was like gold. But I knew my mother was struggling with money, and the more I helped her the more I felt good inside. At least I knew the money would help her with the smaller children.

She once said to me, 'Lilla, you have a heart of gold. I know if you were rich you would look after everyone, including me.'

I used to think, If you only knew, Mamma. If you only knew what I am going through. But I never dared to tell her. I didn't want her to worry about me. I didn't want to hurt her. So I kept my mouth shut and pretended that everything was fine.

One night, very late, I was working in a massage parlour run by a woman. She was the madam. I heard a knock on the door and got up to answer it, because it was my turn. I opened the door and a tall man asked me if I wanted to have sex. I said no, because I felt sick. This was true. That night I got my period and had a sore tummy. In this massage parlour there was me and Trish, a beautiful woman with black hair. She wore a mini skirt with a little white top, so I sent her to this client. She didn't hesitate. She needed money for drugs too.

In that parlour, we had a bodyguard, a fat man, with a big fat belly, who loved to eat junk food. He always dressed in a suit, and was sitting on a chair next to me. His job was to be there for us girls and protect us from crazy clients, or clients that only wanted to have sex and didn't want to pay for it.

I heard a knock on the door and it was my turn to open it. I said to this client, 'Please take a seat. I will get another girl. Tonight I feel sick.'

He nodded and smiled, so I assumed that he was happy with that idea. I went into the lounge room and asked Trish (she was the girl who took me into her home when I was pregnant with Chantelle) to take care of him. At first she didn't want to do him because she had just had a client, but then she changed her mind and went to look after him.

Time was going by. An hour passed and I asked the bodyguard, 'Why is Trish taking so long?'

'You're right. Good question. In the book she signed for half an hour.'

I was terrified. 'You'd better go up and see if she is all right.'

But as soon as I said that, I heard a big roar from up the stairs, and this mad man came into the lounge with a baseball bat. He hit the bodyguard on the back and then pointed his finger at me, saying, 'Do not touch her. She is sick.'

Then he made a run for it, down the hallway and through the front door. I was in shock. I wanted to find out how Trish was. The police came quickly and found Trish tied up on the bed, covered in blood. She had been bashed by this mad man with a baseball bat. Police untied her quickly and took her to the hospital. She almost died, but she made it. She stayed in hospital for three weeks, to recuperate from her broken bones. If I hadn't been sick that night, it could easily have been me in the hospital, not Trish. The police never found the man who did this. Trish was so scared by that attack that she decided to stop working altogether. My disability saved me over and over again.

I was dying, little by little, and even the money wasn't good enough for me. I would go from nightclub to nightclub, searching for somebody new or something new. I loved the adventurous side I had. I was not scared to try new things. I was not scared to come very close to death. Many times I was hoping to die and end it all. But then something so very small would wake me up from this reality, and I would snap myself out of it, ready for another adventure.

I came across so many men and women as desperate as I was. Some did make it, and many did not. Life in the streets is all about looking after number one. Now and then I would come across someone I felt comfortable with, and I would tag along with them, until I became bored and left to meet new people.

I witnessed so many fights, bloody fights and stabbings. Police cars chasing so many drug dealers. It was easy to deal drugs in St Kilda. Fitzroy St had a bad reputation in those days.

I became a regular visitor at the Alfred Hospital or St Vincent's Hospital. Whether because of a drug overdose or motorbike accidents, Alfred Hospital and St Vincent's Hospital became my second homes.

On one occasion I took too much heroin and was very close to death, but somehow I made it to the hospital in time. Again the doctors saved me. This must have been my fourth suicide attempt. The doctors automatically sent me into a mental institution. I stayed there for about six hours, and while everyone was having lunch, I managed to run away in my white gown. I don't know why no one stopped me. I left the hospital in my white gown, opened at the back. I went across the road into a back yard, and on the clothes line I saw men's clothes, pants, shirt and underwear.

I didn't touch the underwear, but I stole the shirt and the pants, changed, and hitchhiked to St Kilda, back to Fitzroy Street. After seven years everyone knew me quite well, and I was liked by so many street kids like me, and shop owners. This kind of life was always on the go. There was no turning back. I had to find a way to stop all this, but my naïvety and lack of information made me believe there was no hope for me. I was going to die. The question was: When? And how?

I was scared, always so scared. Working in the massage parlours began to make me very paranoid. There were many stories of young prostitutes being killed, sometimes two girls per night. I did not want to die like that. If I was going to die, I wanted it to be my way. I didn't want my life to be taken by a mad person.

There were rumours that the mafia was going to take over all the massage parlours in St Kilda, and many of the girls quit because they were too scared to work for the mafia. Many working girls were there one day and gone the next. The working industry was changing for the worse. Most girls were complaining to the bosses that they were taking too much money, but if you complained you would get hurt. I never spoke to anyone in those days. I just did my job, as they told me to, and minded my own business. I always felt too guilty to even open my mouth, and I always believed that my opinions were not worth listening to.

My anger and my fears helped me to stay in control. Although many times I truly believed I was going to lose my mind. Heroin helped me a lot through those bad times. I had no emotions or feelings when I was on heroin. I was just existing.

I was bashed in the street twice, once when I was going to the pool room upstairs. I never made it, because a girl grabbed my hair from behind and started bashing my face and my stomach. Blood poured from my left eye. I'm sure I needed stitches, but she kept on punching me. Then she punched my calliper and screamed. This gave me an advantage and I started screaming too. People came downstairs to see the commotion, and I was saved by two girls. That night the three of us slept in the park, after the biggest hit of heroin.

I loathed the streets. I loathed all the men and women who were struggling with me. I thought, Why isn't anyone changing their lives? Why do we all have to suffer like this? These were the questions that kept going through my mind, over and over again. Why, why and why?

The second time I got bashed was at a nightclub with my sister Isabella and Nino, a pimp I met on the streets. I liked him. I thought he was very handsome, tall, dark and muscular. A great physique. I had sex with him a couple of times, and I thought he looked like a movie star.

As we sat sipping our beers, he turned to me and said, 'I'd like to fuck your sister.'

When he said it, I saw red. I picked up my full glass of beer and tipped it on his head. Next thing I knew, he pushed me on the floor and started to punch my face. He was sitting on me, just punching me. With my arms I tried hard to ward the punches off, but I copped a couple of beauties. It took five people to get Nino off me.

'Why did you do that?' he screamed.

'Next time you say something about my sister, show more respect, you fucking pig.'

He was so angry he tried to punch me again, but two guys held him back. Otherwise I would have copped the second round. The next day I had a black eye and a bruise on my chin. That was the first time I stood up for my sister. I got bashed for it, but it was worth it.

Chapter 24

April 13, 1980—The birth of my son Dean.
I was twenty-two years old.

I WAS DRINKING EVERY NIGHT of the week. I didn't need money to get drunk. I would walk into a pub, sit down and start looking around, hoping someone would get me a drink. I always had that angry look, ready to kill anyone who came my way. I never looked at anyone, for fear of being looked at, but it never mattered. People stared anyway.

When I sat down, so many men stared at my face; but when I walked, so many men ran away from me. But after a couple of days I would need another fix. Heroin was the only drug that saved my sanity. I had made a pact with the devil, and it was up to me to keep that bargain.

I started standing on corners, so men would stop and ask me how much. I would lean over and my breasts, still clean and very pointy and so sexy, would make the men tremble with passion. Some gave me money for nothing. They just wanted to look at my eyes. Some gave me money just to touch my breast; only one, not both of them. Some men gave me money for a kiss. But a kiss always was and still is a 'no' for me, unless the guy is extremely good looking.

'Confusion', digital art by Lilla Benigno.

I had sex with singers, judges, lawyers, young lost men, and young, gorgeous, good looking men, and so many men that made me sick inside. My drug use was becoming unbearable. I was losing my mind. The more drugs I took, the more I wanted to commit suicide. Withdrawal from heroin, alcohol or pills can be so painful, and incredibly scary, especially if you decide to do it on your own. I did this many times, and it was the worst pain in my life.

One night after working I went to Fitzroy St to score my drugs. I saw someone there I used to score with, a skinny guy with pimples all over his face. I would feel sick in my stomach every time I saw him. He rushed up to me and said, 'You want to score?'

'Yeah.'

'Give me the money.'

I suddenly had a bad feeling. 'No, you get it first, then give it to me, and then I will give you the money.'

This bastard insisted I give him the money, so I did. He could see I was hanging out. He saw I was very sick, shivering and sweating, hardly able to breathe. I hadn't had a fix for about two hours, and I was ready for another one, because the heroin I'd had was shit.

He took the money and ran off. I stood on the curb and waited and waited. Two hours went by and this guy didn't come back. I started to cry. I was broke, because I gave him all my money. Without the heroin I knew I was going to feel very sick within an hour.

I cried louder and louder, hoping someone would come to my rescue. And someone did. I heard a voice behind me.

'Hey, hey. What's wrong?'

It was a gorgeous looking guy, with curly, light brown hair, blue eyes, a white shirt, and gorgeous lips. He looked like an angel, and for two seconds or more I thought I was in heaven.

I lowered my head and screamed, 'I just got ripped off. I got no money. I got no place to sleep tonight. Nothing.' I cried again.

'Hey, you can come and stay with me tonight, if you like. I live with my grandma.'

I looked at him and suddenly felt calm. 'Really? I can stay with you tonight?'

He put his soft hand under my chin. I looked at his eyes and he looked at mine. Suddenly all the anger and anguish I was feeling was gone, all gone.

'Yes,' he said. 'You can stay with me tonight. Now come into the pizza shop and I will get you something to eat.'

I was very hungry. He held out his hand, and helped me up from the gutter. He held my hand tightly, so I wouldn't fall over. He saw how I was walking but it didn't seem to bother him. I felt incredibly at ease with him. His name was Greg. Tall, handsome, curly hair, incredibly attractive, gorgeous physique, and a beautiful smile and manners. He made me a Margarita pizza and a hot chocolate. While I was eating I watched him, smiling at him all the time. I was thinking, Why is he so beautiful to me, and why is he helping me?

At midnight, at the end of his shift, he went to the back of the pizza shop and returned looking more gorgeous than ever, without the white apron. He was very handsome.

He fetched his car so that he could take me home with him. I wasn't feeling sick at all. I felt good, because I met this guy, studying during the day and working at night to pay off his student fees. He was so gentle, polite, caring, and attentive.

Greg lived in a small cottage in Malvern, one of Melbourne's inner suburbs. I didn't see much of the house. We talked in the lounge room for hours, about his grandma, and about my family. He showed me albums of his family. His mum and dad were both killed in an accident when he was nine years old. He had lived with his grandmother ever since. He was twenty-five and I was twenty-two.

The more we talked, the calmer and more serene I felt. I was in the most beautiful place on earth. I had never felt that calmness before. As we talked I asked him, 'Why haven't you got a girlfriend? You are so beautiful.'

He put his head down, then looked at me and said, 'I was waiting for someone like you.'

My heart felt as though it was going to explode. I was so happy. No one had ever said anything as beautiful as that, no one. We looked at each other for a couple of minutes. I wanted to forget about all the rapes. I wanted to forget about all the things I had been on the streets, and Greg was doing that for me. I was living in the moment with him. He was so kind and gentle, and I was the one who instigated the first kiss. I couldn't help it. He was the first man who had manners, who was gentle and kind. He was so beautiful, I wanted to kiss him so badly, but his lips were a great start. He was such a soft kisser, so beautiful and tender. Who needed drugs when I could feel this for free?

Our kiss went on for a long time. Then he asked if I wanted to sleep in his bed, with no sex of course. I said yes, without thinking of the consequences. What I was feeling for Greg was incredible. I could tell he really didn't care about my legs. Then finally we did have sex.

That night was the most incredible sexual night I had ever had. I felt so light and free. It was passionate yet gentle love making on his part. I adored how he touched my face, and how the butterflies in my tummy were going insane, feeling these beautiful, incredible, loving emotions. He brought me into the present moment. I felt so alive and safe. I felt real love for the first time. I wanted to cry and did. While Greg was touching my body, tears rolled down my face. He saw my tears, wiped them off and started kissing me more passionately than ever. Our kissing went on for eternity. I didn't want it to end. I loved his body, his hands, his face, his heart. His gentleness was extraordinary. He was an angel for me. Finally, early in the morning, we fell asleep in each other's arms.

A few hours went by and I woke up. Greg was gone, and fear set in. What was I going to do now? I didn't want to go back to work in the massage parlour. I hadn't told Greg that I worked there. I kept this secret because I was very ashamed.

I saw a note on the pillow. It said, 'I have gone to university to pick up a test. Wait for me, then we can have lunch and go out.'

An hour later he came back, very happy. 'Want me to take you to get some breakfast?'

I screamed at him, 'No! Can you take me back to my sister's place?'

Greg was puzzled. He didn't understand why I was so put-out. 'When do you want to go there?'

'Now.'

I looked down. I just wanted to get out of there. He was way too nice, and I was not a nice person. I was a drug addict. I was raped by many men. He didn't know any of this, and I was too scared to tell him. He was way too nice to be involved with a loser like me, someone who had been struggling for years, and who had no knowledge or understanding of love. He was way too beautiful, and I didn't want to tell him my horrific stories. I wanted to run away from him. I didn't want him to end up with someone not so nice. I wouldn't know how to handle him.

I had nothing in common with him. He was a student, he loved fishing, and he loved reading. I hated these things when I was young. I was not into that at all. I was rough. I liked to take risks. I was not good enough for him. I felt like a fraud. If he knew what I had gone through, I was sure he would have left me. And so I left him instead. When he dropped me off at Isabella's place, he gave me his phone number. He still wanted to keep in touch with me. But as soon as I got out of the car, tears in my eyes, I ripped his number into small pieces.

A couple of weeks later I found out I was pregnant with his child, but when I went back to Topolino's Pizza I heard he had left that job, and the owner didn't know where he went. I never asked for his surname. I decided to go through with the pregnancy, hoping that this time I could keep the baby and give it another go.

Working as a working girl was very degrading. I never felt comfortable with it. It always made me sick, but the drugs helped that sickness by blocking it all out. I slowly became a zombie and my mind was not right. I was learning how to survive, not to fall in love. I was not cut out to fall in love with anybody.

I liked Greg very much, but because he was way too nice I had to leave him. I didn't believe I was worthy of his love, worthy of him being there for me and taking care of me. I never wanted people to take care of me, because I thought I always did a good job myself. Sad, but true. Of course, I wasn't doing a good job at all. I was insane. I lost my mind. I was numb.

For that one night Greg made me feel alive and important. He made me feel like a woman, and he treated me with respect and love. When Greg dropped me off at my sister's place, I went straight to bed. It was about 6 am.

A few minutes later I felt cold metal on my forehead. I opened my eyes and, to my horror, I saw two big holes. I was staring down the double barrel of a shot gun. My father pressed this shotgun against my forehead, and kept screaming: 'Where is the baby? What did you do with the baby?'

I was so terrified I couldn't open my mouth. My fear immobilised me from head to toe. I wanted to scream, but words would not come out. I looked into his eyes, hoping maybe he would take this gun off my forehead. Suddenly the door opened and Isabella walked in. In shock and horror, she begged my dad to put the gun down and to get out of the flat. He kept that gun on my forehead for what seemed like hours, but it was only a few minutes. Then he realised what he was doing, and finally put it down.

He looked at me and said, 'You are dead for me.'

My sister managed to send my father back home, then came back into my room.

'You are fucked,' she said, 'totally fucked and insane.'

This was not news to me. I knew that already. But instead of support I received more abuse from everyone.

I knew right there and then that my relationship with my father was broken, unfixable. Instead of getting moral support, I received lots of bad words from him, and distance. Today I understand that my father was not capable of expressing his emotions as many people can. Getting his point across was always more negative than positive. I was really scared of my dad, always had been. Although part of me loved him, there was a big part of me that wished he was dead. Out of my life for good. That was probably the worst day of my life. The family had a big lunch for Christmas, and I was left alone in Isabella's flat. No one wanted to see me, especially my father. I was dead for him, and finally he was dead for me too.

I wished over and over again that my father was different, that he was more understanding towards our problems, but instead I copped a lot of verbal abuse. My father never hit me, he never laid a hand on me, but his words scarred me for life. I knew our relationship was finished. The moment he found out I adopted out my daughter, I was out of his life and he was out of mine. I guess he felt I didn't trust him enough to tell him, or to reach out for his help. But I didn't because I was terrified of him.

My father didn't like us to stand up for ourselves. If we did, he would get so angry and tell us that he knew better, that he was the god of the house. We let him vent all this, but in the end, when we all grew up, we went our own way and left him.

Instead of support I had a gun to my head. My own father wanted to shoot me. It took a long, long time for that memory to leave my head. I dreamed for many years of my father chasing me with a gun. Thank God that in my dreams I could run, and I always ran successfully.

All the things I was doing were really crazy, but I couldn't understand where this madness was coming from. I knew that my family couldn't stand me. I knew they had been brainwashed by the terrible things my father and my mother told them. But I didn't care anymore. I had no family. I only felt close to Mum, Isabella and Stella.

After a couple of weeks I was feeling sick, so I went to see the doctor. He gave me a pregnancy test and it was positive. I became scared. There was no way I was going through another pregnancy all on my own.

Yet I did. I went to a convent in Melbourne, run by beautiful nuns, and stayed there for nine months, with no drugs and no alcohol. I did so many craft activities, and the time went way too quickly.

I had lost Greg. I couldn't find him, but I knew he was the baby's father.

Nine months later my son, Dean, was born, nice and healthy, on April 13, 1970.

I had about three stitches, but that didn't worry me. Finally it was over, and all I wanted to do was sleep and sleep for ever. Giving birth is hard work. A pity we were never given a manual.

I stayed in hospital for a week, then it was time for me to go. As usual I didn't have anywhere to go. The doctors and nurses did everything in their power to find me a place to stay so that I could raise my son.

The doctors kept asking, 'What do you want to do, Lilla? Do you want to keep the baby or give it up for adoption? In your situation we suggest you put him up for adoption, but if you want to keep the baby, we can find a suitable place for you and the baby. The Salvation Army can help you.'

With tears in my eyes, I screamed, 'I want to keep my son!' I was always angry. I could only communicate with anger. That's all I knew.

Two weeks later a big lady, dressed in white, with a white and gold hat that just fit her head, walked up to my bed.

'Hello, Lilla. I have come to pick you up. I have a bed at the Salvation Army, and you can stay there until we can figure out what to do for you and your baby.'

I felt shivers up and down my spine. 'Okay.' We packed up the little things I had accumulated during the past two weeks, and off we went to the Salvation Army.

It was a big place, with so many beds, and so many people lost, just like me. People came in who had been bashed and raped, with children, because they had nowhere to go. So many women who had been battered by their husbands. I witnessed so many people who had totally lost their heads because of drugs.

Matron took me to a small room with one bed in it and told me that this was going to be my room until something better came along. I was happy with it. 'I'm not staying here very long.'

Matron gave me a smile and said, 'Get some rest. We will talk later.'

I was always rude and full of anger. If someone tried to be nice to me I would tell them to fuck off. Matron caught me a few times swearing at the other people, and reprimanded me so many times. But I never listened to anyone. The more people were nice to me, the more I couldn't stand them. But after six months there, something in me started liking Matron. She helped me with my son. She let me sleep in and changed his nappy for me. She fed him for me, so I could get some sleep, because during the night I was always awake feeding him. During the day Matron would give me a good break and let me sleep. She knew I was young, and she knew I was very vulnerable and scared.

Matron always showed her rough side so she could keep everyone safe. But she started to soften up towards me, and we became the best of friends. I started talking nicely to her, and I started thanking her for all the help she was giving me.

But after a year it was time to leave and find my own apartment. With her help I did. I found a nice little place in the Collingwood Flats. Finally I could start my new life with my son. Matron became one of my guardian angels at that crucial time in my life. I still remember her, and she is still in my heart. She will be forever.

Finally I had my own little place, but the old habits were coming back. There I was with a small child, and I went back to work, selling my body to look after him. I was back on the drugs. I was not fit to be a mother. There were so many responsibilities I did not understand. I was overwhelmed by panic attacks.

One night my sister Isabella and I decided to go down to the pub for a few drinks. We met two guys, both of whom were extremely attractive. I liked Frank and my sister liked John. But these two guys put speed in our drinks. Isabella and I were high on speed though we didn't even know it until we arrived back home.

Then Frank, the guy who liked me, laughed and told us what he had done. I was horrified, yet at the same time I liked it. Within a few weeks I was shooting up speed, in the bath, in the toilet. I was not looking after my son. Now I became a speed freak. Off heroin and onto speed.

I knew I couldn't cope, especially when I started using speed. My habit got way out of control. I remember once, in one of my speed episodes, cutting off all the heads of my photos, and making the best collage: pictures of my brothers, sisters, and friends. This lasted hours and hours. Then I started to clean my place and couldn't stop, scrubbing the kitchen, making it spotless, washing the floors, making the beds. I felt great. I had so much energy. I couldn't stop. Then I remembered I had a couple of sleeping pills and took them. Finally I could stop and get some sleep.

I couldn't find a way to be responsible for my son. I wanted to love him, but the more I looked at him the more I felt anger. I was so angry because I kept him. I knew I was not a good mother. The intention was there, to be there for him, to love him, to protect him, but I was way too deep into destruction. I left him once on his own, so I could go out with my sisters and some friends to a nightclub. I was in the nightclub for over six hours. Finally, when my sister took me home, from the car she saw Dean screaming at the window.

'You'd better get up there real fast and look after your son. Why did you leave him alone?'

All I said was a screaming 'Fuck you!'

I knew by now that being a mother was a big job, but my mind was full of terrible memories and traumas. Instead of asking for help I escaped by taking more and more drugs. If it wasn't speed, it was sleeping pills. If I didn't have sleeping pills, I would take heroin. It was a vicious cycle that I could not break.

I went to live with my sister in her commission flat. We fought a lot. We were both young at the time. She had her daughter and I had Dean. But I still couldn't look after Dean. He always cried for food. Even Steve, the guy I was going with at the time, changed his nappies and fed him for me. I was too busy stuffing my body with drugs.

I was not a good mother to Dean, and I knew that, but I didn't know what to do. Even my younger sister Maria told me I wasn't a good mother. We were living in a place called Parents without Partners. We lived there for a year. She told me I was not a good mother with Dean.

One night we went to the pub. Some bikers were there and, after a few drinks I approached one of the bikers and asked him to take me for a ride on his Harley. He said sure, but as soon as we walked out a policeman walked past us. I said hello to the policeman. Next thing I knew, this biker went inside and brought all the bikers outside. They were all ready to bash me. Thank God my sister Maria got me out of that terrible situation.

God only knows what would have happened to me that night. My sister told me that I took a man back home with us, and the three of us were on the same bed. I don't even remember this episode because my mind by now was full of drugs and alcohol. I believe my sister. She was with me for a year. When she ran away from home she came to live with me.

Being a mother was way too hard for me at the time. I was always on drugs. I wanted to escape all the violence and the rapes. But then, I didn't have a voice. I was way too scared to tell anyone what I was going through. Then one day I saw what I was doing to this little boy, and I decided to get help. I decided to give him a good family. I grabbed him and held him so close to me, tears in my eyes, kissing his little face.

I said, 'No more, darling. Mum is going to find you a good mum, I promise.' Hugging him very tightly, we both went to sleep.

Next morning I woke up feeling strong. I was ready to get help. I didn't want my son to be treated badly by me or anyone anymore. I wanted him to have all the love he needed and deserved. I knew I was not a good mum. I knew I needed help. My head was full of hatred towards all the rapists. I felt guilty about selling my body for drugs. I wanted my son to be well looked after, and to have everything he needed, especially love. And I sure didn't have that yet. I was too busy blocking out all my pain, with any drugs I could get my hands on. In the morning I felt so strong, and knew this was the best decision for him and me.

I dressed him, gave him breakfast, put him in a stroller and went to talk to someone at Lifeline. I had to get my son to a safe place. I wanted him to have everything I didn't have. But most of all I wanted him to live in a healthy, secure and safe environment. I couldn't provide that for him. By now I was mentally sick. I was trying so hard to deal with all my own hurt and pain, and my son was not getting the love he needed.

When I arrived at Lifeline I burst into tears. I spilled out my story, about the drugs, the prostitution, the men, and especially about the rapes. I talked also about going out and not being responsible for my son, leaving him alone so I could go out to get my drugs. Doing so many crazy things, and simply not loving him the way he needed to be loved,

After I fostered out my son I was more lost than ever. I worked on the streets, in a special corner where men could see me clearly. I worked with drag queens, and they made sure nothing ever happened to me. They became my friends. But the streets were becoming more dangerous, with prostitutes disappearing. Some were bashed or murdered by evil men. Many were being ripped off. Men would have sex with them then run without paying.

This frightened me. I didn't want to be killed. I was tired of being raped and not even getting paid for it. Many men treated me like dirt, treated me as if I was a parasite. I was humiliated by the looks they gave me, and it was time to find a place where I wouldn't get hurt, a safer place to sell my body for my drugs. If I made lots of money I could help my mother too.

I was working from one massage parlour to the next. I always had money now, but my drugs became more important to me. And my mother. Whenever I had lots of money I would get my fix of heroin, catch a taxi and give the rest of the money to my mother. I gave lots of money to my mum, mainly because I felt so sorry for her. I wanted her to buy for my little sisters all the things I never had.

I remember one night a handsome man, big, stocky, with lots of muscles, wanted to be with me for sex. He paid and I went to his room, took my clothes off and started having sex with him.

Suddenly he pulled out a gun, put it to the side of my head and whispered in my ear, 'Now, I want you to do anything I like, and if you scream I will shoot your gorgeous face.'

I went into shock, but I needed to get out of there fast, so I lied.

'I'm really dying to go to the toilet. Please, let me go and I will come back real quickly, and we can do anything you want.'

I was amazed when he said, 'Yes, okay. Hurry up.'

As soon as I was out of the room, with no clothes on, I went down the stairs as quickly as I could into the lounge room. Rocky, my security guard, was there and I screamed out, 'Quickly, Rocky, get that guy out! He's got a gun and he just put it to my head.'

Rocky ran up the stairs and grabbed this guy and the gun.

'This gun isn't real,' he said to his friend.

I was so relieved, but I still received the biggest shock. I honestly believed he was going to kill me. Rocky and his friends threw this person out without his clothes, then threw his clothes after him.

That night Rocky stayed with me. There was no sex. He just held me close. He knew that what I had gone through was terrifying. We went to sleep hugging each other.

Rocky was the only pimp who was fair to me. He treated me with respect, and sometimes love. We had sex a few times. This was like it had been with Peter, fast, and then off he would go and do his business.

For me sex was not the passionate love that many describe. For me sex was torture. It was a nightmare. I saw so many dicks in so many forms. Some were bent, some were so small, and some were so big and ugly. I always found dicks rather disgusting, and I still feel the same. Dicks make me sick. They look like little snakes, and when they get hard part of me always feels like chopping them off and giving them to the dogs to eat. That was my mentality when I used to work. Selling my body to these ugly men— and even good looking men—made me feel sick. It made me feel as if I was the worst person in the world. Why would anyone want to marry a person with a disability?

But Rocky was good to me. He treated me with respect, not like a slut or a whore. He treated me like a normal person and that is why I liked him. I loved him.

Whenever I needed something to eat he would get it for me. If I was thirsty he would buy me whatever I liked. Rocky always told me I was beautiful, and I believed him. I was very gullible and way too young to understand. Every time someone told me I was beautiful, my first thought was, 'They feel sorry for me.'

I never believed in any of the compliments I received. Now I carried so much guilt, and that in itself made me uglier than ever. I hated myself so much that every time I looked in the mirror I felt like vomiting.

I remember asking Rocky once, 'I wonder what would happen if I axed my legs.' Rocky looked at me and responded, 'Don't be silly. If you do that you will die.'

'I don't care.' And I really didn't care. My mind was always on one thing. I didn't want to be disabled. I wanted to be normal.

But working for Rocky became way too risky.

The police were there almost every week, and all the girls were getting tired of being busted. I was busted a few times, but sometimes they let me go. They warned me that if I didn't go back home I would end up in jail. Hard head me, I never went back home. Instead I kept going back to Rocky. Rocky was Italian, and his personality reminded me of my older brother Paolo. I really believed I was in love with him. But I also saw another side, which was serious, and scary too. Rocky always carried a gun. He said it was only for protection. I loved it. It was little, and I wished many times I had one too.

But I had to leave Rocky. I had to leave that scene. I grew tired of the police. I grew tired of girls getting bashed by clients and pimps. I grew tired of being ripped off by clients. And girls too. I wanted to end all this. I wanted to try something new, something completely different for once in my life. I wanted to be normal.

Chapter 25

My best friend Carol. I was twenty-four years old.

I WAS SO LOST, with nowhere to go. I felt like a loser. I wanted to get off the streets, but I didn't want to go back home. Moving from one massage parlour to the next was the only way to look after my habit. Street after street, not knowing where I was going to be, or who I was going to meet. I would go to places where I knew there weren't many people, and I would sit for hours wondering what to do or where to go. The only thing that kept me going was my own fear, and the excitement that finally I was free.

One day I met Carol. She was working in one of the massage parlours. It was a dirty massage parlour in Fitzroy Street, Fitzroy. In those days Fitzroy was much like St Kilda, but a lot of prostitutes felt safer working indoors than on the streets. There were so many working on the streets, and so many fights to pick the best corner. I preferred to be inside for my own safety.

Carol was much taller than me. Her hair was so curly I thought she'd had a perm, but later I found out it was her natural hair. Curly, and so much of it. It suited her face. She was incredibly attractive, with beautiful

Painting by Lilla Benigno.

eyes the colour and shape of a cat's, and high cheek bones. She wore no makeup. She didn't like it. She said she felt false wearing it. Her smile was beautiful, with perfect teeth, just like my mother.

I couldn't stop looking at her. The first thought that went through my mind was, Why is she a prostitute? She is too beautiful to be one.

All the girls were beautiful. Most were over eighteen, but some were younger. Somehow the police always found out and dragged them out of there.

Some girls had been on heroin for many years, and they looked like walking zombies. Their habit was much worse than mine. I used to have three to four shots a day, sometimes more. But I witnessed some girls having a shot of heroin ten or more times a day.

Carol and I become friends instantly. We laughed, we talked, and we both worked so hard. One thing Carol needed to work on was her self-esteem. She used to complain about her weight. To me she didn't look fat. It suited her because she was tall, taller than me anyway. I am five feet two, and Carol was nearly six feet tall. She was a little bit chubby, but it suited her because of her height. I always tried to make her feel better, but when she'd had a lot of alcohol she used to cry about it. She would make the issue bigger than it really was. Nevertheless, there were parts of her that she loved, and she tried hard to compensate with that for the negative.

Carol also had a heart of gold. She helped me so many times, especially when I fell over, which I did many times. Carol and I were alike. She didn't like her weight, and I didn't like my legs. Because of this we become best friends, and started hanging around together twenty-four hours a day.

We were both crazy. We would go to the shops, steal wigs and sunglasses, and make a run for it. Well, for me it was not a run; more like walking as fast as I could without losing my balance. Then we would get into Carol's car and drive off.

Neither of us liked working in the massage parlours. She was there because the money was good, and she could get everything she wanted. I was there because I was crazy, and I needed money for food and drugs.

One day, out of the blue, we decided to do something totally insane. We decided to buy a book of one-dollar scratch and win tickets. It cost us each twenty-five dollars. We bought coffee and sat in the park, scratching away. There were so many tickets, and suddenly we hit the jackpot! Altogether we won nearly $1000, and in those days that was a lot of money.

She looked at me and said, 'Have you ever been to Queensland?'

'Hell no, but should we go?'

She smiled and said, 'Yes, let's do it. Let's get a plane. We have enough money here to get a ticket, so let's do it.'

Two days later we were on a plane to Queensland. The plane took us to Brisbane, but neither Carol nor I liked Brisbane, so we started to hitch a ride. A big truck stopped, and the driver asked us, 'Where do you girls want to go?'

We exchanged a look and said to him, 'Up further, from Brisbane. Do you know a good place?'

The truck driver, tattoos everywhere but with a heart of gold, replied, 'Cairns? Would you like to go there? I'm going there. I can give you a ride.'

Neither Carol nor I had ever heard of Cairns, but we both said yes. The poor driver had to pick me up and put me in the truck. There was no way I could go up those big steps. It took three days of travelling. One night the truck driver had sex with Carol and I heard everything. He paid her, too.

Thank God he didn't want to have sex with me. He was way too ugly, but with a big heart.

We arrived in Cairns, and Carol and I were amazed how beautiful it was. Such a small place, with lots of backpackers and tourists. We had landed in heaven. We thanked the truck driver and off he went, but Carol and I went to a cheap motel and settled for the night. We had the best sleep.

I was trying hard to get off heroin, and I was feeling sick because I was doing it cold turkey again, all by myself. The shivers and the sweats made me so sick, and my bones were always very sore. But I started drinking instead to stop the pain.

We found a woman who was prepared to give us both escort work. She liked Carol a lot because she was not disabled, but she gave me some jobs too. They paid me and I would give the money to the woman, who was like our boss. But one night, Carol and I put all the money on the table, without giving the woman her money.

Carol said, 'Should we make a run for it?'

Looking at all that money and not wanting to pay that woman, I quickly said, 'Yes, let's do it.'

We both had men in our motel. We used to take backpackers there and have lots of sex, and drinking and fun with them. But this night we didn't want to wake anyone. We were going to run away from Cairns, with all the money. By now Carol had another little car. It worked really well although she bought it for only $600. Our car was packed. Carol looked after the money, and I was sitting in the front seat biting my nails. She always told me off for doing that.

I was full of panic when Carol, out of nowhere, said, 'We can go back to Melbourne, or we can go to Shepparton.'

I said I wanted to go to Melbourne. I wanted to spend my money on heroin. My head was there all the time: heroin, heroin; nothing but heroin.

After travelling for a week by car we arrived back in Melbourne, and I told her to drop me off in St Kilda. She screamed at me. She didn't want me to go back to drugs again.

'Now you give me my money,' I said. 'What I do with it is none of your fucking business. I'll meet you here again in a few weeks.'

She was very angry with me. Nevertheless, she gave me my half of the money, which was about $900. That night I went and scored my first smack. By then I knew how to shoot it up by myself, hit after hit. All the $900 went into my arm.

Again I was in and out of hospital, overdosed on heroin; but now this was not new to me. I was used to that terrible, ugly life.

I saw Carol again after I used all my money on heroin. She never asked me what I did with the money, but I think she knew. When she picked me up, the only thing she said to me was, 'You look like shit. When was the last time you had a wash?'

'I don't remember.'

With that we went to another motel. I had a shower. I was coming off heroin again and feeling very sick. By now my withdrawals were worse than before because I was taking more doses of heroin.

The next morning we had to leave that motel in St Kilda and Carol, out of nowhere, came out with this question. 'Want to get away from Melbourne? Should we go for a long drive to Shepparton?'

I was always open to new adventures and said quickly, 'Yes, let's do it, right now.'

Carol screamed so loud.

I screamed very loud too. 'Let's gooooooooooooooooooo!' And off we went to Shepparton, a nine hour drive. We were both very pumped about this trip.

But first we went into Myer, in Melbourne, and I stole a blond wig and a pair of cat sunglasses. For once in my life I wanted to play the rich woman. Carol, with the money she took away from Cairns, had bought herself another beautiful, sporty little car, with only two doors. But it had a V8 motor, made lots of noise, and was fast. I put on my wig and she laughed. Then I put on my glasses and we were ready for this trip.

With my wig on and feeling like a millionaire, I watched all these gorgeous guys going past with their flashy cars and screaming at me and Carol, 'Hey, beautiful, where are you girls going?'

Carol would scream out, 'We are off to Shepparton. You can follow us if you like.'

We would both laugh and race off these guys; and I would wave to them, loving all the attention.

One guy screamed out to me, 'You are an actress. What is your name?'

I looked at Carol. 'He thinks I'm an actress. What a zombo head.'

Carol would say, 'Lilla, you are really beautiful. I wish you knew how beautiful you are. You are also funny, and very adventurous.'

Carol always used to say beautiful things to me. We would pick each other up. Whenever one was feeling down, the other always said or did something to make it better, and it always worked. We hardly argued, Carol and I, but when we did, it was about drugs. She didn't like me using heroin. She always tried to stop me from taking it. I used to get so angry with her, standing up for myself, but hurting her with my words. I didn't know there were other ways of dealing with fights. I was very young and learning something new every day.

Carol and I were nearly in Shepparton. It was a long drive, but worth it. We laughed, listened to very loud music. We both loved music. We waved to so many guys. When we finally arrived in Shepparton we realised it was a very small town. We were hungry from the trip and tired. First we decided to get something to eat at the local pub, the Shepparton Hotel. As soon as we walked in, all eyes were on us. Half a dozen people were having their lunch, and I became so nervous that I nearly tripped. We found an empty table and I grabbed a seat as fast as I could. We were very tired and ate our meal quickly. Then we went to the Shepparton Motel to unwind and get some sleep.

The weather was simply perfect. I could feel the sun soothing my skin. I always loved the sun. I always felt happier when the sun was out. If the sun wasn't out, I used to feel very depressed.

We found a nice little room with two single beds, took off our clothes and went to bed. We slept all day. We woke up at 8 pm and went to see if there was any work there for us.

We heard about the Three Stars massage parlour. They needed two new girls, and we needed the money, so we decided to see the boss, the pimp. She was a very classy woman. We were both tired of working for pimps. Sure she was our pimp, but she was a woman and she was really nice to us.

Carol and I didn't have a place to stay at the time. After a while, living in a motel can be extremely expensive, so we asked the boss if we could sleep at the massage parlour. We would be responsible for opening and shutting the place. The boss liked that idea, and agreed after a bit of hesitation. Her main fear was that we would get busted. Nevertheless, she said we could sleep there until we found a place.

One night I caught something from a man, crabs, and my vagina was very itchy. Carol said to me, 'Put some Mortein on it, and they will die.'

I did. I found a can of Mortein and sprayed so much that my vagina was burning. I screamed. Carol came into the shower, laughing her head off. She helped me get all this Mortein off my vagina. She scrubbed it so hard with the soap that I was in tears.

'How much did you put on?'

In pain, I said, 'I sprayed it on at least ten times.'

She laughed. 'You're so crazy sometimes, Lilla.'

Finally the burning stopped. I'm sure those critters in my vagina did die at last.

Unfortunately, one night Carol and I were busted by the police. So many police barged in and went through almost everything. 'Who is the boss here?' they asked.

We were both scared. We didn't want to say who the boss was. If we did, the real boss would have killed us. So we said nothing. You cannot tell the police who the boss is. If we told the police, we would have to testify in court, which we didn't want to do. Never tell the police who owns the parlour. That was one rule we had learned from past experience.

Carol and I just wanted to make our money and run away. The next morning, we woke to hear this headline on the radio: 'Two women, twenty-two years old, Lilla and Carol, were arrested last night, living off their earnings. Both face a court hearing on...' They named the date.

Carol and I looked at each other, and Carol said, 'Want to make a run for it? We got lots of money. Let's run away.'

I felt a sudden excitement; and fear too. 'Let's do it,' I said. 'Let's run away. They'll never find us if we leave now.'

We quickly packed our stuff and off we drove, away from Shepparton, leaving the court behind, leaving the Three Stars parlour behind, but taking with us lots of money. We were so ashamed that the whole town knew who we were: two prostitutes who were busted by the system. We ran away from it, just like Thelma and Louise. We knew it was wrong, but we were excited and ran back to our freedom.

But of course, I ended up back on the streets again, searching for heroin, spending all the money I had on drugs and alcohol. Again I wanted to die. I wanted so desperately to change my life, but I didn't know how.

Because of the drugs, I stole the cheque book of my older brother Paolo, and wrote so many cheques so that I could get my heroin. The day the police picked me up I was having lunch at Topolino's Pizza. They grabbed me gently because they knew I couldn't run, and took me to the Saint Kilda police station. I was there for hours. They kept asking me whose cheque book it was. They even had cameras which showed me entering the bank and changing the cheques. I could see it was me because I limped so badly. Although I wore a hood, you could see from miles away that it was me.

The policeman asked me, 'Is this you?'

I looked at the pictures and the videos. 'Yes, it is me.'

I was sent to court, and received a twelve-month good behaviour bond. The judge ordered me to stay in Pleasant View, a rehabilitation centre, for a few months, and to attend groups so that I could get off heroin, until I was well enough to return to the community.

When I arrived at Pleasant View I didn't know what to expect, but I was happy I was doing something good for myself. I wanted to get off drugs. I wanted to stop drinking so much alcohol and having sex with men. I was prepared to do anything to change.

But of course, three weeks later I was kicked out. The staff didn't find it funny when I got everyone drunk on cheap wine. I had bought a big bottle and sneaked it in, contraband. Nearly all the patients got drunk.

One of the patients punched me in the mouth because I was screaming. I was blind drunk and the punch didn't hurt me; but getting kicked out sure did. That night I went to a motel with a crazy man. I was very scared of him. He told me he had killed someone, and I believed him; but that didn't stop me from having sex with him. The next day I left him, while he was sleeping. There was a bad smell of death around him.

Back on the streets, I once again overdosed and ended up in a mental institution. I was there for almost two weeks again. When I left there, that same night I moved in with a man I had met there. He was extremely mad, talking to himself all night very loudly, cursing the world, although no one was in the room. I went to sleep full of fear, but the next morning I knew what to do. I gathered my stuff and got the hell out of there. Somehow I managed to carry my small suitcase down five flights of stairs.

I went back to selling my body, back to the heroin, back to the pills, back to sleeping with so many men for a bed to sleep in, or for food or sometimes even a shower. My life was getting worse by the second. There I would be, after a big hit of heroin, looking like a dirty old woman, ripped jeans, dirty jeans jacket and sneakers; short, spiky hair, angry, lost; sitting next to a friend in the gutter and talking shit. I always thought I was really intelligent when I had a shot of heroin. It was not true. Drugs made me think I was intelligent, but I wasn't at all.

After my time in Pleasant View, I never saw Carol again. I lost contact with her. I only knew her by her first name, but I knew that was not her real name. She had played a big role in my life. We had lots of fun together, and we made lots of money too. The best part was running away, which we did twice. Thelma and Louise were caught in the end, but Carol and I were too quick and too smart.

I heard from other junkies that when they'd had enough of living that kind of life they would go to a rehab so they could get off the drugs and start a new life. I knew it was going to be very hard, but I was left with no choice. I was tired of selling my body for drugs. I was tired of looking like a bum. I was tired of depending on drugs to give me that false high. I was tired of all the rapes and the bashings. I was tired of losing my friends because they died of an overdose or were killed by guns because of drugs. I was tired of hiding away from people I had ripped off over and over again.

This was not a life. This was misery. This was hell, and deep inside I knew there was something better than this. I didn't know what, but I was willing to give it a good try. And I did.

Chapter 26

Melbourne Odyssey House; and six months in Sydney Odyssey House. Altogether four and a half years of rehabilitation, getting off heroin. I was twenty-five years old.

ONE DAY I WAS SITTING IN THE GUTTER with my best friend Steve. We were watching people going by. Some were going to work, and some were scavengers, begging money from rich people. Junkies were everywhere. I was one of them.

Across the road I saw a beautiful woman, with long, blond hair, dressed all in black. Her jacket was black, her skirt was black, covering her knees, and she wore black shoes. She looked stunning, incredibly beautiful.

I said to Steve, 'Steve, see that woman across the road with a black suitcase?'

He looked up. 'Yeah, what?'

'One day I want to be like her, Steve. I want to live a good life. I know I can do it.'

'I know you can do it too, Limpy.' And with that he gave me a smile.

'Self-Portrait', painting by Lilla Benigno.

That woman at the bus stop was probably going to work. She looked like a lawyer. This gave me a bit of hope. Now was the time to get off the streets. It was time to get off heroin. It was time to start something completely different.

This woman, who I never met, made me see a little bit of light at the end of the tunnel, because a couple of weeks later I picked up the phone and called Odyssey House. I had heard from another junkie that he went there for a while, and when I saw him again he was straight. He was really happy with his new life, and now it was my turn. I knew that I too could do something about this new life.

This woman that I never met gave me the strength and courage to reach out for help. There was hope for me, and I wanted to try it out. I wanted to be free from this mess I had created. I went to Odyssey House voluntarily. No court, no other people, suggested it to me.

Odyssey House in Melbourne was an enormous place, run by other addicts who had changed their lives and become directors or counsellors. Odyssey House was an institution for addicts of any kind: drugs, alcohol and other addictive personalities. It looked like a castle. It took both men and women, but the sleeping quarters were separate, men on one side and women on the other.

When I arrived in Odyssey House, I was scared of everyone. I was afraid to tell anyone what had happened to me on the streets and what I had done. This turned me into a very angry person. I hardly spoke to anyone, and when I did it was always an accusation, or something I made up in my own head.

I knew this place was going to help me, and I knew it was up to me, but I didn't understand what to do, who to trust, and what to say. I had sold my soul to the devil, and it was hard to tell anyone what had happened to me. It was so hard to trust anyone.

Somehow the word got around Odyssey House that I was a good cook, and the staff decided to put me where the food was. I spent most of my time cooking for other people. I remember one day I made fresh *gnocchi*. I left it out for the night, and cooked it the next day for five hundred people. The sauce was beautiful, tomato sauce the way my mother made it. Everyone loved the sauce but left the *gnocchi*. It was rock hard and no one ate it. I was shocked! I couldn't believe I gave everyone rock hard *gnocchi*. But of course, everyone quickly forgave me, and the rest of my cooking was really nice and no one complained.

One night I really couldn't sleep. I had been there for a couple of weeks. I was coming off heroin cold turkey, with no other drugs to control the turmoil, the pains, the vomiting, the hot and cold flushes. I didn't know what was happening, but I was feeling really sick. My bed was wet because of how much I was sweating, and then freezing. I felt my head was going to burst open, and there would be blood splashed all over the walls.

My thinking was insane. I was too afraid to cry, and I kept thinking of Mum, pretending she was next to me. Sometimes that was my only comfort. I felt a bit safe. Thinking of her calmed me down, but on this night nothing was working, not even thinking of my Mum. I got up, sweating and crying, walked only a few steps and sat right next to the window, looking out and shivering. I need something. I need some Valium, something to calm me down. I wondered what in the world I was doing in this place. I put my hands on my face and sobbed. I kept saying in my head, 'I want to go. I don't want to stay here. Please, Mum, tell me what to do.' A woman on level four heard my cries and came to sit on the floor, very close to me.

'Hang in there, Lilla. I know you're hurting. You are going through withdrawals from the drugs. I went through it, and I experienced what you're experiencing right now.' Then she said, 'Come here.'

I went closer and she gave me the tightest hug. I kept crying while she held me. When I stopped crying she asked me, 'Want me to give you a hand to go back to bed?'

She held my hand and slowly I went back to bed. She covered me with my blankets, and touched my forehead gently.

'You will be fine. Try to get some sleep. We have an early start in the morning.' I closed my eyes, and that was my first good night's sleep. Only four hours, but the best hours I had slept in a long time.

I began feeling so much strength within me. I wanted to do this program. If not for myself, then for my mother. I wanted her to feel proud of me one day. Slowly but surely my recovery picked up speed. I was learning to say please and thank you. I started learning about honesty. I would watch people talking in groups, not understanding why they talked like that, full of honesty. Some would cry in front of us. But I was tough, or so I thought. I kept my walls up. I still didn't trust anyone.

Months went by and my recovery was very slow. I was learning new things: how to speak, how to express emotions and feelings. Sometimes I felt like returning to the streets. All this was way too hard.

Some nights I would wake up and sit on the floor near a long window and cry for hours. I wanted my recovery to speed up. I couldn't see my changes. I wanted to see them, feel them, like everyone else, but I couldn't. On the floor I was a bitch, calling people names or giving them dirty looks.

There were too many people in Odyssey House, but we had to somehow work together. If anyone brought drugs into the house, we would all have to thoroughly clean the house. And this was not a normal, one or two bedroom house. I am talking about three storeys with lots of rooms; never-ending rooms and beds and classrooms. It would take three or four days to clean the whole house, so contraband was a disaster for us all.

By now I had no callipers. I had thrown them away many years ago. Sneakers were the only shoes I could wear, and I had to put tissues inside the right shoe to make it comfortable enough to walk in.

Odyssey House was a big place. I didn't like the stairs up to our bedrooms. I slowly became used to them, but one day I fell down. I cried, and the staff took me to the hospital. My right ankle was dislocated, so I had to wear a plaster for three weeks. No more stairs for me. Now my bed was downstairs, until my foot got better.

I was learning how to speak, but sometimes the staff became frustrated with me. Now and then in a group the staff member in charge would turn and ask me, 'And how things are going with you, Lilla?'

I would always say, 'Aw, I am good, good.'

But some of the others would talk to the staff and tell them I was not good at all. I would lash out at some of them. If I spoke one-on-one with a male, I would be in trouble. If a male looked at me strangely, either sexually, or just looked at me for no apparent reason, in the groups I would tell that male off.

Some people were puzzled by me. I never did things the way I was supposed to. The more they told me what to do, the more I would tell them to fuck off. After living on the streets for so many years, and having gone through so many traumas, there was no way I would trust anyone. I didn't even trust myself.

One day Mr Marco took me outside to the gazebo and started asking questions about my feelings.

'So, Lilla, tell me what happened in the streets? Did you get raped? Did you get bashed? And how did you feel when these terrible things happened to you? Tell me about your family, your children, and why did you decided to put your son in foster care.'

The more questions he asked, the more I would be quiet. I didn't understand why he would ask all these questions. I couldn't answer him because I couldn't label my feelings. I couldn't label the torment I felt inside. I couldn't explain why I made those terrible decisions regarding my children. I did what I did to survive. But now that I had this wonderful person, Mr Marco, the big boss of Odyssey House, trying his best to help me, I had no trust. I couldn't talk to him at all. In the end, he became very frustrated with me. What he said I will never forget.

'You did get hurt a lot by so many men, I know that. You ran away from your family, and for ten years you've been living a terrible life. But it will end one day, and I will help you.'

I couldn't even look him in the eyes. With my head down I thought, 'Why can't I talk? Why can't I express how I feel? What is wrong with me?'

When Mr Marco left me alone in that gazebo, I started to cry. I was frustrated that no words would come out, only tears. Although I was in Odyssey House I found it extremely hard to talk about my experiences. I was too scared to open my mouth. I pushed my experiences to the back of my mind. There was no way I could say anything about them. No matter how hard people in Odyssey House tried to get it out of me, I could not talk. I was numbed out. Inside I was dead.

Gradually, as time passed, little by little I learned how to trust, how to talk; not much, but I was trying so hard. I wanted to tell everyone what had happened to me on the streets, but my mentality was still: 'If I told anyone I was gang-raped or bashed, they would come and kill me.' I was afraid of being killed, which was why it was too hard to tell my story.

I began to move up levels. During pre-treatment I had a session in front of staff during which I would have to tell them why it was time for me to move up levels. This was so hard, especially when they asked questions about my recovery. I couldn't answer them. I didn't have a voice. Everything I said seemed stupid, so I preferred to shut up rather than have them see me as a stupid girl. But the staff still moved me up levels. When I reached level one I was so happy! Now I could have my make-up and my hair drier; and in level two you could finally have visitors. But no one ever visited me.

At level three you can sit in a group and be the leader of that group, and ask everyone how they are coping. Reaching level four was like a graduation. You were cured. No more drug dependency. You could leave Odyssey House forever. Unless you took up drugs again, and then you were back in and had to start from scratch. You were given only three chances. If you ran away more than three times, the staff would never let you back.

I blew my three chances. Once, during pre-treatment, after a couple of months I ran away without telling anyone, and went back onto the streets. More drugs. I was admitted a second time after a few months, and I was going better because I knew the rules. I met some wonderful friends. But again I ran away while everyone was in bed. I went back to Saint Kilda and back into drugs. The third time I was doing so well. I started from scratch again, pre-treatment, and then level one and, one year later, I moved to level two.

Level two was wonderful. I could smoke lots of cigarettes, and I could order people around. I was like a boss, giving people duties to do and writing reports. Level two made me feel so important. While I was on level two the staff decided to put me on the front desk to answer the phone. I learned how to do it quickly and became the telephonist of Odyssey House. It was the best job ever. I loved it.

I loved seeing Mr Marco first thing in the morning, all dressed and ready for his business. He was a short man, well dressed, with a black suit and a black tie, black pants and black shoes, his hair flicked back and looking very clean. He would ask me with a big smile, 'Any messages for me, Lilla? And a very good morning to you.'

I have never forgotten how he used to treat me, with respect and dignity. He always made me feel special and he was always caring. I felt like a little girl around him.

But now and then my womanhood would come out, along with my flirtatious behaviour. But Mr Marco never criticised me for it. He accepted me as I was and always told me how much I was changing. It made me feel appreciated, and to hear that I was getting better made me feel over the moon.

Two more years went by and I was more involved in Odyssey House. I was starting to feel that I was changing. I was smiling a lot more, and especially when I saw Mr Marco. To me he was like the father I never had. Although he was rather attractive, I only saw him as a father figure. One day while I was having breakfast, Mr Marco walked in.

'Good morning, Mr Marco,' I screamed out, and gave him a big smile.

He walked over to my table and said, 'Good morning, Lilla, I have a surprise for you. Finish your breakfast and meet me in the front foyer.'

I was very excited. 'Really? Please tell me what it is.'

Mr Marco smiled again and said, 'It's a surprise'.

I had a lot of respect for Mr Marco. He was trying so hard to get inside my heart, to get me to talk about my traumas. He wasn't successful, but at least he tried.

I finished my breakfast quickly and went to the front foyer. A black car was waiting for us. Mr Marco opened the door for me and said, 'In you go. Time to go.'

He sat in the front and I sat in the back. Another man drove the car. Mr Marco and this man started talking but I didn't understand what they were saying. There were too many big words for me. I started fantasising about the surprise he had for me.

My fantasy didn't last very long. Very soon we stopped. Mr Marco opened the door and said, 'We are here. I will take you in now.'

There were three steps, and Mr Marco gave me a hand up. When he opened the door, a man in a white suit greeted us both with a big smile.

He was a dentist. Mr Marco took me to the dentist to fix my tooth. I had lost it when I had my motorbike accident. I lost half of it when it came through my top lip. After about two hours, he gave me a mirror. I was stunned. I looked pretty with my tooth fixed, and Mr Marco said, 'Now you look a lot better and you can smile as much as you like.'

I gave him a big hug. 'Thank you so much. No one has ever done anything like this for me.'

He patted my head. He knew what I was talking about. 'Come on, let's go,' he said. 'And show off your new smile.'

I was so happy. I looked and felt pretty. I could smile without covering my mouth. I was so grateful to Mr Marco, and I still am today. The tooth that Mr Marco fixed for me I still have, and I am still smiling.

Odyssey House gave me a glimpse of light at the end of the tunnel. I started to participate more in the groups. I learned if I had a problem with someone to write it down, and then in groups to voice what we felt. It was our chance to voice the problem without getting interrupted and without arguments. I learned to speak up a little bit, and not to blame other people for the things that happened in my life. I learned about friendships. I learned how to trust some people, and how to voice my opinion, while also respecting other people's opinions. I learned that I could cook. I learned that I could keep myself clean, shower, and take care of my body. Everything was new to me, but I started to like it. Sure, I would become frustrated from time to time, and even fight and argue with other people, but finally my passion to live a better life was getting stronger and stronger. My dream was always to reach level three or four, but level two was already an indication of big changes in me.

I knew I was ready by now to move to level three. Every month the staff would move people up. This time Mr Marco was in this special group. Everyone was there. I didn't want to sit down because I had so much to do, but I decided to see who was moving up the levels. They called so many, but not me. I had been in level two for two years, and I knew I was ready to move up to level three, but it never happened.

That day I threw the book on the floor, went into the office and told the staff there that I wanted to go. I'd had enough of this place. I wanted to be free. No more regulations, no more telling people what to do, no more office hours or writing reports on other people's behaviour. I wanted out. I wanted to leave, all because I was not moved to level three when I felt I was ready.

One older guy screamed at me. He was in level three and had been now for over three years. 'What, are you going back onto the streets to sell your body again, so you can go back to your dear drugs?'

'You can't fucking tell me what to do. If I want to leave and do all those things I will, so fuck you, you bastard!'

He saw red and was just about to hit me, but another woman stopped him. 'Let her go. She will die like a prostitute.'

When she said that I slapped her face. She was shocked. Two guys were holding me because I wanted to rip her hair out. Instead, I left everything that was mine behind. For the third time I ran away from Odyssey House, Melbourne, knowing that Mr Marco was going to be very angry with me, and feeling that any chance of recovery was gone for me. I was a loser. I knew there and then that if I did go back onto the streets I would die.

On the streets of St Kilda I started using heroin again. I'd learned a belly full of new things in Odyssey House. Now even the heroin had no effect on me. It felt different. Every time I took it I would have a panic attack. I knew I had changed for the better. I knew I didn't need that drug anymore to live a better life. I knew that all the things I learned in Odyssey House were for one reason only: to help me get better.

I was different. With my body full of heroin I was thinking of Odyssey House, about the new friends I had made. I was thinking about Mr Marco, the Director; how he was there to help me, how he wanted me to change and feel good about myself. But instead I let him down, not once but too many times.

My head was full of new thoughts. I didn't want to be another day on the streets. I wanted to leave that life behind. And I was so tired, tired of walking, tired of crying, tired of looking for a place to stay, and tired of being tired. I wanted to live a new life. I knew it was there, but I had to be strong and go back to Odyssey House to learn more about me and other people.

So I went back. I felt so ashamed for leaving. I could have been in level three by then if I hadn't left. But I had to restart the program from the beginning, pre-treatment. In pre-treatment you have no privileges. You receive only fifteen cigarettes a day. If you run out you can't ask anyone for a smoke. You have to wait until the next day. Somehow I always made mine last.

Living on the streets had become part of my past. But of course, all this took a long time. I knew I didn't want to take heroin anymore. I already ran away from Odyssey House two times, but this one last run away was the third time and now I blew my three chances with Melbourne Odyssey House, so this time the staff sent me to Sydney Odyssey House and I lasted there for six months. I knew by then I was ready to leave. I was changing, learning to live without drugs, and I started to like it. I started to feel better within, and I knew it was time to try to live on my own without any drugs or men.

After four years in Melbourne Odyssey House and six months Sydney Odyssey House, I felt I was ready to move on, to go on another journey. This time my journey was all about recovery. The day I left Odyssey House was the day I finally learned how to grow up, a little bit. I wanted to see if I could carry on this recovery on my own.

I knew deep inside that I could make anything possible if I put my mind to it. Mr Marco always said that to me, and he always reassured me that I was not stupid. I was intelligent, but because of my traumas I didn't trust anyone, and I kept all those traumas inside. I was too scared to tell anyone about what happened to me on the streets. But Odyssey House opened my heart a little bit. They taught me about acceptance, and taught me that there is a better life with no drugs. In the end I believed it. I knew it was possible.

In the end I realised I was not a bad person. I was very sick, and all I needed was someone to guide me and show me a way out. Odyssey House did that for me. It was the best rehabilitation centre. They persevered with me despite my tantrums. Everyone there, especially Mr Marco, never gave up on me. They always stood by my side, so I could get well.

After leaving Sydney Odyssey House I went to see my sister. Her door was unlocked, so I went in and, because I had travelled many hours by train, I went straight to sleep in her bed, under the covers. I woke up with Mark (my sister Isabella's ex-husband) on top of me, having sex with me. He was raping me and I kept pushing him off, but he was too heavy. This wasn't the first time he had raped me. While I was living on the streets he always raped me, but this time I was fighting and screaming.

'Get off me, Mark, get the fuck off me. I just came out of Odyssey House. Why are you raping me? No more!'

He came inside me, and I felt sick.

When he got dressed he said, 'Keep your mouth shut, slut,' and walked out.

I was mortified. Again I was raped. I couldn't stand Melbourne anymore. I had to do something quickly. I dressed and went to see my mother. With tears in my eyes I asked if she could lend me some money so I could get away from Melbourne. I sat on that chair and sobbed, and told her everything, how many times I had been raped.

I told her about the bikers, and about Mark, raping me over and over again for many years. I told her of the rapes that happened while I was in bed sleeping one night, and she couldn't believe it; but I saw her tears rolling down, and she said to me, '*Aspetta*. [Hang on.]' She went into her bedroom and put her hand under the mattress.

She came back, sat down and grabbed my hand. 'I have been saving this money. I don't need it. Go away from here, go far, far away, and let me know where you go as soon as you arrive there.' She put in my hand a bundle of money, all tied up with a rubber band.

While I was crying I said, '*Ma quanti soldi mi stai dando?* [How much money is that?]'

'$250. Get the bus. Go somewhere away from Melbourne.'

I cried more. I couldn't believe my mother was giving me that money.

I got up and hugged her so tightly, crying and thanking her for the money. I remember saying to her, 'I promise, one day I will give it back to you.'

'*Ma ti ricordi quando tu mi hai aiutata? Ora e' il mio turno.* [Do you remember how many times you helped me? Now it is my turn.]'

More tears and, yes, remembering the times I used to get a taxi to give her money to help her with my little sisters. I did give her lots of money, but always felt proud and happy and never wanted anything in return.

Only once did I ask something in return and that was a kiss, and when my mother gave me that kiss on the cheek I gave her $250. I never dared to tell my mother where the money came from but I always felt in the back of my mind that she knew, in a way.

But when she heard about all the rapes I'd endured, she changed. She became my Mum. Not only because she gave me the money to run away, but also because for the first time I saw her feeling my pain, my hurt, and the humiliation I went through. She wanted to help me, and she did.

It was then that my love for my mother began. It was then that I saw how powerless she felt in the face of what I had gone through. It was then that I felt closer to her than ever.

Whenever I went through a trauma, whether being raped or bashed, I always called my mother's name out loud or in my head. Whenever I felt pain from each rape, I would console myself by thinking about my mother, being in her arms, fantasising about having her with me. She was on my mind always. I prayed to my mother to make it all stop, and that she did.

God didn't work for me anymore. The only person that always answered my prayers was my mother. This is when my relationship with her changed. I fell in love with my mother. I started to see her so differently. I started to love her laughter more and more. I wished I could be there with her all the time, but just the thought of going back to Melbourne, the fear of being raped again, was way too strong.

Whenever my sisters asked me to come back and stay with them— 'My home is your home'— my excuse had always been that Melbourne was way too cold for me. But if they knew the truth, they would have understood better why I never wanted to go back there.

I told my mother not to tell anyone about all the rapes, and she promised she wouldn't say anything to anyone. She kept this secret. If my father had known what had happened in the streets, he would have died of a heart attack. If my sisters or brothers had known, I'm sure they wouldn't have been able to deal with it. This was way too big. This secret was only for my mum. And she took this secret to heaven.

My mother knew I didn't want to go back into the drugs, and she knew I was so tired of being raped and bashed. She gave me the keys to freedom. She saved my life. My mother became my god.

When I said goodbye I hugged her so tightly. I looked up at her and smiled. I went to the city by cab and asked the driver to take me to a travel agent.

I remembered going with Carol my friend for a holiday in Cairns, and my first words, when the woman at the travel agent asked where I would you like to go, were, 'I think I will get a bus ticket for Cairns.'

Chapter 27

January 28, 1987—The birth of my daughter Caroline.
I was twenty-nine years old.

THE BUS TO CAIRNS was departing at 7 pm. I was eager to go, but I had about an hour before boarding so I called my mother from a phone booth. As soon as she picked up I said happily, 'Mum, I bought a bus ticket to go to Cairns. It's always hot there. It will be good for my legs, Mum.'

'*Ma dove e' Cairns?* [Where is Cairns?]'

'*Sul nord Queensland, molto, molto lontano da Melbourne.* [Up north Queensland, far away from Melbourne.]'

'*OMG, stai attenta, non parlare con nessuno telefonami quando arrivi la.* [OMG, be careful, and don't talk to anyone and call me when you arrive there.]'

'*Sette giorni nel autobus mamma, sette giorni e si' ti telefono quando arrivo.* [Seven days, Mamma, seven days and then I will call you when I arrive.]'

I loved talking to Mum in Italian. That was the only way I could keep my heritage alive and get better with my Italian. I didn't want my heritage

Lilla Benigno and her daughter, Caroline, aged six months.

to disappear for good. I had already lost so much of my soul, but not my identity. I wanted to keep that.

Seven o'clock came, and the bus arrived on time. I was the second to go up the three big steps, nearly lost my balance, and showed the bus driver my ticket. Then I sat next to the window. That was my seat number and I was happy, because I wanted to watch everything, all the places we were going through.

The bus started to fill. A band of four musicians, all dressed in black, hopped on board. The first guy was tall and handsome. He had chains hanging from his jacket, wore tight black pants and his hair was all stuck up with Vaseline. His eyes were black from the black pencil he must have used, and he had a white-powdered, ghostly face. His lips were slightly red, but it didn't look like lipstick. It was their real colour.

In his right hand he held a bottle of whisky, my favourite drink. As he passed me I asked, 'Have you got Coke with that?'

This tall, dark, handsome musician replied, 'For you, princess, yes I do. And I will make you a special drink later.' He smiled.

'Ok, I'm in.' I smiled back.

He sat three seats behind me on the right. I was on the left near the window, so I couldn't see him anymore. A few minutes later a cute couple took the seats next to me, the woman in the middle. The guy looked like a model. They started talking in Spanish. Great! Now this is going to be such a boring ride, with two people I can't understand. I put my earplugs in and started listening to my music. I heard, over and over again, 'What's Going On?' by Toni Childs. I used to love her and still do. The best singer around in the seventies.

My legs were hurting. If I keep them bent for a long time, my feet start to get cold and all circulation stops. Then they get really sore. But after five stops, the couple next to me left the bus. I had three seats for myself, and I put my legs up and went to sleep.

During the second day on the bus the scenery was beautiful. I saw so many mountains, and I love mountains. The bus stopped now and then so we could go to the toilet or buy some munchies to keep us awake. I don't think anyone wanted to sleep. We were all too curious. I was so happy to be finally leaving Melbourne. I was so happy to be leaving my past behind. I didn't realise that wherever I went my memories would always be there to haunt me. And they did.

The next day, the singer of that band came and sat in the middle seat. He told me he was going to Brisbane to do a gig. He was the singer. With him he had his scotch, with a can of Coke and a small plastic glass. He introduced himself as Frank. I told him my name and we shook hands. He gave me the first drink of scotch and Coke and it went straight into my head. I was feeling a bit dizzy but happy, so I asked him for another one. He made me another, and the more I was drinking, the more I wanted to have sex with him. He was good looking, charming, beautiful, and sex came into my mind. Next thing I knew he kissed me, and I made sure to kiss him back, passionately and roughly. He stood up and pulled his pants down, and I could see the bus driver watching everything.

'Get down,' I said to him; and suddenly there we were, having sex on the bus, in and out; kissing, not kissing; moaning and doing our best not to scream too loud. A couple of heads turned to watch us, but no one objected. They turned back and minded their own business. Then suddenly he came. I didn't. I was too drunk for that. But he did.

He climbed off me and pulled up his pants. Half an hour later the bus stopped, and he and the all band left the bus. We had arrived in Brisbane. I waved goodbye. I wonder if I will ever see you again, I thought. But I never did.

There were three more days on the bus for me. Nearly everyone left, but there were still five of us. Finally, at 10 pm, we arrived. I was extremely tired. Even though I'd had my legs up on both seats they were still very sore, but I managed to get my suitcase and leave the bus.

It was night time, and I heard some people screaming and fighting, not too far from the bus stop. I sat on my suitcase. To my left I saw a bunch of black people swearing at one another and screaming.

Then suddenly it hit me. Where in the world was I going to go? I started to panic and then to cry. A gentleman got out of his taxi and asked me, 'Where do you want to go?'

'I don't know. I'm from Melbourne, and I don't know where to stay for the night.' I sounded so scared and cold. 'Who are those black people and why are they fighting?'

The old man, with white hair and a white uniform that looked more like a hospital uniform than a taxi uniform, looked at me and said, 'Those people are called aboriginal. There's some good ones and some bad ones. But don't you worry, they won't hurt you. Come on, get in. I know the perfect place for you to stay for the night. At least you will have a bed to sleep in and breakfast too.'

'Oh, thank you so much.' I felt relieved and safe.

I got into the taxi and this kind person took me to the Budget Accommodation. He helped me to settle into a room. I paid for the room, which was only $15 a night. The driver took my suitcase because he saw I couldn't walk too well, settled me there for the night and left. I went to bed and slept right away. I knew I had a big day ahead of me tomorrow, but doing what?

I didn't sleep well that night. I kept being woken by men who were drunk and talking very loudly, right next to my window. I screamed out, 'Shut up!' and all the noise stopped. Now I could sleep in peace.

The next day I called my mother in Melbourne. There were no mobile phones in those days, only public telephone boxes. 'Mum, I've arrived in Cairns. I'm so scared. I don't know anyone. There are black people everywhere, Mum.'

'*Vai a Social Security. Sistema tutte le cose e vedi se puoi trovare un bel posto.* [Go to Social Security. Fix everything up, and then see if you can find a little place to stay.]'

After calling my mother I felt stronger than ever. I knew what I needed to do. I went back to that cheap motel and packed my little suitcase. The lady at the counter had a cigarette hanging from her mouth and her hair was in a bun. She looked up. 'Yes, dear, what can I do for you?'

I kept thinking, Wow she has lots of wrinkles. But I asked, 'Can you please tell me where Social Security is? I need to tell them I am here and I need some help.'

The lady took the cigarette in her right hand and stood up. 'Luv, only two blocks down. You can walk that far, yes? That's where Social Security is.'

I thanked her, smiled and said goodbye.

I was glad Social Security wasn't very far and, yes, I could walk that far. Luckily my suitcase had wheels and I could wheel it and hold myself up too. Whenever I was tired I could lose my balance and fall, especially now that I wasn't wearing any callipers to support my legs.

When I arrived at Social Security (now called Centrelink) I took my number and went to sit down. I had nothing with me, only my pension number to say who I was and my bankbook. In those days there were no credit cards.

My turn came and the woman on the counter fixed my payments for the next two weeks. I was ready to go, but where? I asked the woman behind the counter if there were any good places for girls like me to stay. She didn't know, but she told me about Lifeline and the Salvation Army. I didn't want to call them, so the man who was sitting beside me said he had a spare room at his place in Gordonvale. I didn't know where Gordonvale was, but he said he had a motorbike and an extra helmet, and if I wanted to go with him I could. The rest would be very cheap. I jumped at the idea without thinking.

'Okay, sure, let's go.'

He saw that I couldn't walk properly, so he picked me up and put me on the back of his bike, then put the spare helmet on my head. It fit perfectly. I liked it, because there was a plastic cover that came down so the bugs wouldn't get into my eyes.

The ride seemed to last forever. My arse was so sore from sitting on the bike. He wasn't going very fast because I begged him not to, but eventually we arrived at his place. We were both wet from the rain, lots of rain. He gave me a towel to dry myself and told me where I could sleep. It was a small room, very clean, with one single bed already made, with sheets and a beautiful red doona. There was a single cabinet, small and blue, with a lampshade, also blue, just in case I felt like reading before going to sleep.

I stayed with this man for four months. It was hard for him to take care for me. It rained every single day for four months. I couldn't go anywhere. I was stuck in this unit, with this lovely man, who loved to cook. He always cooked for me too. It felt as though he became my father. But one day he had had enough, and asked me to go and live somewhere else.

I moved to three more places before I found a great hostel for women only. You could stay if you were pregnant, but as soon as you had the baby you had to find somewhere else to go.

In the meantime I would call my mother and let her know every little thing I was doing. She was really happy when she found out I was pregnant. I wasn't happy, but she was, and I couldn't understand why. Later I did.

Every second or third day I called my mother. If I didn't hear her voice after four days I would have panic attacks. And my mother always picked up the phone and always talked to me. There was not one day that she didn't pick up the phone.

I was only two and a half months pregnant, but this time I didn't want to have an abortion. I thought the father could have been the singer I met on the bus. But no. I still believe the father of my daughter is Mark. His rape produced my daughter. I couldn't live with that. I couldn't believe it when the doctor told me I was pregnant.

Fortunately I found a great hostel run by Mr and Mrs Buffie, both lovely people. Mr Buffie worked to maintain the place. If a bulb blew he would fix it. If the electricity went off, he would fix that too. He could fix everything. He was a very tall man with a gentle heart. His wife was a lot shorter than him and she, too, had a very kind heart and a lovely personality.

The hostel suited me just fine. All I had to pay for was my food and the rent. I was happy with that because I had money left. I started going out with my new friends. I was liked by everyone except Belinda. She was the fattest person alive, and she and I would have screaming matches, which I always won. I couldn't stand her. She would sit in the lounge all day, watching all the soapies on TV and eating lots of junk food. She used to think she was the queen of that hostel but she wasn't. I was.

Belinda dared me to take off my jeans and show my legs. At first I told her to fuck off; but then something inside told me to go upstairs, steal someone else's shirt, and put it on. I came down the stairs slowly, without the jeans.

All the girls who were there at the time clapped, and I won the bet with Belinda. She also clapped, and gave me $20.

'Well deserved,' she said. 'It took a lot of courage to take those stupid jeans off.'

I smiled at her. 'I felt better and cooler without them too.'

It was then and only then, for the first time in my life, that I didn't care who looked at my legs and feet.

Even Mr Buffie noticed. 'Finally you took those jeans off. Good girl.'

I smiled at Mr Buffie too and said, 'Yes. I did it, and I feel wonderful now.'

I still think of Belinda when I mention this. She gave me the courage to stand up to my disability. I had always been too shy to show anyone my legs, afraid they would say how ugly they were; instead they told me my legs were beautiful. It was my new beginning, showing off my legs. I had been ashamed of all my life. Learning to love them, to accept them.

But of course, that was only the beginning. While I was pregnant I called Steve and Sara, the foster parents who were looking after my son, Dean. He had been with them now for nearly six years. Dean was close to his new family, so I told them I was ready for them to adopt him. I knew he was settled and happy there. So they sent me the papers and, within a couple of weeks, Steve and Sara, who had other children, were happy to adopt Dean.

I was happy too. I was still mentally very naïve. And now pregnant again! How in the world could I look after two children? I couldn't do it. The day I made the decision to adopt out my son was the day I went out and got blind drunk. I felt like a failure, a bad mother. Feelings of guilt returned. Not only did I let my daughter be adopted; but now my son too. I was devastated, and again blamed it all on my disability. The only way to stop these terrible feelings was to go out and get drunk. I mean really drunk, to the point of blacking out.

Time was passing. I still kept calling my mother and telling her how well I was doing, how I was living in the hostel full of girls. There were young girls like me. Some were tourists and would stay for only a little while, but some stayed for many months.

As my stomach grew bigger, a lady I had never met visited me at the hostel. The very first question she asked was, 'Are you keeping your baby?'

At first I thought it was a bit odd. 'I don't know yet. Maybe yes, maybe no. I'm not too sure.'

This lady, whose name was Carmel, said, 'What if my husband and I look after you through the pregnancy, give you anything you want, and when you have the baby you can give it to us, if you want.' She continued, 'I can see that with your legs you will find it very difficult to look after it. I will be willing to adopt the baby, so you can do whatever you like in your life.'

At first the idea seemed really nice. I wanted my baby to have a good family so, without thinking, I said, 'Yes, okay. You can look after me, and if I don't want to keep the baby, you can have it.'

This was the worst thing I could have said. She was around me nearly every day like a bad smell. She would come with salads. She would come with pastries and lots of sweets. Every single day she was in my face, and I was getting more and more irritated.

When I was seven months pregnant, she and her husband, and myself and a few other girls from the hostel, decided to see a strip show in town, just for fun. I loved going out, pregnant or not. That night I got really drunk, and the lady who wanted my baby started screaming at me.

Then this angry person came out of me and screamed, 'Get me off this bus. You are not going to have my baby. I never want to see you again.' I screamed louder and louder. 'Get me off this bus NOW!'

The husband opened the door for me and let me out, just outside the Cairns Base Hospital. He threw me on the grass. I started laughing and remember saying, 'You will never get my baby, and if you try I will tell the police you wanted to give me ten thousand dollars for my baby. Get out of my face before I go to the police.'

They became scared and left, because they knew it was wrong. They knew I was disabled and tried to take advantage of me. I was not ready to make any kind of decision about my baby yet. It was way too early for that.

I had lots of cravings while I was pregnant with my daughter. The best ones were for an ice cream known as the Heart. Sometimes I might have five a day. Sometimes I craved mashed potatoes, or soup, or mangoes. Mr Buffie always gave me mangoes, and I loved them. I was always grateful to him for that.

One day I went to have a shower, but when I closed the shower door I heard another shower: it was between my legs! I screamed out, 'My water broke. Help! Someone please help me!'

Mr Buffie picked me up in his arms. He knew I couldn't walk at all. They called an ambulance, which took me to the Cairns Base Hospital.

At last this baby was going to come out! My pains weren't severe. I was starving, and as soon as I arrived at the hospital, they gave me lunch.

One of the nurses told me not to move from that bed, because the floor was wet. But I thought, Fuck what the nurse said. I know I'm ready to walk over to the other bed. So I got up from the bed and started walking towards the other one. The next thing I knew I did the splits, like a ballerina. My right foot slid and I fell over. The nurses rushed in, and the nurse who had told me not to move told me off.

Now four of them were holding me, and they put me into the labour bed. I was ready to have this baby. I felt a strong need to have the biggest shit, but the nurse told me not to push. She told me to hold it, but all I wanted to do was push.

Two doctors came in, and one tied my legs up in the air. A little voice said, 'Push, push NOW.'

I started to push. Oh my God, my vagina felt as though it was ripping apart. I was in such incredible, indescribable pain.

Then the same voice said, 'Push harder. Now, push harder.'

My body tensed, ready for the biggest explosion. The head was out. Oh my God, how painful, and only the head was out.

The same nurse screamed out, 'This is your last push, NOW.'

And I pushed it out. I received a couple of stitches. Then one of the nurses came over.

'It's a girl,' she said. 'She is so beautiful. Do you want to hold her?'

I was crying, but then I looked at the nurse and said, 'No, I'm not ready to see her yet.'

I was happy the baby was out, but I was mixed up in my head. I didn't know what to do. I had only three days to think about this.

On the first day the doctors came in and asked me, 'Are you keeping the baby, Lilla?'

'I don't know yet.'

I kept thinking I had nothing for this baby. I had no cot. I had no place to stay. I had nothing. What was I going to do if I kept this baby? I had already made a mess with two other children. I had a big decision to make and I was really mixed up. I didn't know what to do. The fear of not being a good mother entered my mind over and over again.

On the second day the same doctors came, one young and one old, with a couple of nurses.

'Have you come to a decision yet, Lilla?'

I looked at them angrily. 'Leave me alone. No, I'm still thinking about it.'

The next day different doctors came, with other nurses. I could see they were getting impatient. 'Have you decided yet what you are going to do with the baby?'

I had an idea. 'I want to call my mother. I want to hear what she says, then I will make up my mind.'

I hadn't seen my daughter yet. It was the third and last day, time for my biggest decision. I went downstairs to the phones and called my mother. '*Mumma, tre giorni fa' ho avuto una bambina cosa posso fare?* [Mum, three days ago I had a baby girl. What do I do?]'

She was so happy. 'Keep her, Lilla.' Normally my mother never called me Lilla, but Letteria. 'Not only she will be company for you, but you will learn a lot from her too.'

I started screaming with happiness, 'Okay, Mumma. I'm going to see her right now. I'm keeping the baby.'

Quickly, in my wheelchair, I went to the fifth floor. I screamed out to the first nurse I saw, 'I want to see my baby. I want to see my baby now.'

There were three nurses, with big smiles on their faces. One of them hurried to fetch my daughter and put her in my arms. I felt so calm. I felt so beautiful inside. All fears of this and that went out the window. I couldn't stop looking at her. I was there with this baby in the present, observing her little eyes and her little nose; her little mouth with no teeth. She looked a bit wrinkled, but to me she was beautiful.

Then the doctors arrived with big smiles. One of them said, 'I see you have decided to keep your daughter. Well done. I will call a women's shelter here in Cairns. These great people will help you a lot with the baby.'

'Yes, okay, and thank you so much for waiting. That phone call with my mother was really important, and now I'm happy to keep my child.'

Chapter 28

Keeping my daughter, learning to be a mother with all the advice of my mother, 1987.

MY DAUGHTER CAROLINE was born on 28th of January 1987. She was only a few days old when we arrived at the women's shelter. On the first of February, Joanne, a dark lady from Papua New Guinea, came to see me. I had never met a dark person before, but she was so nice. She bent down and said, 'Are you ready to see your new home?'

With a big smile I said, 'Yes I am.'

Joanne made me comfortable right away. I liked everything about her: how gentle she was, how kind she was, and how she picked up my baby with lots of care.

I won't say the name of the women's shelter to protect them and respect all the women who were going through their own traumas. The shelter was an escape for them and kept them safe. For me it was the best shelter. The staff gave me so much support and I will never forget them for that. I was now a new mother. I had a baby a couple of days old, and I was prepared to embark on this new journey.

'My Daughter Caroline', painting by Lilla Benigno.

I was scared at first. I had nothing for the baby, but Joanne and Mary, the two main women who looked after the shelter, helped me so much. They understood that this was new to me. During the night, while the baby was crying, one of the older aboriginal women would pick up my daughter, feed her and change her nappy for me. I didn't know what to do. I didn't understand my role as a mother. I had never been successful as a mum before. Some of the other women helped me.

Sometimes Joanne would come in and do her shift, and my baby would cry. Joanne would pick her up, give her a bath, change her completely and feed her for me. She would let me sleep in, because I would be awake with the baby, not knowing what to do. I only knew how to feed her with a bottle, not too hot and not too cold, then burp her. Then I would go back to sleep.

One day Joanne said to me, 'Today I will show you how to bathe little Caroline.'

I was so scared but I said, 'Yes, please. I want to learn.'

She got the bath ready for me, a little red bath that looked like a toy. She told me to always use my elbow to test the water. It mustn't be too cold or too hot. This was my first lesson. Then I learned how to hold the head of the baby while I sponged her everywhere, slowly, slowly, and made sure no soap got into her eyes.

Joanne was very patient with me. She was kind and beautiful, such a tall lady, heavily built but with a heart of gold. After two weeks I told her I wanted to go to Melbourne to show the baby to my mother. She helped me with the tickets, and before I knew it I was heading to Melbourne. My daughter was too small to travel, but I had a strong desire to show the baby to my mum.

When I arrived in Melbourne everyone was there to greet me, Stella and my mother and a couple of my other sisters, all happy to see me. I was so happy to see my mum. I saw that right away she loved my daughter. But my daughter had become sick while she was on the plane, and I immediately took her to the Royal Children's Hospital. She stayed there for two weeks. She had caught an infection, and the doctors gave her antibiotics. I was so scared, but my mother kept telling me that everything was going to be all right, and she was right.

When I went back to my mother's place I was tired of sleeping on the chair next to my daughter, so I put her on Mum's bed and went to lie down. My mother thought I was sleeping, but I was just resting on the lounge. I saw her go into the bedroom where my daughter was lying on her bed. She didn't know I was watching her. She picked up my daughter and she kissed her.

'You are so beautiful,' she said, and held her in her arms for some time. I had tears in my eyes.

I could only stay in Melbourne for three weeks. Two of those weeks my daughter spent in hospital, and the week after that we spent with Mum. She was so good. My little girl was now healthy, eating and sleeping well. When I said goodbye to Mum, this time I didn't want to leave her, but I had a place just for me in Cairns, and I wanted to go back and start looking after my daughter.

I went back to the women's shelter and stayed there for over a year. Then Joanne and Mary thought it was time for me to get a nice little unit of my own and live with my baby. That was very scary for me, but I was also excited. For the very first time I was going to look after my daughter on my own. Caroline and I found a cute little apartment, with one bedroom. I loved it right away. Joanne and Mary helped me to move in. It was already furnished, with a double bed, a TV, a little table, with a small sofa, a stove and a fridge. I had everything in there and I loved it. This was such a great novelty for me, to be on my own, and to look after my daughter.

I couldn't stop kissing her. I kissed her while she slept, and I kissed her while I changed her clothes. I knew now how to bathe her, and she always looked clean, well fed and with a clean nappy. I made sure I did the things Joanne and Mary had taught me. I did everything in my power to become a good mum.

After a while I moved in with a few friends, because living on my own was hard for me. First I moved in with Sandra and her children in Holloways Beach. I lived with her for a while, learning more and more about how to be a good mum.

I wanted to prove to everyone that I could bring up this baby alone, that I was strong enough, disabled or not. I could be a good mum.

At times I would relapse. I would get a babysitter and go out and get drunk. Being a mother was very difficult, and at times frustrating. I had to let out some steam, and the only way I knew how to do that was to go out and get drunk.

My nightmares about my traumas haunted me, but I never wanted to go back onto heroin. Instead, I started drinking. Even moving away from Melbourne hadn't helped. The turmoil inside was sending me crazy. I was insane, and I had no clue how to reach out for help. Sometimes I would take my baby to the pub and drink until I blacked out. But one day I went too far. I left the baby under the table. I forgot all about her and went home.

When I woke in the morning I panicked. I dressed quickly and went back to Rusty's Pub, searching for my daughter. Then I saw an older aboriginal woman holding my baby. She told me she had taken her back to her place and looked after her. They knew she was mine and they were my friends. When I blacked out I would not remember what had happened the night before. My drinking was getting out of hand, and I needed help fast, before my daughter was taken away from me. A few months later I decided to go back to Melbourne to visit my family.

One night, my older brother Paolo had a barbecue for everyone, and left a bottle of scotch right next to my chair. I hated Melbourne. It always bought back those terrible traumas. I sat outside with Mum, and while she was talking to everyone else, I kept drinking. The more I drank, the more she told me off.

'*Ancora? Ancora che bevi??* [Still? You still drinking??] Stop it.'

I got really drunk and started saying bad things to my mother and my brother Paolo. I became hysterical. The memories of the rapes were driving me insane. I couldn't get them out of my head. But I couldn't talk about it to anyone. Only Mum knew.

I went inside Paolo's new house and vomited all over the floor. Bet, Paolo's wife, a beautiful woman with a heart of gold, was really sympathetic, but my brother Paolo slapped my face to shut me up. I was screaming out to everyone that my brother-in-law had raped me, but no one wanted to hear it and I was too drunk to make any sense.

A couple of days later I left Melbourne and returned to Cairns. I was using alcohol to stop these traumas, but instead the alcohol would drive me more insane. It would make me do things I didn't want to do. I needed help fast.

I had been in Cairns now for almost four years, and my daughter Caroline was slowly growing. Every second day I would call Mum and ask, 'Mum, how do I cook *polpette*?'

'Mum, how do I make meatballs?'

Or, 'Mum how I can make *pasta e patate* [pasta and potatoes]?'

Now that I was living on my own, whenever anything was new to me I would call my mother for help. When my daughter cried and I didn't know why, I would call my mother. She always had the answer. I would follow everything she told me to do. Especially when my daughter was very sick, I used to get so scared and would cry over the phone to my mother. She would explain to me what to do, and how to do it, and then my daughter would be okay again.

At Christmas time, instead of buying my daughter one Christmas present, I would buy her thirteen presents, and I would put in each card my sisters' names, my brothers' names and my mother and my father. I bought the extra presents so she felt that all her aunties and uncles and grandparents were there for her. But one day I got caught. My daughter was eight years old at the time. She saw all those presents on the bed, which I was wrapping for her.

'Mum,' she said, 'all those years, no one has ever sent me a present, true? You are the one who has been buying me all these presents?'

With tears in my eyes I told my daughter the truth. 'Yes, Caroline, I have been buying all those presents, because I wanted you to know that all the family cares for you.'

She gave me a big hug. 'You don't have to do that, Mum. One present is enough for me.'

I felt sorry for her, because I wanted her to know that all the family in Melbourne loved her. And they did, they all loved her. Once my sister Stella sent her a package full of beautiful things, and she was so happy about that. Stella my sister once also sent me a present for my birthday. I didn't want my daughter to think badly about my family. Living so far away from them was incredibly hard but, at the same time, it was the best decision I had ever made.

One day I was feeling a bit down, tired of doing the same things, tired of being a mum, tired of being so far away from my family. So I decided to call my mother again. 'Hello?' 'Mumma, what you doing?

'*Ma chi e?* [Who is it?]' She didn't even recognize my voice.

But I was so happy to hear her voice. 'It's me, Lilla. *Che fai?* [What are you doing?]'

'Not much. I just had dinner.'

'What did you have?'

'*Bello sugo con polpette e uova e pane bello caldo.* [Beautiful sauce with spaghetti meatballs, eggs and warm bread.]'

I was so tired of eating shit food. It was either cereal, eggs, potatoes, or tomatoes. I always tried to make nice food for my daughter, but I felt I was a bad cook. When my mother told me she had beautiful sauce with meatballs, eggs and warm bread, I saw red. I suddenly wished I was back in Melbourne, as my cooking was terrible.

My face changed and I screamed into the phone, '*Ti odio, ti odio.* [I hate you.]' I said it as a joke.

My mother started laughing. '*E te? Cosa hai mangiato?* [And you? What did you have for dinner?]'

I was so ashamed to tell my mother what I had for dinner. How could I compare it to a beautiful *sugo*? My dinner was shit. '*Due ova scaffedute.* [Two rotten eggs.]' That's what I had for dinner.

My mother went into a rage of laughter. The more she laughed, the more I screamed, '*Due ova scaffedute e tu mangi il sugo con polpette e uova.* [I had two rotten eggs, and you had spaghetti with meatballs and eggs.] Noooo!'

We laughed for nearly two hours. Our laughter was coming from our guts. Mum loved to tell this story to the rest of the family so she could laugh more about it. Me too. It's probably one of the funniest times I ever had with my mother. When we laughed we really laughed, and that's one thing I miss about her so much.

My mother became my biggest influence, even though I lived so far away from her. I loved when she answered the phone. I would talk to her in Italian about everything I went through, and she would turn it around and make me laugh. Sometimes our conversations were very long, and when I received my phone bill, I would freak out. Sometimes it was $700 or $800, and it would take months to pay it off.

My mother knew that if she didn't hear from me it was because the phone bill was too high. And as soon as I paid it off, the first person I would call was Mum. She taught me how to cook over the phone, and how to wash the clothes. I used to wash black and white clothes and different colours all together, and sometimes the white shirts would be black and I would call my mother in tears. She would make me laugh, and that's when she told me I had to separate the washing, black with black, white with white, sheets on their own and towels on their own.

I called her once and asked her how to make *arancini*, and she came up with so many things I had to do that I wrote it all down. *Arancini* are balls of rice with mozzarella and ham inside. They are made into balls and fried. This was the most difficult food I have ever made. My daughter Caroline loved them, but I swore to her I would never do it again. It was too much work.

My mother never knew how to say 'I love you'. Every time before I hung up I would say, 'I love you, Mum,' and my mother, with her broken English, would say, 'I love you too.' Just to hear her say that was like gold to me. It was as though I hit the jackpot. After each conversation I made sure to say, 'I love you', and I loved hearing it back from her. It was just beautiful.

My love for my mother grew so much stronger when I arrived in Cairns. I was scared, and I was still very young, but this time I had a little girl to look after. Thanks to my mother, I learned how to make lunch for my daughter and take her to school. I always made lunch for my daughter, every single day.

I went to Lifeline to do a course on how to talk to your children without anger, and how to be there for my child appropriately. I still remember the woman who helped me on this course. Her name was Frances and she was magnificent. She taught me how to listen to my child, and how to support her, especially when she was sick. She showed me how to solve her problems in a better way. That course was the best thing I have ever done. It taught me to stop being so selfish and start putting all my heart and soul into raising my daughter with great beliefs and strong morals. After six weeks I received my certificate. I felt so proud of myself, now I was learning how to deal with my daughter, how to listen to her, and how to be there for her appropriately.

Once, after so many years, I decided to find out what had happened to my best friend Rita, who I had left back in Italy.

One day I was talking to a co-worker at Sea Swift. She was Italian too, Maria. She was a great worker. She was a bit stocky, but had the biggest green eyes. She was always trying to show me how to become fast on the computer. I had to enter at least five thousand pieces of information each day, and when I began working there I could only enter five hundred.

I was slow, and later I found out why. My eyes were going on me. I couldn't see properly. Everything was either double or fuzzy. No wonder I couldn't work fast. Maria gave me a number to call in Italy, and she said I could find news about Rita that way. I called that number, but instead of asking about Rita I asked if I could have Anna's number.

She had been in the convent with us too. We were also friends, kind of, although I did pick on her a lot.

When I finally called Anna she was so shocked.

'*Anna, ciao, sono Io Lilla, ti ricordi di me?* [Anna, it's me, Lilla. Do you remember me?]'

'*Certo che mi ricordo di te, come stai? Cosa fai?* [Yes of course I remember you. How are you and what are you doing now?]'

I talked to Anna for a while, told her I had a daughter, and that I was looking after her on my own. Told her how I never got married, but had been engaged a couple of times. Then I asked her, 'Are you married?'

'Oh no. I am not married. My brothers won't let me.'

I found that a bit odd, so I went on and asked her the most important question of all. '*Anna, dove Rita, cosa fa'? Lei e' sposata?* [Anna what happened to Rita? What is she doing? Is she married?]'

Anna stopped talking, so I said, '*Anna, Dai' dimmi la verita' cosa e' sucesso a Rita?* [Anna, please tell me the truth, what happened to Rita?]'

Anna finally told me the truth about Rita. '*E' morta Lilla, si e' ammazzata.* [She died, Lilla. She committed suicide.]'

I stopped talking. I wanted to ask Anna why she committed suicide, but I couldn't. I went into shock.

I said goodbye to Anna and went to my bedroom. The white cat I had at the time was sleeping on my bed. I hugged the cat so close to me, and bawled my eyes out for a long time.

All the memories of Rita came back to me, the laughter, how naughty we were, how mischievous we were, and how close we were. It was like a tape running over and over in my head. I couldn't stop crying. Why did she commit suicide? Was life so bad for her in Italy that she wanted to end it? Did people look upon her as a freak, like me? Is that why she did it? All these questions were going over and over in my head.

My eyes were sore from crying. I couldn't see properly, so I lay there on the bed, face up, staring at the ceiling, flooded with so many memories of me and Rita. I had even thought of going back to Italy, once, to steal her and bring her back here with me. But now that flew out the window.

I know I hadn't seen her in years, but Rita had always been on my mind and in my heart. I hope now that she is in a better world. No more pain for her, no more insults from anyone. Rita is finally free, up in heaven, and no doubt I will see her again when I die too. Rest in peace, my gorgeous, beautiful soul. I will always love you, no matter what. Rita was my best friend and she still is, living or not. I have wonderful memories of her, and they are enough to keep me going with my life.

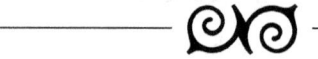

Chapter 29

*March 1989 —First time at the Addiction Help Agency.
This place slowly restored me to sanity. I was thirty-three years old.*

SURE, I HAD LEFT MELBOURNE, and now I had a newborn child, but my traumas were haunting me, and I knew I never wanted to go back to heroin again.

I heard about the Addiction Help Agency from a friend of mine, who was living there at the time. I was so tired of leaving my daughter everywhere so I could go out and get drunk.

When I went and spoke to Ellen, she suggested I become an inpatient, a live-in resident. I would pay only for food and a cheap rent, and I would receive lots of therapy. I went home and packed everything up, and went to live at the Addiction Help Agency.

At first I didn't understand what the program was all about, but I knew it was going to be quite a challenge to release the anger I had inside me. I had to find a way to do it. I sat in those meetings listening to others share their stories, their traumas, and slowly, slowly I learned how to express my feelings too. I especially learned to name my feelings. I didn't know what sad was. I didn't know what intimidation or abuse were. I didn't know the

Painting by Lilla Benigno.

real facts about rape and sexual abuse. I sat there for months, and was more eager than ever to learn about my real life, not the masks I had worn for many years. All those masks were like an onion. Bit by bit I was peeling off my covers. I was learning not to be false. For once in my life I was learning how to be true to myself, to be real and honest.

I shed so many tears and punched the big punching bag, with gloves on, so I could let out all this rage I had within me.

I met one of the most wonderful therapists. Ellen was taller than me, slender and petite, with high cheek bones and a beautiful smile. She always dressed like a business woman. I loved her clothes, and she always looked very classy and very respectable. I had never met anyone like her before. She had such a strong personality, and sometimes I was scared of her. But deep within, I knew I was in the right place. She took my hand and slowly we started to work on changing a lot of my ideas.

I was so screwed up. I didn't know anymore what was right and what was wrong. All I knew was that I wanted to learn. I wanted to find out about me, who I was and what I had become. I wanted to undo all the pain and hurt that I had caused so many people, including myself.

I couldn't run anymore, I was defeated. I was bankrupt, emotionally, spiritually and psychologically. I was numb. I felt nothing anymore, except a little love towards my daughter; but not towards me. I didn't know how to love myself. I had to find a way. I wanted to learn. I was desperate.

My brain was full of negativity. I wanted to let it go and find a way to communicate with people, instead of using the old tactics, such as manipulation, sleaziness, and dishonesty. I wanted to be real. I wanted to feel my feelings. During a session with Ellen she asked me if I loved my body, and for the first time in my life I said, 'No, I don't.'

Her next question was, 'Lilla, have you ever seen your full body in a mirror?'

I looked at her in disgust. 'Hell no. I would never do that. It's way too ugly.'

I started to cry, and Ellen came closer to me. 'Tomorrow,' she said, 'I will bring a mirror from my place, and we can have a session about your body.'

I was scared. I didn't want to do it. But I looked at Ellen with tears in my eyes.

'Okay, I am ready for it.'

Ellen came to the rehab the next day all smiles. She made herself a cup of coffee and called me into her office.

Ellen looked beautiful, as always. 'We have a lot of work to do, Lilla,' she said, 'but first, let's go upstairs. I have a surprise for you.'

I lived upstairs, sharing my room with another woman, Sylvia. But Ellen took me to a smaller room. She opened the door and there it was, a long, tall mirror. I looked at her, petrified. I didn't know what she wanted me to do.

She brought two chairs from the kitchen into the bedroom, shut the door, and asked me to sit down. Then she started talking.

'Lilla, remember the other day when you asked me how you could love yourself? Well, this is the first step. I will be here to support you, but what I would like you to do is undress. Take all your clothes off and stand in front of this mirror.'

I looked at her in shock. No way was I going to take my clothes off and look in the mirror. I had never done that before. I might die if I saw my body naked. I wanted to run away right there and then. I wanted to escape from all these confrontations. But instead I was stuck on the seat. I couldn't move, paralysed with fear.

I had never seen my body naked, and this was going to be quite a challenge for me, but something within me wanted to do it, wanted to find out what I really looked like. I have always hated mirrors, and I was going to try something new and scary for the first time in my life.

Ellen kindly said, 'I will leave the room. I would like you to take off one item at a time, first your T-shirt, then your pants. If you're wearing a bra, take your time and take that off too; and last, your underwear.'

I kept thinking what a big job it was, but I wanted to do it, although my heart was beating so fast. When she left the room, I started doing what she suggested.

First I took off my T-shirt, looked at my breasts for a little while, and felt such a strong sense of shame. I quickly took off my pants, looked at my legs, and they made me sick. So I took off my underwear, and there I was, naked, in front of a full length mirror. I was naked, bare, nothing on my body. Then I started to observe the details of my body, my shoulders, my arms, my breasts, my tummy. When I got to my legs, I started to cry. Then Ellen knocked on the door and asked if she could come in. I wrapped the towel around me. I didn't even want Ellen to see my body. She walked in.

'You are wonderful, Lilla. This is the first time you've seen your body. I'm so proud of you. Your legs are part of you, all your body is part of you. I would like you to look at your body for ten minutes every day for two weeks. You think you can do that for me?'

With tears in my eyes, and happy to hear she was proud of me, I nodded. I was prepared to go through that, for two weeks.

The first time it was so hard, and the second time it was still very hard. I didn't mind looking at my breasts. They were the only thing I liked about my body. I have never worn a bra in my entire life. Bras, for me, are evil. Every time I tried to put one on, I felt as though I couldn't breathe. So I never bought one and never wore one.

A week went by, ten minutes every day, looking at my body, and the more I did it, the more comfortable I felt. I had never been able look at my legs. When I did, I started to cry. They repulsed me. They made me sick. But slowly I started to look at them differently. I also started looking at my feet in a different way. And then something started to happen. I was falling in love, for the first time, with my legs. I kept looking at them in the mirror. Much of my hate towards my legs was lifting, was leaving me. I started to like them, at last.

Ellen gave me the biggest gift of all. She taught me how to love everything about me, not just my breasts, or my eyes. It was the whole package, legs, feet, arms, hands; my bottom, my hair, my vagina, my fingernails. My body become my best friend.

It was the beginning of a new love affair for me, not in a vain way. A deeper love towards myself. Now that I was learning to love my body more instead of rejecting it, it was time I did more hard work. This concerned my emotional side, which was stuck in a rut. I also wanted to change this desperately, so it meant more hard work, and I surely was ready for it.

I had accumulated a lot of false beliefs in the streets. I was also angry all the time. But I knew deep inside that I was a nice person, and I would go to any length to change my old behaviour. I was an emotional wreck, paralysed by my own fears, feeling things I had never felt before. My life was built around blocking out my feelings: don't show them to anyone. Wear a happy face in front of anyone who crossed my path. I fooled and lied to so many people about how I truly felt.

I started going to lots of meetings, and I noticed that I was becoming addicted to them. At first, whenever I was asked to share, I would start sharing a little bit of my drinking and drugging story, and then I would start crying. I felt no one had ever heard me before, and now I had so many people wanting to listen to what I had to say. That made me feel more at ease, and I was learning to trust. I was learning how to put my jigsaw puzzle together again.

While living in AHA, I was introduced to other groups, such as NA (Narcotic Anonymous), ACOA (Adult Children of Alcoholics), SA (Sex Anonymous) and Alanon (families that shared stories about their alcoholic mothers or fathers). All these meetings gave me a deeper understanding of myself, of how screwed up I was, mentally and spiritually.

I was moving forward. Now I was unstoppable. This strong need to change was with me twenty-four hours a day. Now and then I could see glimpses of my recovery, and it made me feel so amazing inside.

I stayed in AA for ten years. The longest I stayed sober, completely sober, with no drugs or alcohol, was five years. They were the hardest but the most rewarding years of my life.

I held on to AA because I was terrified of being a bad mum. I had done so many wrong things in my life, but my biggest desire was to be a good mum to my daughter. I didn't want her to go through the same pain and sorrow I went through. My goal was to change myself so I could be strong and do my best to protect her and look after her, as a real mother should. I didn't want to drink anymore, and I wasn't. I didn't want to have sex with men so I could feel beautiful, so I stopped that too. I didn't want to manipulate people for money and food so I could survive. That stopped too.

I was changing. I was becoming responsible for myself and my daughter. I was making new friends in AA, especially men. I met so many AA members. Some of them were wonderful, but some I could not stand. Yet I learned to tolerate them because my need to change was far more important than anything in this world.

I remember when my daughter was only four years old, and she was going through something that I didn't understand. She kept on washing her hands every few seconds, and I asked her, 'Why do you wash your hands all the time? What's wrong?'

Her sad little eyes looked at me and she replied, 'I don't know why I do it, Mum.' That was when I thought, Okay, time to get help to be a better parent.

My daughter saw me crying many times, and I didn't know how to tell her it was not her fault. I had to find a new way to communicate with her. I had to find a way to make her feel safe and loved. I didn't want to be like my parents. I wanted to learn about feelings and emotions. I wanted to teach my daughter how to express herself. I wanted to break this cycle. I was determined to break it and I did.

I went to Lifeline and asked one of the counsellors if they had a course on how to become a better parent. They did, so I put my name down. I was so happy about it. Finally I was going to get some insight into how to be a better parent.

A week later I started the course. It lasted for eight weeks, and I learned so much, especially about how to talk to my daughter, how to be there for her, and how to make her feel safe and loved.

Doing the parenting course gave me a sense of confidence and so many new tools for becoming a better mother. I received my certificate, stating that I had finished the course, and I was proud of myself for doing it.

Life started to change. I started to change.

But now and then I felt that this recovery was driving me crazy. I tried so hard to do the right thing, but then the thought of escaping again and getting drunk would return. Instead of being honest with myself, I would go out and get drunk.

I relapsed many times in AA, not because I wanted to, but because I felt that AA was becoming another institution for me. I wanted to try and live my life, instead of depending on this program for the rest of my life.

By now I'd had enough of institutions, from the time I was small. I wanted to break free. I wanted to see if I could handle my life without AA. It worked for a while, but then my drinking would get out of hand again. This meant blackouts, hospitals, a broken chin, blood all over my clothes, smashing my three-wheel motorized wheelchair into everything, just to be a nuisance. A rebellious menace without a cause.

One night I got really drunk and went to the Pier, upstairs, to a very classy cabaret, and I saw Bert Newton with his wife Patty. They are celebrities here in Australia. They have done many TV shows. I wanted to say hello to Bert, and if I wasn't drunk I wouldn't have done what I did.

So, with my bike, I drove fast towards Bert Newton's chair and banged it really hard. He nearly had a heart attack. Bert Newton's nickname was 'Moon Face' and as soon as I hit the chair he turned to me, eyes full of fear. I screamed out, 'Hi, Moon Face, I'm your biggest fan.'

Bert was very nice. He laughed but I knew I had offended him, and I could see that Patty was not very happy with me. He asked me where I was from. But a moment later a security guard came and asked me to leave.

'Why? I love Bert Newton,' I screamed. 'This is the first time I have ever seen him in person. Leave me alone.'

But the security guard calmly asked me again to leave. Before I did I said to Bert Newton, 'I loved all your shows and you always made me laugh. I wish I was not this drunk, but today is my birthday and I am allowed to get drunk.' I lied to him. It was not my birthday. 'I'm sorry. Didn't mean to smash my chair into yours. I hope you are okay.'

With a big smile Bert said, 'You're okay. I hope you have a lovely birthday. Bye now.'

With that I was escorted out by the security guard. On my way home I was busting to go to the toilet, but instead I pissed on my bike. I was so drunk that I couldn't get to the toilet in time.

I had so many drunken episodes that even today I don't remember most of them. But another night I remember going to the Nest nightclub. At the time it was the best place to be for good music and live bands. I liked the look of the singer right away. I told him to get off the stage and he did. He came over to me and I asked him, 'Want to come to my place? And then you can come back and play again.'

I was surprised when he said, 'Yes. Give me a minute. I'll tell the guys where I am going.' My place was just around the corner. I was so drunk again I didn't care about anything. All I wanted was to have sex with him. We had passionate sex for about an hour. It was the most intense sex I had had in a long time. We both came and, with that, we dressed and went back to the nightclub. He sang again.

I stayed there for a few hours, and by now I was close to blacking out, so I went to another night club, Johnno's Blues Bar. There was another live band, and I knew everyone there. The bouncer lifted me out of my chair and took me upstairs. I went straight to the bar and got myself a triple scotch and Coke. I started listening to the music and wanted to dance, so

I stood up, with hardly any capacity to walk. But a good looking guy came over to me. He looked like James Dean, my favourite actor, and started dancing with me, and holding me so I wouldn't fall.

That night I took this man home and had sex with him. It wasn't as good as with the singer because by now I was extremely drunk. While he was having sex with me I blacked out and went to sleep. When I woke up in the morning he was still there. My hangover was killing me, but he was so damn good looking that I slowly woke him up and we had sex again. That was the last time I saw him.

When I got drunk my intention was always to pick up a man for the night, have sex with him, then go out again, find another guy and have sex with him too. Sometimes I would have sex four times a night. Alcohol always gave me a strong desire for sex. But without alcohol I was frigid, and I hated sex so much. I would go back to AA and tell them all how I busted again. I would tell them about the Bert Newton episode and about all the men I was having sex with. I even had sex with a lot of AA members. Some of them were very good looking.

An old timer told me to wait for two years and stay sober for two years before having a relationship but, of course, I broke all the rules. I didn't want to wait two years to have sex. I wanted sex right then. And that I did. Part of me believed I was a sex maniac, but that wasn't the case at all. The alcohol would give me the courage to have sex with all these men. Without it, I couldn't at all.

I even went to Sex Addicts (SA) groups. I listened to many stories from real sex addicts, and then I realised after a few months that I was not as bad as them. I was not going from window to window in the night time like a peeping tom, watching women or men undress. I wouldn't blow all my money on sex. Alcohol yes, but not sex. I wouldn't think about sex twenty-four hours a day. So after a while I decided that SA was not the right group for me.

I did go to Adult Children of Alcoholics, because my father was an alcoholic. He was a binge drinker, but he still managed to abuse us emotionally and psychologically. Those scars are the worst to fix. After a while I got tired of ACOA too.

I was going from group to group, trying so hard to find all the answers all at once. Then one day a very dear friend of mine, who is now passed away, said to me, 'Lilla, time always heals everything. Give it time. Don't rush'; and that was when I learned to take my time with my recovery.

After one year of recovery Ellen decided it was time for me to try and find a new place to live, and she helped me to find a nice little granny flat in Grafton Street, Cairns. It was a small, two bedroom unit, with a fridge. There were no doors in the bedrooms. One had a double bed, and the other, smaller room had a single bed for my daughter. As soon as I saw it I fell in love with it.

I then met Mary and her son Doug, the same age as my daughter. She was then five years old, and they played a lot together. Mary was a beautiful woman, with long curly hair, incredibly attractive, and now and then her ex-boyfriend would come around to spend time with his son. They still had a great relationship, mainly because of their son. They were like best friends.

But one day I lived through the biggest cyclone, my first cyclone in Cairns. I was incredibly scared. The sound of the wind was so loud I started having panic attacks. The warning said it was category four. I looked at Tim, Mary's ex-husband, and started to really freak out.

I screamed, 'We are going to die! We are going to die! This is way too big, Tim. No, no, no!'

I started crying uncontrollably. I didn't want my daughter to die and I didn't want to die either, but the winds were incredibly strong. When I witnessed this huge tree in front of Mary's house bending, that was when I lost it completely. I couldn't see past this fear. I nearly passed out. My own fear sent me into a frenzy, and I started screaming louder and louder. Suddenly Tim slapped my face, and I stopped screaming. He slapped my face because I was hysterical. I had lost it.

When Tim hit my face I quickly went quiet. Looking back I'm so glad he did that. I really believed we were going to be blown away somewhere into the darkness. The house was moving from side to side. It felt as though it was going to break in two any minute.

And then, with the last warning, the biggest warning of all, Cyclone Steve was now a category five. This was the biggest category, but for some reason I took category five a lot better than four.

There was a kind of acceptance. If I was going to die, then let it be. If it was my time, okay. I was ready.

The strong winds went on for hours. We could hear roofs being pulled apart. We could hear pieces of metal being thrown into the road and turning somersaults. The electricity went off, and the winds grew stronger and more violent. The terror was incredible.

My daughter fell asleep on me, and I kept praying that nothing would happen to her or me or Tim or his son Doug. Pray, pray, pray, with my eyes shut, holding my daughter tightly to me, feeling helpless and hopeless. But hanging in there, and doing my best to be strong for my daughter. That night was the most horrifying night I ever encountered here in Cairns.

The next day Tim, the children and I went for a drive to see the damage. Apart from small trees blown down and six inches of water in my flat, there was no damage to our house. Many of my things were wet, but that was fixable. My daughter's first three-wheeler pink bike, that I had bought her for Christmas, was still there, undamaged. I was happy about that, because it cost me a lot of money and I knew she would love it.

We saw the damage that cyclone did to our city: houses ripped apart, roofs blown off, big, broken trees on cars; floods everywhere, water inside shops, lots of picnic areas under water. Practically all of Cairns was under water. It was a major disaster. Cyclone Steve was the biggest cyclone.

It nearly killed me and my daughter, but we survived.

Although Cairns, this small city, experiences extreme weather—heat and rain—I still think it's the most incredible, peaceful city I have ever lived in. Living in Cairns is like living in paradise. People are extremely friendly, artistic and business orientated. The key attraction of Cairns is the Great Barrier Reef. Billions of tourists love to go there and watch all the different species under water. I went to the Great Barrier Reef and totally loved it. I saw so many different-coloured fish. It was a different kind of paradise, more alive and so vibrant. I was blown away. I still remember all the colours of so many wonderful fish.

I loved living in this granny flat. My daughter Caroline loved it too. She had a playmate, and she was always outside playing with him. We were settled and happy. Although now and then I would relapse, I still kept going to AA. At the time AA for me was like a life saver. Whenever I felt down or depressed I would use the meetings to change my mood, and to listen to others' problems, and how they were learning to live the twelve steps program.

Chapter 30

Sexually molested by a priest two days before Christmas 1992, and I was thirty-four years old when I was raped again by a friend I knew.

ALCOHOLICS ANONYMOUS was slowly starting to work for me. I was starting to change. I was starting to be a better mother to my daughter. AA played a big role in my becoming a better parent, to be there for my daughter whenever she needed me. But one day something terrible happened. I met Father Michael through AA at one of the meetings that were held at the Cairns Base Hospital. After the meeting he came over and introduced himself to me, but I kind of remembered him from when he baptised my daughter when she was six months old.

Father Michael would come into my home and help me with money, or bread or milk. Many times he took me to AA meetings, because at the time I didn't have any way of getting around. I used taxis a lot, but that was money I sometimes didn't have.

Father Michael and I became very close. I talked to him a lot about my past. I even confessed to him about all the men I had gone to bed with, and about me selling my body for my drugs. I trusted him completely. I told him so much of my story, and he was there for me many, many times. Whenever he would see me struggling with money, he would give me $50 to see me through until my next pension. When he could afford it he would give me more.

I left my door unlocked most of the time, but there was a big gate which Mary kept locked so no one could get in. But this morning she must have forgotten to lock it.

I woke up to find Father Michael sitting on the chair right next to my bed. He was watching me while I slept. I sensed someone was in my room so I woke up and turned around. He gave me a fright.

Digital art by Lilla Benigno.

'What are you doing here, Father Michael, is everything okay?'

He looked at me, and while I was stretching my arms to wake up a bit better, he pinched my right nipple.

I looked at him and shouted, 'What are you doing? Stop it.'

'But they are so beautiful. Your breasts are really beautiful. Can I do it again, please? Let me touch it again.' And suddenly with his left hand he grabbed my right breast full on.

I pushed his hand away. 'No, you can't. STOP IT.'

I tried to get away from him. With my right arm I grabbed both of my legs and put them on the ground so I could get up, trying to get away from him. Suddenly I lost my balance and fell backwards onto my bed. He stood up and threw his body on top of mine. I tried to push him away.

'Stop it, Father Michael,' I screamed. 'Please. STOP, STOP, STOP!'

When he fell on top of me my head was at the level of his chest, and he kept pushing his hard-on against my stomach. I couldn't breathe. He kept on going up and down, as if he was having sex with me. I struggled but I couldn't push him off. He was too strong. When I finally turned my head away from his chest, I screamed, begging him to stop.

My screams woke my daughter who was sleeping in the next room. She came into my room. When I turned my head, I saw my daughter and said, 'Caroline.'

It was then that Father Michael stopped, when he saw my daughter. He quickly got his body off me and said, 'I'm truly sorry. I didn't mean to do it.' He ran from my little granny flat, and I was left there in shock.

I couldn't believe what had just happened. I said to my daughter, 'Come here, darling.' I gave my daughter a big hug. 'It's okay. Mum is okay.'

But I wasn't. I was trembling and in shock.

Two days later Father Michael knocked at my door. I was very abrupt with him.

'What do you want now, Father Michael?'

Now there was no way I was leaving my door unlocked. It was locked all the time. But it was made of glass and I could see who it was.

All he said was, 'A secret admirer gave me this envelope to give it to you, to help you with your Christmas.' I let him in, looked at him, and felt disgusted by what he had done two days earlier.

'Tell me, who is this secret admirer?'

He couldn't even look me in the eye. 'I promised this person I wouldn't tell you who he was.' He continued, saying, 'Open it only when I leave.'

I took the envelope without looking at him. 'Goodbye, Father Michael. Now you can go.' And he did.

I opened the envelope and found $500.

I had a strong feeling that this money was not from a secret admirer. It was from him. He stole it from the church. He was my secret admirer. I felt like a prostitute all over again, but at least now my daughter and I could have a good Christmas. I bought her lots of presents, and a Christmas tree. I didn't spend a dime on myself. It made me sick inside knowing that the money came from Father Michael.

The money was for keeping my mouth shut. He sexually abused me. He took my trust away once again. And he was a fucking priest. For that, although he is now dead, I will never forgive him. This man, a Catholic man, who baptised my daughter, who gave me so many rides to AA, sexually molested me. Today, I can never trust another priest.

After the accident I had on 17 January 2014, so many memories came back, but the worst was of Father Michael. I did go to the police to report this incident, and it was then that I found out he had died. If he hadn't been dead I would have done everything in my power to lay charges against him. The police woman who looked after me that day was incredibly helpful. She gave me a few numbers to call, so I could deal with this trauma. I was very sad that I didn't get the chance to slap his face, and today I am still being counselled over this incident.

He died the same year I received my Diploma of Visual Arts—2008.

Any spirituality I had in me was gone. This sexual assault left me scarred for life. I do believe in a Power greater than myself, but I am sure it is not God, it is not the church. Every time I go past a church I remember this incident as if it happened yesterday. Maybe one day I will be able to forgive, but I still have a lot of anger.

The questions that go through my mind were: Is it because I was disabled that he thought he could get away with doing that to me? Confessing to him about all the abortions I'd had, because of all the rapes I had been through, I was very scared to tell anyone about it, and I felt that Father Michael would maybe help me to get rid of the guilt I had been carrying for years, so I told him, I had six abortions. I also spoke to him about all the men I'd been with, and working in those terrible places to keep my drugs habit alive. Why did he think he could get away with what he did?

If he was still alive today I would have had enough courage to confront him, to ask him why he took advantage of my vulnerability and my disability. He is dead, and somehow I have to find a way to forgive him and let him go. But right now I have every right to be angry with him.

Maybe a letter from the church would be the beginning of my forgiveness. I hope one day I will get that, because I feel that what he has done to me was totally inappropriate and disgusting.

After the incident with Father Michael a few months went by, then I received a phone call from a friend of mine whose girlfriend had committed suicide four weeks earlier. He asked me to go to his place after my AA meeting. For some reason I felt he wanted to talk about his girlfriend.

He would come and pick me up. I said, 'Okay, that sounds great. I'll see you at 7.30 pm at the Parramatta School.' The AA meeting was held there. We said goodbye and left it at that. I felt sorry for him. I thought he needed someone to talk to.

Seven thirty came and the meeting was great as usual. I used to love going to AA at that time. I needed and loved every meeting and met so many fantastic people. I walked out of the meeting after saying goodbye to everyone, and there he was in a small bus. It looked like a hippy bus. It was the only transport he had.

Gary was tall, dark and handsome, a very intellectual and intelligent person and so charming in front of the girls he liked. But behind doors he was a very different man, abusive, not only emotionally but sexually.

One day I went to say hello to him and his girlfriend in the old flat where I had been bashed years earlier. It felt very weird returning to that unit. His girlfriend looked petrified. They must have been fighting when I walked in. Gary ordered her to go into the bedroom. He didn't ask nicely. He asked her as if she was his slave. She looked awful. She was the sister of a friend of mine, and she looked terrified of him. Every time she looked at him from the side she would lower her eyes. She looked so dirty, in a white T-shirt, with black marks on her dirty underwear. There were also black marks on her arms and her legs, and some on her face. Black dirt and tears. She had bruises on her arms and legs. This was why Gary told her to go into the bedroom. He didn't want me to see her like that, but it was too late. I had never seen her like this before.

Months later we heard that she had hanged herself at the cemetery. The next day someone who was going to work saw the body hanging from a tree. Everyone was in shock, and in my guts I felt something was not right. Why would she kill herself? This question was going through my mind.

At the funeral, when he went past me, I gave him a look as if to say, 'I know it was you.' I hated him so much. When he smiled at me I thought, You fucking prick. How can you smile at me, while you are walking out of the funeral?

He was creepy and I knew to stay away from him, but part of me wanted to know why he wanted to take me to his place. As soon as he helped me up into his minibus I knew something was very odd. He wasn't driving properly. He was drunk, swinging his minibus from side to side, but finally we arrived at his home. He asked if I wanted a beer and I said to him, 'You just picked me up from an AA meeting and you ask if I want a beer?'

Very rudely he said, 'Suit yourself.'

'Why did you bring me here? Want to talk about something? Are you okay?'

'Come and lie down in my bed next to me, and I will tell you everything.'

I was scared now. He was up to no good. 'Can you please take me home now? I'm very tired.'

'Yes, okay. I will take you home, but I am way too drunk to drive. Please come and lie down with me until I get sober, and then I can drive you back.'

'NO! I don't want to.' The more I said 'no', the more he insisted. In the end I said, 'Only five minutes, then please drive me home.'

I lay down on the bed with him. He wanted to kiss me, but I kept saying, 'No, don't, please!'

Then he turned violent. He climbed on top of me, took off my undies and put his dick into me so hard that I screamed. And I kept screaming, 'Get off me. You're hurting me. Get OFF me.' The more I screamed, the more he kept going. He put his hand over my mouth so I couldn't scream, and all the memories of the other rapes came back. All the eyes of the other men who raped me many years ago came back. After hurting me so hard with his dick—up and down, but really down and hurting me like hell—he finally came and got off me. By now I was crying.

'You fucking bastard. Is that why your girlfriend committed suicide? You bastard.' I put my undies on and ordered him to take me home.

In the minibus he was very apologetic, but I couldn't look him in the face. He made me so sick I wanted to kill him. I thought my days of rape were finished, but obviously not.

When I was home I rang a very dear friend of mine, Stella, and told her the story. She told me to call the police, but I said, 'No. I'm scared, so scared, and I'm in so much pain.' After talking to her I cooled down a bit, had a shower and went to bed sobbing.

A week later, at an AA meeting, I told everyone that I had been raped seven days ago. The meeting stopped and all the women told me to go to the police. With their help, this was the first time I ever went to the police to tell about a rape. The next morning I felt as though I had a spiritual awakening. I couldn't believe I had finally stood up for myself. I had finally gone to the police, with wonderful support from other AA members.

I went to court, but I lost. He was found not guilty because I told the police a week after the incident, and by then he had gotten rid of all the evidence. So the police had nothing to charge him with. They had no evidence so they let him go. This time the system was not on my side because I was too late and too scared to say anything about this rape earlier.

But that day it felt not only as though I took Gary to court, but also all those bastards who had raped me years ago, even if I didn't win the case. I was happy because finally I had a voice. Finally I was not scared to tell the police if anything like that ever happened to me again. Finally I started to trust the system. They did take good care of me. The police had a feeling that he did rape me, but they couldn't prove it.

After that I was more cautious with men. I started to recognise who was an abuser and who was not. I learned to listen to my gut feeling.

Whenever I felt I was in the wrong place at the wrong time, I would do something to get out of that situation very quickly. I started to believe that I had been attracting these people so that I could learn to speak out. Now I had a voice, and I was going to use it whenever something bad happened to me.

I didn't tell my mother about this rape by Gary, or the sexual abuse from Father Michael. It would make her too sad. Every time I was hurt my mother was always on my mind. Even now that she has passed away, I know she is watching over me.

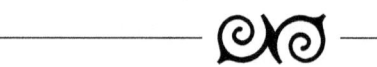

Chapter 31

1993—My new freedom called 'Gopher'. I was thirty-five years old.

WALKING FOR ME had always been such a huge struggle, especially when I went out. I found it hard to walk long distances, and fell over more than usual. It was especially difficult when I needed to do the shopping, and with a little girl it was even harder. I could never hold my daughter in my arms while I walked or I would lose my balance and fall over very quickly, and probably hurt my daughter in the fall. Thank God my daughter learned to walk at around eight months, and things became a little easier for me. The pram was like gold for me, and it helped me walk a little further.

Sometimes everything would get to me, especially how difficult it was for me to get around with my daughter. I used to cry in bed at night, praying and wishing that something extraordinary would happen to make life easier for me and my daughter.

One particular morning I woke up feeling very happy. It must have been all the crying I did the night before. I really felt like going to an AA meeting. In those days I used to go regularly, sometimes to eight or nine meetings a week. I loved them, and I was learning a lot, especially about patience and tolerance.

Happy Lilla—finally I am free!

This particular day, when Alex dropped me off, James and a girlfriend of mine, Donna, decided to pay me a visit. These were friends I met in AA. James was holding a guitar. He loved to play and sing, and he was great. James looked like a footballer, tall, blond and very handsome, but so crazy in the head. If he was on medication he was a wonderful person, but without medication he would do crazy things, such as going outside with no clothes on, or preaching about his world, which was a crazy world. But, overall, he was harmless, and a joy to be around. He always made me laugh.

Donna was a struggler like me. At last I had found someone my own height, five feet two. Donna would come to AA, and then after couple of months she would bust and would pick up a drink again. The same story as me. I would stay sober for eight months and then I would get itchy feet and want to party. So I would drink again. The longest I stayed sober and clean is five years. No drugs and no alcohol for five years. I loved living that life, and my daughter loved it too. She told me once that those five years were the best years of her life. She also told me that I was very spiritual and so calm. But deep inside I was dying. I felt as though I was in prison. I must have been such a great actress to pull that one off for five years.

Donna had high cheek bones and blond hair, but I could see the roots, and I know blond was not her natural colour. She had blue eyes and a sweet, curvy smile. She came over to me and gave me a kiss on the cheek. Then she gave me a piece of paper.

'Lilla, look at this bike. If you can get this for a little while it will make life easier for you and Caroline. Give it a go. Call them and see what they say.'

I looked at the article and saw a blue, motorized wheelchair, with one wheel at the front and two wheels at the back. The front wheel looked like a Harley to me, and I love Harleys.

As soon as I read the article, I said to Donna, 'Wow! It says I can use this for ten days' trial, and if I like it I can buy it.'

I gave Donna a big hug. I was so happy she had given me the newspaper clip. Donna was busy and couldn't stay. James, after a few songs, decided to leave. Before leaving, Alex asked if I wanted to go to another meeting that night.

I responded quickly. 'Yes, I will be ready. Thanks, Alex. See you then.' I said good bye to everyone and went straight to the phone.

Ring ring ring ring. Finally someone picked up the phone.

'Hi, my name is Lilla. I have polio in both of my legs and I find it hard to walk, especially now that I have a daughter who is almost six years old. I'm calling to find out if you can send me the Gopher in your article, so I can try it for ten days. If I like it I can buy it.'

I knew I wasn't going to buy it. Where in the world was I going to get $3250?

The voice at the other end was male and husky. He sounded old. 'Ma'am, where do you live?'

'Cairns.'

'Okay, we can send the bike over for ten days' trial and, if you like it, we can discuss payment arrangements.'

I thanked him so many times, and then I hung up.

I was so happy that I was getting a bike, even if it was only for ten days. I didn't care. If it was good for me and my daughter, and if it meant freedom to do more and more in my life, I would try anything.

A week went by after my call to the Gopher Company. The next day, at 10 am, a big truck pulled over in front of Mary's place. I opened the door and screamed out to my daughter, 'Caroline, the bike has arrived, the bike is here.'

Then I screamed out to Mary, who was having breakfast upstairs. 'Mary, the bike has arrived.'

Mary gave me the biggest smile and came down the stairs. Doug, her son was behind Mary, and Tim came down the stairs too. Caroline stood next to me, holding my hand, and finally we saw the bike. We were amazed how beautiful it was. It was brand new, still wrapped in plastic; plastic on the tyres and the knobs at the front of the bike. The man who dropped it off handed me some forms to sign. He showed me how it worked and gave me a manual. But the main thing he told me was, 'Charge it up before you use it. It takes at least a few days. This Gopher is new, and it isn't charged.' He plugged the charger into the bike and the other end into a socket on the wall.

I was so happy. I thanked him, and off went the truck. Mary, Doug and Tim all had a good look at this beautiful, blue, three-wheel bike. I remember Tim saying, 'Now you can go and drink as much as you like, and you will never fall over again.'

'Yeah, what a great idea.' We both laughed it off.

But I felt as though I was in dreamland. I kept looking at the bike, but I was scared to touch it. I didn't know how to ride it, but I knew I would learn fast.

Three days went by, and the lights on the charger were both green. That meant the bike was charged. It was time to take my daughter for a long ride. I was both scared and excited. Our first trip was to the Cairns Esplanade. I was so happy not be stuck at home. I was happy I could go out whenever I wanted. I was so happy to finally take my daughter to the park, and enjoy watching her having so much fun on the swings.

Right there and then my life changed. Not only did I have freedom to go anywhere, but I had freedom within, because I didn't have to ask for a ride from anyone to go shopping or to AA. I could do it on my own. This was another new journey. My legs took me to so many places, but they always made me fall over, alone or in front of people. Now I didn't have to fall anymore. Now I had the biggest freedom ever, in the form of a new brand new bike called 'Gopher'.

Once I became stuck in the middle of the road. Something went wrong with the bike while I was trying to cross the road. Suddenly all these cars were coming my way. Some people were beeping the horns. I became so scared and started to cry. Then a car full of young men stopped the traffic for me, and two of them pushed my chair all the way home. I was so grateful to them. I found out later that the batteries were run down. If the bike wasn't charged it wouldn't go, but all this was so new to me. I had to remember to plug my bike in every single night. I never wanted to be stuck on that monstrous, busy road.

We would go at the Pier Market Place. We would ride to where the boats were, and look at each boat. We would have lunch out. I would go to more meetings. My life changed dramatically. Not only was I changing mentally and spiritually, but for the very first time in my life I had total freedom. The kind of freedom that so many people with normal legs take for granted.

I could explore whatever I wanted. I would go for long rides with my daughter, taking her to the parks. I could take her to school in the mornings and pick her up afterwards. I could be there for her school dances. If she was sick I could quickly take her to the hospital. If I wanted to see a friend I didn't have to hesitate. I could just get on the bike and go.

On the eighth day I started to panic. I loved this gopher way too much to let it go. But I didn't know how I was going to pay for it. That night I cried and cried until I fell asleep. I prayed so hard to my mother, mentioning her name over and over again. 'Mum, please send me a sign. Tell me what to do. I don't want to let this bike go. I can't. If I do I will be back in my own prison.' Now that I'd had a taste of not relying on other people for anything, I wanted so much to find a way to keep this bike. It was like my saviour. It was like my invisible husband. I didn't want to let it go. I kept praying and praying so hard, and crying. I had only two days left, and if I didn't come up with the money, the bike would have to go back where it came from, back to Sydney.

But what could I do? Who could I turn to for help? These questions went through my mind. I didn't have much time left, and I cried for a long time, praying over and over, begging Mum to send me a sign. Anything, and I would do it.

In the morning I woke with an idea. I would go to the Cairns Post, the local newspaper, and tell them my story, and see what happened from there.

I dressed in a white dress. Whenever I wore white I felt lucky. I got my daughter ready. At the time she went to kindergarten. They used to pick her up in the mornings, and drop her off at 3 pm.

Off my daughter went to kindergarten, and I travelled with my new bike to the Cairns Post.

I was very nervous, and all I could say to the lady at the counter was, 'I want to see someone please. In two days this bike will go back to Sydney. Can I please talk to someone, who can put my story in the paper?'

The woman was so polite and understanding. 'I know the right person. Go over to the lounge and I will get him for you.'

I quickly thanked her and zoomed off to the lounge.

A very handsome man came my way. He introduced himself to me. 'Hi, my name is Bob. How can I help you?'

I shook his hand and smiled. 'Hi, my name is Lilla. I have had this bike now for eight days and I have only two days left. Then it has to go back to Sydney unless I find $3250. I haven't got the money. I am a pensioner and a single mum. I wanted to find out if someone could help me to keep this bike. It's my freedom. Without it I will lose my independence, and I don't want that. I love my freedom too much.'

Bob, tall, dark and handsome, wearing stylish, brand-name clothes, looked at me and said, 'Okay, here's what we're going to do. I want you to come back tomorrow with your daughter, so we can take a couple of pictures for the newspaper. Now just give me your details, and why it's difficult for you to pay for the bike.'

I spoke with Bob for over an hour. I agreed to show up the next day with my daughter.

At 10 am the next day I was there with my daughter. Bob came down the stairs with a big camera and started taking pictures of us, while she sat on my legs on the bike.

The next day, my story came out in the newspaper, on the second page. It was a big article about why I needed help with the bike.

I was out, minding my own business with my daughter on my lap, going to Woolworths. I bought a few things, and suddenly I heard a voice screaming, coming towards me.

'Lilla, Ms Lilla, everyone has been looking for you.' The tall man was speaking so loudly that I became scared.

'What's wrong?'

He looked at me with wide eyes, full of excitement. 'Your story in the newspaper has touched so many people in Cairns. The first donation towards your bike was $500 from someone who doesn't want to be named. Now everyone, shops, businesses, children, mothers and fathers, are all donating money so you can keep the bike.'

I was in shock. I started to cry. I couldn't believe what was happening.

This man gave me a big hug. '4CA, the radio station, would love to give you an interview.'

I had never seen a radio room before, and I was so scared. I wanted to say, 'No, I don't want to be interviewed.' But when I heard that so many people were donating for my bike I felt so grateful and so moved that I didn't hesitate. I wanted to do the interview.

At 4CA I was interviewed by one man, and all I remember is thanking everyone for the kind gesture. Then the big news. All the money for the bike was raised, $3250. The radio station sent the cheque to the manufacturer of the bike in Sydney, and also gave me an extra $50.

That night I took Caroline out to a restaurant with that $50 and we celebrated our victory. I was told I was going to be seen on the television on the news, but I didn't care. I was too happy to watch myself and my daughter on TV.

The waiter of the Italian restaurant came over and said, 'You are on the news. I want to congratulate you on the good news.' I thanked him, but I never got a chance to see myself and my daughter on TV because I was too busy celebrating my new freedom.

The bike was ours, finally, after so many tears, so many ideas. The people of Cairns were my angels and still are. They gave me my freedom, and I am still very grateful to each person who made a donation towards my bike.

Life was so beautiful. I loved living in Cairns, although I was missing my family desperately. Sometimes I would feel so alone, especially at night, but I always called my mother just to hear her voice.

Now that I had more freedom with this new bike, I would go out more and more, just to get drunk. The pressure of being a mum was a bit too much for me. I was never responsible with anything and, all of a sudden, I had to learn to pay the bills, clean the place, and look after my daughter. I had to make sure she had food, play time and sleep. That became my new life.

My life was changing, but the demons of my past were ripping my soul apart. On the outside, I managed to put up so many masks, and tried so hard to keep my daughter happy. But on the inside, I was fading bit by bit. Although this bike gave me outward independence, inside I was dying little by little.

Chapter 32

Trauma while I was sleeping, my daughter was nine years old.
1996—Second time at the Addiction Help Agency.
I was thirty-six years old.

AT THIS PERIOD IN MY LIFE I was feeling pretty happy. I was going to so many groups, AA, NA, SA, ACOA, and I was changing for the better. I was staying sober and meeting lots of good people, people who had been through the same experiences.

I was very sociable. Sometimes, when the meeting was finished, a group of us would go to The Esplanade for coffee, and talk about our experiences. Or we would go to a restaurant, or to barbecues. It was a beautiful life. I was learning new things about myself. I was learning how to feel and laugh without taking drugs or alcohol. I was finally learning how to cry without believing that I was going to die from it. I was learning to build new friendships, learning how to fall in love without using sex as a tool.

All these things were so new to me, but I loved this change. I was finally living a life I felt good about, instead of feeling shame and emptiness.

I was missing my family and one day, out of the blue, I received a phone call from my younger sister Michela. She gave me the wonderful news

Digital art by Lilla Benigno.

that she was going to visit me in Cairns. I was so happy, so excited. I was counting the days, hours and minutes. It was like winning the lotto. I really wished that Mum would visit, but she was scared of cockroaches. She always said that if there were no cockroaches, she would have visited. But I think that was just an excuse for Mum. She was scared of travelling.

When my sister arrived I wanted to take her everywhere, show her all of Cairns. Michela was my height, with long, blond, curly hair. I always loved her hair, her big blue eyes, and a face like an angel, with a petite nose and high cheek bones, and a beautiful smile. She was incredibly beautiful.

When she was small and I was living at home, I loved playing with her. I loved chasing her with my callipers, which she was scared of. I was very close to Michela, because when she was born Mum let me hold her all the time. I loved feeding her too. She was a beautiful baby. I loved to kiss her. When she started walking— Mum screaming out to Dad with lots of excitement, and me, standing back and watching her taking her first steps—I felt so happy for Mum and Dad, and for my sister too.

We had a lot of catching up to do. She looked wonderful, still very beautiful, and so funny. I loved her personality. She is nine years younger than me. I loved the way she talked. We laughed and talked, and I was so happy that she had come to spend time with me. I would feel lonely, but having my sister here with me was just beautiful.

One night, while we were all in bed sleeping, the phone rang. I hesitated to answer it, but then I got up. It was Vic, my sister's boyfriend. He asked me where she was and I told him she was in bed, sleeping. I had no clothes on that night. It was really hot. In Cairns sometimes the temperatures can go up to forty degrees, and it was one of those hot summer nights.

When I finished talking to Vic and hung up the phone, I had the weird feeling that someone was watching me outside, through my curtain in the lounge room. I looked out the door, but saw nothing. I heard a little voice in my head, saying, 'Lock the door.' Then another little voice said, 'Nah, go to bed. Nothing bad is going to happen.' So I did. I went back to bed with the door unlocked. I went under the sheet and tried to go back to sleep.

A few minutes later, I heard footsteps running into my bedroom, and I saw a figure flicking on a lighter. They had long, curly hair, and I thought it was my sister.

'What are you doing, sis? Go back to bed.' This person, who looked like they were kneeling at the end of my bed, stood up and left. I wondered if my sister was sleepwalking, or if she'd had a nightmare.

Then I heard the footsteps, louder than ever, and this time they were running. Next thing I knew, someone hit the right side of my face with a hard object, and I felt warm liquid running down my face, and covering my other eye. Now I couldn't see anything. I screamed out, 'Oh my God, what's happening?' I felt this person taking off my sheets and felt his hands all over my body, my breasts, my legs, my face, and my breast again. I wanted to scream, but nothing came out. I was immobilised with fear and pain.

Then sound came from my mouth. 'Help! Help! Someone help me.' I shouted louder as this person touched my body, harder than ever, and hurting me, especially when he grabbed my breast. I screamed out, 'STOP! STOP! STOP! NO, NO, NO!'

Then I heard my little girl, who was awake now from all the noise. 'Leave my mummy alone,' she screamed.

As soon as she said that, he stopped. He dropped the object he had hit me with and ran. I can't run, but I did manage to get up, walk to the front door, and go outside, with no clothes on, screaming, 'YOU FUCKING BASTARD!'

Then my sister was awake and in shock, looking so scared; and my daughter, who then was only ten years old, saw me with no clothes on and with blood all over my face, my hands and parts of my body. I managed to call Alan, a very close friend from AA. He came very quickly, called the ambulance, and I was taken to the Cairns Base Hospital. I needed five stitches in my eye. The doctor warned me that I would go through a hard time, and that I might suffer post-traumatic stress disorder (PTSD).

I did. It was the worse experience of my life. During the ten years I lived on the streets nothing like this had ever happened to me. I didn't know how I was going to deal with this trauma. It was the most shocking trauma I have ever experienced. Not only did this person invade my privacy, but he was never caught. The police found no trace of this person, and I was left to deal with this shocking trauma for a long time.

When I arrived home two days later, after spending time in hospital, I was a mess, and so was my sister. She wanted to leave right away, and I thought it best she did. At least she could be with the family and get support from them. I didn't want her to stay. I was incredibly sorry that she had to witness that. It was simply shocking.

After my sister went back to Melbourne, it was time to get back on my feet again. It was hard. I couldn't stand living in that place anymore, but I couldn't just pick up my daughter and run. Where would I go?

My best friend at the time, Lizzy, helped me out so much. She took my daughter in and told me she was going to look after her until I received help getting over this. She was pregnant herself and going through her own problems, but she was kind enough to look after my daughter for a couple of weeks.

Instead, I picked up the booze again, after being clean for almost two years. With my patched, stitched eye, I went out and got drunk, or off my face with other substances, such as sleeping pills, Valium. Anything I could get I would take, just to stop the movie that played in my mind, over and over again, of when I was bashed.

If this person hadn't heard my daughter's screams, I'm sure I would have been raped, and maybe killed. He hit me really hard, and his hands were really strong. I had no strength to push him away and fight. He was too strong for me.

Life became worse for me. I was having thoughts of killing my daughter and myself. My anger turned to rage. What kept going through my mind was that he must have known that I was disabled. And why didn't I lock the door? I was beating myself up, over and over again.

I kept going to the hospital. I wanted pills to make me better. I couldn't cry. I had really bad thoughts going through my mind. I want to kill myself. I want to end my life. I don't want my daughter to live in this ugly world. These thoughts were getting louder and stronger. I was going through hell, but I felt powerless, scared. The only way I could stop this madness was if the hospital staff locked me up on the sixth ward. Where all the mad patients are. And they did. At least I felt a bit safer. Doped off my brain with pills, but safer.

I didn't last too long in hospital. Within two days I saw a little bit of sanity. I decided to call a staff member from the Addiction Help Agency. I didn't want to keep taking lithium. It was strong and I was losing grasp of my own reality. I was going into a darker world where there was no way out. I was too scared to go back there, and I didn't want to rely on drugs or pills to make me better. I wanted to get through this by sharing what I was feeling, not by being drugged up twenty-four hours a day.

I have had many bad experiences with antidepressants. I have watched so many of my friends who took them lose their spark of life. They were not the same people, and I sure did not want to become one of them. This was and still is one of my biggest fears, and this gave me the motivation to reach out for help elsewhere.

I was so happy to see Frank, another counsellor from the Addiction Help Agency, when he picked me up from the mental ward. He gave me a big hug.

'Come on, Lilla, let's go and deal with this the proper way.'

The nurse gave all my pills to Frank and told him that I needed to take them for a while. In the car, with tears in my eyes, I asked Frank, 'Do I have to take those fucking pills?'

'Not if you don't want to, Lilla, but we do have a lot of work to do. Are you ready for this?'

Crying, and so damn confused, I replied, 'I'm ready, Frank. I am.' I cried all the way to the Addiction Help Agency. This was where my truest recovery began.

As soon as I arrived at the AHA, Frank and Ellen and I went into a private room. She hugged me, and I sobbed and sobbed until no more tears would come out. I was dried up.

I cried so much that I was too exhausted to talk, but Ellen did the talking for me. She reassured me that I was going to get through this, with her help and the help of all the other people at the AHA. The first thing Frank did for me—and he made sure I watched him doing it—was to throw all the pills down the toilet. One bottle after another into the toilet.

Then Frank said, 'Lilla, you can flush them all down if you like.'

I looked at Frank with tears in my eyes and said nothing. But when I flushed the water, I knew I had to work really hard to change these feelings and get back my spirit. Because it was broken, too many pieces; and I had to find a way to put it all back together.

First I had to get my daughter into a safer place, as I was way too screwed up emotionally. My only thoughts were about how I was going to kill myself. I went to court and asked the judge to help me foster my little girl out for a year, so I could get counselling every single day. The judge was surprised by this request, but he understood completely and even praised me for this action. It was approved, and my daughter went to foster care for one year, so I could get all the help I needed emotionally and psychologically from the Addiction Help Agency.

I didn't trust myself around my daughter. I was scared of my thoughts. For the first couple of weeks it was best that I didn't see her. But as I was progressing and feeling a bit better, visitations became regular, and those ugly thoughts were disappearing bit by bit. Thanks to Ellen and Frank. They were the people who restored me to sanity again.

I was improving, but I still felt incredibly scared. One of the residents at the AHA had a beautiful dog named Ralph. A German shepherd, such a gorgeous dog, he helped me through this rough time. I was allowed to take him shopping with me. He was allowed to sleep at the end of my bed.

That was the only way I could get some sleep. Every time I shut my eyes I could see this violent act, over and over again. It was sending me crazy. But the more I expressed it to Ellen, my counsellor, the more I began to let it go, bit by bit.

Ralph was my hero. He helped me through this terrible emotional and psychological ordeal. Ralph played a big part towards my recovery, and although he is now passed away, he is still in my heart, and always will be. I miss him. My friend Luke owned Ralph and he was kind enough to let him sleep next to my bed for many months, until I started to recover.

And yes, little by little I was recovering. I was doing really well. My visitations with my daughter increased, and I was learning to let go of a lot of my rage, by screaming into the pillow, or punching the punching bag, with either a bat or my hands with gloves on. I was releasing all these crazy emotions.

Whenever I went out I was scared to look at men with long, blond hair. If I saw a man with blond hair I would get a shiver down my spine, believing he was the person who had bashed me. I was terrified I would come face to face with him. I talked to Ellen over and over about what I was going through, always repeating myself, because I didn't want to live with this fear. I knew it was unrealistic fear, but in my mind it was so real, and I was so confused.

Once I learned that fear was based on 'false evidence appearing real', I knew that I could deal with this, and maybe one day let it go.

While living at the AHA, my best friend Lizzy, who looked after my daughter for a few weeks before she went into foster care, took a bad turn with her own pregnancy. She went into labour. The birth was at home. She had the baby, but a few hours later she died. Lizzy had complications with her blood, and she was in intensive care for a few weeks. Finally she was taken off life support and passed away.

Lizzy and I were best friends for four years. Whenever I sank into a huge depression, she would leave her home and lie next to me, on my bed, holding me tight, and always reassuring me that one day everything would be okay.

I was too busy dealing with my own trauma and Ellen didn't want to tell me about Lizzy, but I found out the hard way. I went to visit her in intensive care at the Cairns Base Hospital. I went with Frances, another resident at the AHA.

When we arrived at intensive care, I had a big bunch of flowers for Lizzy. I hadn't seen her for a couple of weeks and I was dying to see her. When the nurse came she told me the bad news that Lizzy had passed away early that morning, at 5 am to be precise. The flowers I was holding flew up in the air, and I started screaming and crying. The nurse took me to a small room, and she apologized to me for not breaking the news more gently.

I remember how she had said it. I had asked to see Lizzy, and she immediately said, 'I am so sorry. Lizzy passed away early this morning.' Lizzy was only thirty-three years old and the baby only a couple of days old.

I was devastated for several years. It took me a long time to get over Lizzy's death. I used to think she was going to come and see me any minute. I lived in denial for many months, before I learned to accept that she was really gone. I couldn't believe what was happening: the bashing, and now Lizzy.

Lizzy left behind two gorgeous children, Mark and Molly, and her partner Joe. He was also devastated. I went to the funeral and saw the baby lying on Lizzy. Lizzy looked all blown up, and it didn't look like her anymore.

I was going to miss our talks, our laughter. She was my dearest friend, and now she was gone forever. I was devastated for many months, but Lizzy's death took me away from my own trauma for a while. Now I had to grieve my best friend's death, and that was so hard. I nearly gave up a few times, wanted to run away over and over again. But instead I stayed at the AHA and did my best to deal with it all.

At the funeral I made a promise to Lizzy that I would never pick up a drink or drugs ever again, and that promise held for five years. I was changing, and becoming spiritual in every sense.

Lizzy's death was a big blow for me, but it gave me the courage to move on, to deal with all the stuff I was going through, and prepare to get my daughter back and start my life all over again.

When I felt strong enough to move on, I went back to the courts and asked to take my daughter back into my care. The same judge was sitting, and he was so proud of me. He granted that Caroline be allowed to come back home with me.

Chapter 33

Going back to school, at TAFE College—1997-2008.
My gift to my mother and my family, also to my children: my son Dean,
my daughters Chantelle and Caroline, and all the people of Cairns.
Finally in 2008, I proudly received my Diploma of Visual Arts.

I WANTED TO GO BACK TO SCHOOL. I wanted to learn more about life and other new things, so I went to the TAFE College in Cairns. I studied different subjects. First I wanted to become a receptionist, and I passed. Then I studied accounting, and I passed.

As a result of the receptionist course I had two jobs. I worked at the Ambulance Service as an Administrator Officer AO2. The contract lasted for six months. I really loved working there. My job was to put all the information from the night before into the computer. Sometimes the load was incredibly heavy, but my manager was wonderful and very patient with me. After a couple of weeks, I knew how to do the job very well.

Then I got another job in Grafton Street, under contract again for six months. This is where I met so many wonderful people, such as Marcy and Paul. I worked under contract as a project officer for Paul. I loved it.

A collection of paintings by Lilla Benigno.

Marcy and I became friends, and she wanted the whole world to hear me sing. Soon there I was on the stage, singing and playing the guitar in front of all these people. Most of my songs were Italian, but I wrote a few English songs too.

I went with Marcy to the Ingham Italian Festival and sang two or three songs on the stage, and everyone clapped. It was the best feeling ever.

I used to eat lots of Nutella before I sang. Somehow Nutella gave me a better and stronger voice. Once I had about five big spoons full of Nutella and I won the second prize in a song competition. I was over the moon. I wanted to carry on with my singing, but I also wanted to try other things.

I never got stuck in one place. I wanted to learn more and more, because I knew I had lost so much when I lived on the streets. I had lost so many years of learning, and my head wanted to try new things every couple of years.

My daughter was now about thirteen years old, and we were getting better. I cooked every single day for her, or we would go out to restaurants and celebrate anything, especially my successes.

Months and even years went by, and I was learning more and more. But one day, I again sank into a big depression. Although I was learning all these new trades, I felt I wanted to do something big. I had proved to myself that I could learn and become somebody. I was tired of being looked down upon by so many. Now it was time to rise up and be someone, for me, not for anyone else.

I decided to go back to TAFE, and try something completely different. My daughter was doing really well at school. She was becoming more popular, and even became the president of the school. She loved school.

I was still going to AA, but I wasn't drinking anymore. It had been a few years, but my depression came back, and when my daughter went to school I would go crazy in my mind, wondering what I could learn. What could I do that would fulfil my life, and make me happy? So one day, while I was very depressed, I paid another visit to TAFE. For some reason my bike took me to the art section, hoping that someone would give me advice on how to become an artist.

Tammy was an art teacher. She was and still is very successful with her art. Her work is well known all over Australia, and overseas too. Her work is magnificent. Her latest work was on display at the Casino, and most of it was sold. It wasn't cheap either.

Tammy said to me, 'Now, what can I do for you?'

I sat there with my head down. 'I don't know what you can do for me, but I want to do something with my life. I am so depressed. I cry every day, and I'm tired of that. I don't know anything about art, but I want to learn.'

I started to cry, tears rolling down, looking at Tammy, hoping she had a great answer for me.

'Okay why don't we put you down as a beginner for your first module? That way you can find out if you'd like to do art or not.'

'Really? I can do art too? Yes please, I want to do it. When can I start?'

Tammy walked around to my gopher. 'Come with me. Let's get all the paperwork done. If you like you can start next week.'

I wore the biggest smile. I followed Tammy to the administration department and proceeded to fill out forms and sign papers, so I could start my art course.

I met so many wonderful teachers in that art school, too many to mention. The students, too, were all amazing. Everyone helped me achieve my dream. Before I knew it I had progressed from one module to five, and that's when I decided to go for my Diploma of Visual Arts.

After six months of painting, I had my first exhibition at the Tanks Art Centre in 2003. I couldn't believe it, my first exhibition! I did all those paintings, thanks to so many wonderful teachers. I was on cloud nine every single day. I was so happy every morning, knowing I would learn something new in this art school.

I'd only had six months of school my whole life, before I landed in the streets. Now I was getting distinctions. I got five distinctions in my exams, and finished all my exams with amazing marks. So I decided to go all the way and get my Diploma of Visual Arts. I never thought this could be possible for me.

I called my first exhibition 'Beauty behind Darkness'. That night, 250 people showed up, and I sold four paintings. Weeks later I had sold all forty-eight of my paintings to the public and my friends. I was on a roll. I couldn't wait to tell my mother and show her how well I was doing. But after the exhibition, disaster struck the family.

One morning, 22 April 2006, as I was getting ready to go to college, a picture of my mother fell on the floor. I picked it up, looked at it and kissed it. Two minutes later the phone rang.

It was my brother Paolo. 'Lilla, I think you'd better come to Melbourne. Mum is very sick.'

'I can't come right now. I've got no money, and I'm doing an important course.'

My brother was kind and offered to buy a ticket for me, but I didn't accept it. I told him I would get the money and come soon.

I started freaking out. I had to find the money quickly. It was my off-pension week too and by now I was already broke, although I had everything I needed.

I quickly called Lukey, my best friend for over ten years or more. He and I dated for two years. It was a great relationship, even when it ended. Lukey was very handsome, with a heart of gold, a man who always liked to say it the way it was, living in reality, not in a fantasy world. He was accepting of his accident, which left him a quadriplegic, relying on his wheelchair to get around.

Lukey never showed his soft side, but he would do beautiful things to make me feel at ease and talk to him. He and I are still very close. Our friendship is the most wonderful friendship I've ever had. Every weekend he still comes over to visit me. He still brings me fruit or chocolate. He is like a brother. His love for me and my love for him is something I've never experienced before. I call it unconditional and respectful love.

I told Lukey about the situation. It was the worst call I'd ever had. Time stopped for me. I needed to go to Melbourne, and I had to do it fast. Lukey didn't hesitate. He gave me the money and I bought the tickets. Two days later I was in Melbourne.

My sister Isabella picked me up at the airport and drove me straight to the hospital. Isabella was scaring me, saying things like, 'Mum is going to die. I can feel it, sis.' She kept repeating this while she was driving.

'Stop it, Isabella. She is strong. She will make it. Shut up! Stop it.' Isabella nearly started crying and I stopped her. 'Let's be strong. She will pull through. Mum is strong. You know that. I know that. Let's think positive.'

Finally we arrived at the hospital. Everyone was there, all my sisters, brothers, nephews, nieces, and suddenly it hit me. Fuck, this is serious.

I hugged everyone. Stella asked how I was, and the rest of them told me that Mum might not make it this time. She'd already had triple bypass surgery and other operations. She had diabetes, and the doctors had even cut off a couple of her toes. My sisters and brothers did their best for Mum, but in the last few years she had been getting worse and worse. Sometimes I wouldn't hear from her for months.

My sisters Stella, Isabella and Michela looked like ghosts. They were incredibly scared. But for some reason, I felt okay. I guess I had learned how to block out my feelings; I had learned from the Addiction Help

Agency how to control my feelings in a more appropriate manner. I wanted to be there for my sisters. Everyone was freaking out. Even my brothers. We all tried our best to comfort each other.

When I went into intensive care I nearly fainted. Luckily, one of my sisters found a wheelchair and she wheeled me in. I looked at Mum in shock.

She had tubes everywhere. The operation she'd had just didn't make her better. It made her worse. She was breathing through a machine. I stared at her, with tears in my eyes. I was thinking, 'Mum, what are you doing? Come on, get better. We have to go to Italy. Get better, Mumma.'

I picked up her white and fragile hand with both of my hands and held it. I looked at her hands, the hands that saved my life, the hands that gave me life, and the hands that she loved to look after so much. She always loved her long, well-painted nails. She always admired her hands and nails. Not like me. I have been biting my nails since I was twelve years old and I'm still doing it. My mother loved her hands and I did too, but this time it was a different hand. Pale, it looked like a mannequin's hand.

I felt a knot in my throat. I knew that Mum was not going to make it. I knew that she was going to go to heaven. But each of us, my brothers and my sisters and everyone else, kept our hopes up, tried to lift each other up. We were united. There was so much love for each other. No arguments. Just love and fear.

The doctor called the whole family into a small room. As soon as he started talking I knew my mother would not make it. I knew it was her time to go.

This idiot of a doctor, trying in his silly big words to explain what was happening. We knew she didn't have much time left. I was dying inside. Oh my God, this is real. Mum is going to leave this world. How am I going to cope without her? How in the world will I go on? I'm going to die without her. It's not her time yet. My head would not shut up. While the doctor was talking I turned to one of my sisters.

'Mum is going to die,' I said. She looked at me and didn't answer. She knew it too.

We each in turn went to see Mum. I went in a few times. I kept talking to her in my head, hoping she would listen to us.

Pippo my younger brother came in. 'Mum, can you hear me?' Mum swung her head from side to side.

Then I asked her, 'Mum, it's me. Can you hear me too?' Again she swung her head from side to side, meaning yes.

Pippo and I looked at each other. He quickly went to fetch the others. 'Mum can hear us. Look, I'll show you.' He did the same thing and everyone was going crazy.

Then I said out loud, 'Mum, I love you. Get better, fast. You can do it. You are strong. Stay strong and come back to us, Mum. Please!'

But when Pippo told the doctor what had happened the doctor said, 'People on life support can still hear you, but they can't come back.'

And that doctor was right. My mother was gone. But her spirit was still there, and she knew that we were all there. She knew that even I was there.

After a few hours the doctor told us they were transferring Mum into a smaller room, and that they were going to send a priest in. We followed a man who pushed Mum's bed into a small room. He left all the plugs in, and the box that showed her heart beating. I didn't like the sound of it and I hated watching it.

When they put my mother into this little room we surrounded her bed. I chose to hold her head. I held her head with both of my hands. I didn't want to let her go. I kept kissing her forehead, and saying in my mind, Thank you, Mum. Thank you for everything you did for me. Thank you for my new life. Thank you for my daughter. Thank you for rescuing me from that terrible period in my life. Thank you for loving me and giving me your courage and your strength. Thank you, thank you. I love you so much. All these thoughts were going through my head. I was in shock. But because of the Addiction Help Agency, by now I had learned how to deal with shock, by recognising it and by being in the present. That was helping me so much.

A stocky man, who seemed so rude to me, barged through the door.

'It is time for you all to say goodbye to your mother. We will remove all the wires in five minutes.'

Five minutes? What's he saying? Why is he saying that?

My sister Michela screamed out, 'Get out of here!' But one of my brothers calmed her down.

Five minutes went so quickly. This stocky man, short, nothing to look at except that he knew what he was doing, came over to my mum and roughly took out all the tubes. Then he switched off the machine. I was still holding my mother's head, and I could still hear her breathing. But after about six breaths, it all stopped. I felt her last breath in my hands. A couple of my sisters screamed out. My brothers were all in shock. Me too.

One by one everyone left, after an hour or more. But I still held her head and gave her one more kiss on the forehead.

I said softly, 'I will always love you. Your body is gone but not your spirit. You are always with me.'

And with that last kiss, everything became slow motion for me, her death, my brothers and my sisters.

I had to be strong. I cried, yes. But I didn't cry enough. All my sisters and brothers and their families—everyone in our family… We were all in shock. We couldn't believe that Mum had died. Couldn't believe she was gone. But I felt a strong sensation coming over me, and it was then that I knew that Mum was not gone at all. Only her body; not her spirit. I felt it.

I felt the warmth and the strength, the courage, to be there for my sisters and brothers. The courage to get up at the funeral and say a few nice words about my mother. The courage to see that my mother's pain was all gone. She didn't have to suffer anymore. She went to a better and everlasting place, and I know I will see her again. I know that. My mother passed away on May 6, 2006.

A few days later we all went to the funeral. The coffin was beautiful and my mother looked gorgeous, well dressed; a little puffed up, but I remember when my friend Lizzy died that she too was a little puffed up. All my brothers and sisters were around the coffin.

My sister Michela put a bag of pasta inside the coffin. I smiled and she said, 'She did make the best spaghetti didn't she, Lilla?'

'Yes, she sure did.'

I took off the ring my mother gave me years ago and put it next to her feet.

'Here, Mum, this is my ring, the one you gave me. I'm giving it back to you so you can be with me forever.' Then I sat next to my younger sister Anna.

I had looked at Mum's face long enough. I couldn't believe she had died. I couldn't believe they were going to shut the coffin soon. Everything was happening for me in slow motion. I was observing everyone's pain, and grieving. I had some kind of inner strength and I didn't know where it was coming from. Then I heard the door open, and I saw my daughter Caroline. She came to the funeral too, and I was so happy to see her.

My brothers shut the coffin and a priest walked in. He was rambling on and on about so much bullshit. I kept on looking at everyone and thinking, Who in the fuck got this damn priest? Then, after about an hour or more talking about shit, things I was not interested in, the priest asked, 'Would anyone from the family like to get up and say goodbye to this woman?'

I thought, How fucking rude! He could have said 'our mother'. I looked at everyone, all my sisters and brothers, but they were all in shock, as was I. But something in my head screamed out, Get up and say something! With my legs trembling—they felt like jelly—I got up. I was so scared. I asked Anna, my younger sister, to help me up the steps. She was so sad, and I felt so sorry for her, but she gave me a hand up those three steps.

I felt so strong within. I felt as if I had become another person. All those fears were gone. I was saying goodbye to my mother. In my speech I thanked her for helping me with my decision to keep my daughter. I thanked her for everything she did for me and everyone. I thanked her for all the spaghetti and nice food she made for us. In the end I said, 'I will always love you.'

I was not angry with anyone, just disappointed that none of my brothers or sisters got up to say anything to Mum. But I understood that they were all in shock. They couldn't believe that Mum had passed away. They were scared and vulnerable.

My anger towards them didn't last long, because I understood that each member of the family had done their best to look after Mum while she was alive. In their own way, each did something to make my mother better and more comfortable. There was no one who was better than any other. They all tried, in their own way, to look after my mother and love her unconditionally.

Mum loved us each in a different way. She was a brave mother, and a courageous woman, full of love for everyone. She was a woman who overcame many obstacles on her own. My mother was a loving and compassionate woman, always there for other people when they needed help. Her family was everything.

When my mother passed away, she gave me three most important gifts: courage, love, and the strength to keep going forward. For that I will always be grateful. I still pray to her every single night, and many of my dreams are coming true because of her. My mother hasn't left us. She is still here with us.

A week after the funeral I returned to Cairns. I had been in Melbourne for three weeks. I was stronger than ever. This time I knew what I needed to do. I wanted to get my diploma, not only for me, but for my mother too. I was in the second year of my diploma, and I was more determined than ever to carry on. All my grieving went towards my diploma.

But when I first came back to Cairns I went crazy. I couldn't believe my mother had died. I couldn't believe I wouldn't hear her voice over the phone again. I went on a rampage of hard drinking, smashing my bike into cars, in and out of emergency at Cairns Base Hospital. Crying every time I got drunk. The one person I was learning to admire and love with all my heart and soul was gone. She was really gone, and I felt lost, confused, and so damn depressed. But I had to find again the courage and strength to carry on, not only for myself but for my daughter.

I turned all my grieving towards my Diploma of Visual Arts. It normally took two years to get the diploma. It took me five years, but I did it! Finally, in 2008, I received my Diploma of Visual Arts. I received five distinctions for my essays on art, and the rest of my marks were fantastic.

I held my last exhibition, called 'Women who taught me how to fly', in 2011.

I was on top of the world when I received my diploma and I still am. It's a feeling that never leaves me. I am proud of all I have achieved. I was half way there when my mother passed away. I came back and worked even harder. I know that my mother would have been really proud of me. I was sad that she wasn't here to see it. But I know she would have said, 'Brava, brava, Letteria. Well done.'

My father passed away one year after my mother. He had already had an operation on his lungs because of cancer, and in the end he didn't want another operation. The cancer took over his whole body. When my father passed away I didn't even cry. I did feel sad for him, but his death didn't affect me as much my mother's.

Chapter 34

My new life, my freedom and my happiness. Present moment.

TODAY I CAN HONESTLY SAY I am happy. I don't have to live that lifestyle anymore, full of guilt and remorse. Everything I went through I had to learn from, the good, the bad and the ugly.

I still have those memories. There are many more things I don't remember. I have put in this book what I do remember. I recently spoke to one of my sisters, and she told me of a few incidents I put myself through, and barely came out of alive. I am still receiving a lot of counselling. But I do feel so much happier, because I have learned to speak about my traumas. I have learned to let them go, bit by bit.

I learned that you cannot play the victim role forever. At some point in life you have to put a stop to it, and learn to stand on your own two feet, disability or not. I learned that even disabled people can be great mums, as I was with my daughter. I made a lot of mistakes along the way with my daughter, but I persevered and dealt with each obstacle, instead of running away.

I learned that no one can make you feel inferior. Only you can do that to yourself.

Painting/Collage by Lilla Benigno. Donated to charity.

When I learned to let go of my anger, my resentments towards my family and my parents, I felt free and alive. I never wanted to grow old and bitter. My goal was to grow old and cherish all I have learned along the way.

I learned how to love again. Not only myself, but everyone around me, especially my daughter, and the children I left behind.

I learned that I am not a bad person, but a very sick person. Through recovery I learned that I too could become a better human being, and especially a good mum.

I learned that everyone who crossed my path taught me how to change for the better. I learned to forgive, but I don't ever forget.

I learned what rape is all about, and how so many men had sex with me without my consent. I have learned to speak up and say no, and stop the cycle of rape and abuse.

I learned how to stop blaming my family for the things I have done. I learned to love my mother again, and cherish her last years on this earth.

Slowly I am also learning to forgive my father.

Everyone in my family has gone through his or her own traumas, and because of that we have something in common. We are all survivors, and for that I truly respect all my family. I love them all with all my heart and soul.

I learned how tough it was to be a single mother, but I also learned how to ask for help when needed. And I receive help, instead of getting angry and going back to sell my body.

I stopped running away. I stopped judging people. We all have a story to tell. I learned that family is number one, before anyone else. And I am like that with my daughter, and the rest of my family.

I learned that giving away my children, Chantelle and Dean, was the best thing I could have done. I'm not sorry for giving them up today, because I gave them the gift of a better life, not a life with a drug addict and loser.

I learned not to beat up on myself because of things I should have done, and things I didn't do. No regrets for me, only lessons.

I learned that disability or no disability, each of us goes through some kind of trauma. It is up to us to deal with those traumas, or give up; and I had never wanted to give up. Today my disability does not bother me. I am not in this world to be liked or loved by anyone, and external things are nothing to me. As long as I feel inner peace, and love for my daughter and my achievements in my life, I am happy. I learned to forgive myself and let go of all the suffering I put myself through. I also learned not to blame anyone for my mistakes.

If I could turn back time would I do this all again? Maybe yes, because I know today I have become a stronger and healthier woman, with so much love to give. I am today the woman that I always wanted to be. I am free.

My daughter Caroline has left home, spread her wings, and learned to fly, living with a wonderful boyfriend, and living her own life. Today I am left with me, but I am not scared. Today I don't run anymore. I enjoy my own company, and I enjoy seeing that people like me for who I am, not for who they want me to be. I love being me today. I love knowing that I don't have to hide or run anymore. I love knowing that I have a voice. I can speak about my traumas, and I am learning to let them go. I love all the wonderful people who walked into my life, and taught me so many wonderful things about the person I have become today.

My love for myself is unconditional. I have never been into vanity, but I do believe today that I am a beautiful person, disability or not. I have made it. I am alive and stronger than ever.

Today I am free, free from the burden I have carried for years. Free as a bird. When I shut my eyes, I can be anywhere I want to be. Today I love my life, and I love me for who I am. My courage, my strength and my determination have led me to a wonderful destination called 'LOVE'.

On January 17, 2014 I had an accident. A car hit my motorised wheelchair, and so many traumas came back from the past. But today I know how to reach out for help. I am still in counselling, and just recently I received incredible help from the Acute Care Team (ACT).

I know today that my traumas cannot hurt me, because I have the courage to talk about them, to express all the pain and hurt I have been through. I keep going. I have no more suicidal thoughts. I feel as if I have been reborn. Life is very precious for me today, and if I need help I know where to go and who to talk to.

I am not alone. I am safe, and I cherish my life, my daughter and all the experiences I have been through. This is not the end for me. This is the beginning of another chapter in my life. I know that my past cannot hurt me anymore, and for that I feel real happiness, and real acceptance of who I am today.

'Me—Italian Woman' by Lilla Benigno.

'Me—Italian Woman' by Lilla Benigno.

Chapter 35

My disability—1958 until the present moment, 2019.

BEFORE GOING ON, let me say what polio has meant for my life.

For many years I never felt disabled. While living in the convent with the nuns for so many years and among so many polio victims, I learned to accept the malady. We accepted each other. We never complained to anyone about our disability. We were all in a similar condition. Some girls were in better shape than others, and some a lot worse, but we had an understanding that when someone needed help, we were there quickly, no questions asked. Whoever or whatever was in our path, we would do anything to remove the obstacle and make it easier for whomever needed help the most.

I never compared my disability with anyone else's. I always looked at it as it was, especially when I was little. Sometimes my mother and father made me feel special. They were there for me when I was little and for that I will always be grateful. When I was sick they were always by my bedside. I was too little to remember, but my mother told me how many times she walked miles just to come to the hospital to be with me.

But when I arrived in Australia, everything changed. This was when I began to see my disability in a very different way. I could see that all

Lilla Benigno, aged twelve, in Australia.

my brothers and sisters had normal legs, but I hadn't. I was comparing my legs to those of my siblings, and I couldn't understand why I was the only one born with these terrible legs. This is when the problem of hating my legs started. Now that I was no longer in the convent with the nuns, I felt so out of place. With my new family, I became aware that I was not the same. It was then that I started to feel very inadequate and incredibly alone.

Something inside me snapped when I realised that I was different. I walked different, incredibly slowly, and because I had callipers on my legs I would swing my legs with my hips to get from A to B.

That was how I walked, and if I didn't watch my steps, I would fall. I had thousands of falls in my lifetime. Each fall was different. Sometimes when I fell on the floor I would cry. Some of my falls really did hurt. In the end I got used to my falls and learned to cope with them all, but I would still become angry inside each time it happened. I would pick myself up, and sometimes one of my siblings would give me a hand.

When I was wearing callipers I could walk better, but the looks and stares brought home to me the cold reality that I was 'DISABLED', and this made me angry and, at times, full of rage. I would sometimes scream at people who stared at me as I walked by. I would shout, 'What are you looking at?' They would turn their heads quickly, pretending not to see me. Some children were curious. Sometimes I could hear them asking their parents, 'Why does she walk like that?' The anger I felt inside was getting out of control. I felt that one day I might explode. But I kept it all in. Now and then I would scream in the toilet, or when I was alone. I would cry uncontrollably. I didn't like being disabled. I wanted to be normal. I wanted to be free. Instead, I was in this prison with no way out. I was locked in a body I used to call 'freak' and 'ugly'.

Sometimes I felt I walked like Frankenstein. I remember watching the movie, and thinking, Maybe one day I will meet someone like Frankenstein and marry him. I watched the way he walked and suddenly saw the similarity. I felt abnormal and incredibly inadequate. The little self-esteem I had was leaving my soul bit by bit. I didn't want to be different. I wanted to be normal and live a normal life. But I knew deep inside that it was impossible. I knew I had to work twice as hard to achieve my dreams and my goals.

For many years I blamed my disability on everyone, especially my family. But as the years went by I started to understand that this life was given to me for a reason, to help me grow, mentally and spiritually. I had to learn to let go of all the anger and concentrate on what I could do, instead of looking at my disability as a curse or a punishment. I pushed my family away. Many of them seemed like strangers to me. It was never their fault or mine. It was not my mother's fault or my father's fault. I was sent into the convent for a reason, and that was to get better, not because my parents or my family did not love me. But after spending so many years in the convent, my anger was misdirected towards my family. I had to change that way of thinking and put it all into perspective.

Coming face to face with these feelings today has given me the courage to become honest with myself. Hopefully one day I will be able to forgive myself for all the hatred. I know I will, but of course it takes time. People say that time heals everything, and yes it is true, time does heal all wounds. I will forgive myself for the hatred I had towards my legs, for using my legs to push people away, especially my family. Forgiving myself will mean coming face to face with my own demons and letting them all go, so I can live the rest of my life in peace.

My legs are my legs. They are unique, different, and very beautiful. This is love. Loving my legs means loving me for who I am, and today I can proudly say, 'I love my legs with all my heart and soul.' I always had the feeling that people never loved me, because of my legs. But today I have a daughter who loves me, not because of my legs but because of the courage and strength I gave her as a gift. So she can pass this on to her own children. Today I have beautiful friends who love me for who I am, regardless of my legs.

Acknowledgements

Thanking everyone for being there for me.

I want to thank my parents for bringing me into this world. I want to thank my mother for being there so many times for me, and for giving me that money so I could run away from Melbourne. She gave me a chance to rearrange my life and become a better person, and a good mother. She also gave me so much hope and strength and courage to carry on. I love my mother very much. Part of me doesn't want to let her go. She is always in my mind and in my heart. When I pray, I pray to her, not to God. I want to thank my father for saving my life when I was little.

And thanks to the team at Michael Hanrahan Publishing for their ongoing support and encouragement. I couldn't have done this without you.

Painting by Lilla Benigno.

www.ingramcontent.com/pod-product-compliance
Lightning Source LLC
Chambersburg PA
CBHW060338170426
43202CB00014B/2812